OpenDaylight Cookbook

Explore how to move from legacy networking to
software-defined networking

Mathieu Lemay
Alexis de Talhouët
Jamie Goodyear
Rashmi Pujar
Mohamed El-Serngawy
Yrineu Rodrigues

BIRMINGHAM - MUMBAI

OpenDaylight Cookbook

First published: June 2017

Production reference: 1270617

Published by Packt Publishing Ltd.
Livery Place
35 Livery Street
Birmingham
B3 2PB, UK.
ISBN 978-1-78646-230-5

www.packtpub.com

Credits

Authors
Mathieu Lemay
Alexis de Talhouët
Jamie Goodyear
Rashmi Pujar
Mohamed El-Serngawy
Yrineu Rodrigues

Copy Editor
Safis Editing

Reviewer
Pradeeban Kathiravelu

Project Coordinator
Kinjal Bari

Commissioning Editor
Kartikey Pandey

Proofreader
Safis Editing

Acquisition Editor
Divya Poojari

Indexer
Mariammal Chettiyar

Content Development Editor
Mamata Walkar

Graphics
Kirk D'Penha

Technical Editor
Sayali Thanekar

Production Coordinator
Arvindkumar Gupta

About the Authors

Mathieu Lemay is the CEO of Inocybe Technologies, a company founded in 2005, a SDN pioneer specializing in real-world OpenDaylight-based deployment solutions, training, and services, and the CTO of Civimetrix Telecom, a company deploying open access networks.

Mathieu has more than 20 years of experience in information technology. At the age of 10, he was programming C++, ADA, and x86 ASM and then got involved in networking from the early bulletin board systems to first commodity internet.

He earned a master's degree in electrical engineering with a focus on wireless and optical telecommunications. Inocybe Technologies has been a member of OpenDaylight since June 2013, and Mathieu is currently a committer to the docs and reservation projects. After nine years of being CEO, Mathieu has acquired intensive knowledge of business administration.

Alexis de Talhouët has always been interested in the way information is transmitted through a network. His background in computer science and networking combined with an interest in new technology naturally guided him to the SDN field.

Jamie Goodyear is an open source advocate, Apache developer, and computer systems analyst with Savoir Technologies. He has designed, critiqued, and supported architectures for large organizations worldwide.

Jamie holds a bachelor of science degree in computer science from Memorial University of Newfoundland.

Jamie has worked in systems administration, software quality assurance, and senior software developer roles for businesses ranging from small start-ups to international corporations. He has attained committer status on Apache Karaf, Servicemix, and Felix and is a project management committee member on Apache Karaf. His first print publication was co-authoring Packt Publishing's *Instant OSGi Starter*, followed by co-authoring Packt Publishing's *Learning Apache Karaf*, and Packt Publishing's *Apache Karaf Cookbook*.

Currently, he divides his time between providing high-level reviews of architectures, mentoring developers and administrators with SOA deployments, and helping grow the OpenDaylight and Apache communities.

To my fiancée, Laura, thank you for saying yes.

To my brother, Jason, you're always there supporting my endeavors, even when it eats into movie/game nights.

I'd like to thank my family and friends for all of their support over the years. I'd like to also thank all the open source communities that have made OpenDaylight possible.

Rashmi Pujar is interested in new technology trends that are shaping today's networks. With a background in networking and telecommunications, she finds ample opportunities at Inocybe to engage her interests.

Mohamed El-Serngawy has experience in virtualization platforms and security, and his curiosity about SDN and cloud computing led him to join Inocybe. He is also interested in software vulnerabilities and playing soccer.

Yrineu Rodrigues has three years of experience in software-defined networking, with a solid background in algorithms and programming languages. Yrineu works for Instituto Atlantico on SDN projects and is a project leader/committer on the OpenDaylight project (Network Intent Composition - NIC).

About the Reviewer

Pradeeban Kathiravelu is an open source evangelist. He is a PhD researcher at INESC-ID Lisboa/Instituto Superior Técnico, Universidade de Lisboa, Portugal, and Université Catholique de Louvain, Belgium. He is a fellow of the **Erasmus Mundus Joint Degree in Distributed Computing (EMJD-DC)**, researching a software-defined approach for quality of service and data quality in multi-tenant clouds.

He holds a master of science degree in **Erasmus Mundus European Master in Distributed Computing (EMDC)**, from Instituto Superior Técnico, Portugal, and KTH Royal Institute of Technology, Sweden. He also holds a first class bachelor of science of engineering (honors) degree, majoring in computer science and engineering from University of Moratuwa, Sri Lanka.

His research interests include **software-defined networking (SDN)**, distributed systems, cloud computing, web services, big data in biomedical informatics, and data mining. He is very interested in free and open source software development and has been an active participant in the **Google Summer of Code (GSoC)** program since 2009, as a student and as a mentor.

I would like to thank Prof Luís Veiga, my MSc and PhD advisor, for his continuous guidance and encouragement throughout my five years at Instituto Superior Técnico.

www.PacktPub.com

For support files and downloads related to your book, please visit www.PacktPub.com.

Did you know that Packt offers eBook versions of every book published, with PDF and ePub files available? You can upgrade to the eBook version at www.PacktPub.com and as a print book customer, you are entitled to a discount on the eBook copy. Get in touch with us at service@packtpub.com for more details.

At www.PacktPub.com, you can also read a collection of free technical articles, sign up for a range of free newsletters and receive exclusive discounts and offers on Packt books and eBooks.

https://www.packtpub.com/mapt

Get the most in-demand software skills with Mapt. Mapt gives you full access to all Packt books and video courses, as well as industry-leading tools to help you plan your personal development and advance your career.

Why subscribe?

- Fully searchable across every book published by Packt
- Copy and paste, print, and bookmark content
- On demand and accessible via a web browser

Customer Feedback

Thanks for purchasing this Packt book. At Packt, quality is at the heart of our editorial process. To help us improve, please leave us an honest review on this book's Amazon page at `https://www.amazon.com/dp/1786462303`.

If you'd like to join our team of regular reviewers, you can e-mail us at `customerreviews@packtpub.com`. We award our regular reviewers with free eBooks and videos in exchange for their valuable feedback. Help us be relentless in improving our products!

Table of Contents

Preface

OpenDaylight is an open source project aiming to be a common tool across the networking industry for enterprises, service providers, and manufacturers. This provides a highly available multiprotocol infrastructure geared to build and manage **software-defined networking** (**SDN**) deployments. Based on a Model Driven Service Abstraction Layer, the platform is extensible and allows users to create applications for communicating with a wide variety of southbound protocols and hardware.

In other words, OpenDaylight is a framework used to solve networking-related use cases in both SDN and **network function virtualization** (**NFV**) domains.

The recipes in these chapters will present fundamental use cases one can solve using OpenDaylight.

A common and widely used network emulator, Mininet, is required to perform various recipes in this book. Prior to any recipe, as a requirement, you will need a running version of Mininet.

What this book covers

Chapter 1, *OpenDaylight Fundamentals*, talks about the OpenDaylight platform. The goal of the platform is to enable the adoption of SDN and create a solid base for NFV.

Chapter 2, *Virtual Customer Edge*, talks about virtual customer edge, which can connecting network entity endpoints to each other and integrating them within the network by allowing some access policy rules.

Chapter 3, *Dynamic Interconnects*, focuses on establishing dynamic connections among network devices within the SDN environment.

Chapter 4, *Network Virtualization*, covers some usage of network virtualization provided by OpenDaylight.

Chapter 5, *Virtual Core and Aggregation*, focuses on fundamental use cases for BGP and PCEP using OpenDaylight SDN controller.

Chapter 6, *Intent and Policy Networking*, covers how **Network Intent Composition** (**NIC**) provides some features to enable the controller to manage and direct network services and resources based on intent.

Chapter 7, *OpenDaylight Container Customizations*, dedicates the recipes to network engineers, systems builders, and integrators—the people who need to make their OpenDaylight deployment integrate even more closely into their organization.

Chapter 8, *Authentication and Authorization*, learns how to use OpenDaylight built-in authentication and authorization functionality and how to integrate OpenDaylight with existing federation systems such free IPA.

What you need for this book

You need to download the OpenDaylight software and select the Beryllium-SR4 release from this link:

```
https://www.opendaylight.org/downloads
```

Also, download the zip or the tarball, and once it's extracted, get into that folder through the command line, and you are ready to play with the recipes.

Who this book is for

OpenDayLight is an open source SDN controller based on standard protocols. It aims to accelerate the adoption of SDN and create a solid foundation for NFV. With over 90 practical recipes, this book will address common problems and day-to-day maintenance tasks with OpenDaylight.

Sections

In this book, you will find several headings that appear frequently (Getting ready, How to do it..., How it works..., There's more..., and See also).

To give clear instructions on how to complete a recipe, we use these sections as follows:

Getting ready

This section tells you what to expect in the recipe, and describes how to set up any software or any preliminary settings required for the recipe.

How to do it...

This section contains the steps required to follow the recipe.

How it works...

This section usually consists of a detailed explanation of what happened in the previous section.

There's more...

This section consists of additional information about the recipe in order to make the reader more knowledgeable about the recipe.

See also

This section provides helpful links to other useful information for the recipe.

Conventions

In this book, you will find a number of text styles that distinguish between different kinds of information. Here are some examples of these styles and an explanation of their meaning.

Code words in text, database table names, folder names, filenames, file extensions, pathnames, dummy URLs, user input, and Twitter handles are shown as follows: "This will list all the nodes under the `opendaylight-inventory` subtree of MD-SAL that stores OpenFlow switch information."

A block of code is set as follows:

```
<node xmlns="urn:TBD:params:xml:ns:yang:network-topology">
<node-id>new-netconf-device</node-id>
  <host xmlns="urn:opendaylight:netconf-node-topology">127.0.0.1</host>
  <port xmlns="urn:opendaylight:netconf-node-topology">17830</port>
  <username xmlns="urn:opendaylight:netconf-node-topology">admin</username>
  <password xmlns="urn:opendaylight:netconf-node-topology">admin</password>
  <tcp-only xmlns="urn:opendaylight:netconf-node-topology">false</tcp-only>
```

Any command-line input or output is written as follows:

```
$ ./bin/karaf
```

New terms and **important words** are shown in bold. Words that you see on the screen, for example, in menus or dialog boxes, appear in the text like this: "If prompted, choose to select the **Insecure connection** option."

Warnings or important notes appear in a box like this.

Tips and tricks appear like this.

Reader feedback

Feedback from our readers is always welcome. Let us know what you think about this book-what you liked or disliked. Reader feedback is important for us as it helps us develop titles that you will really get the most out of.

To send us general feedback, simply e-mail feedback@packtpub.com, and mention the book's title in the subject of your message.

If there is a topic that you have expertise in and you are interested in either writing or contributing to a book, see our author guide at www.packtpub.com/authors.

Customer support

Now that you are the proud owner of a Packt book, we have a number of things to help you to get the most from your purchase.

Downloading the example code

You can download the example code files for this book from your account at http://www.packtpub.com. If you purchased this book elsewhere, you can visit http://www.packtpub.com/support and register to have the files e-mailed directly to you.

You can download the code files by following these steps:

1. Log in or register to our website using your e-mail address and password.
2. Hover the mouse pointer on the **SUPPORT** tab at the top.
3. Click on **Code Downloads & Errata**.
4. Enter the name of the book in the **Search** box.
5. Select the book for which you're looking to download the code files.
6. Choose from the drop-down menu where you purchased this book from.
7. Click on **Code Download**.

You can also download the code files by clicking on the **Code Files** button on the book's webpage at the Packt Publishing website. This page can be accessed by entering the book's name in the **Search** box. Please note that you need to be logged in to your Packt account.

Once the file is downloaded, please make sure that you unzip or extract the folder using the latest version of:

- WinRAR / 7-Zip for Windows
- Zipeg / iZip / UnRarX for Mac
- 7-Zip / PeaZip for Linux

The code bundle for the book is also hosted on GitHub at `https://github.com/PacktPubl ishing/OpenDaylight-Cookbook`. We also have other code bundles from our rich catalog of books and videos available at `https://github.com/PacktPublishing/`. Check them out!

Downloading the color images of this book

We also provide you with a PDF file that has color images of the screenshots/diagrams used in this book. The color images will help you better understand the changes in the output. You can download this file from `https://www.packtpub.com/sites/default/files/down loads/OpenDaylightCookbook_ColorImages.pdf`.

Errata

Although we have taken every care to ensure the accuracy of our content, mistakes do happen. If you find a mistake in one of our books-maybe a mistake in the text or the code-we would be grateful if you could report this to us. By doing so, you can save other readers from frustration and help us improve subsequent versions of this book. If you find any errata, please report them by visiting `http://www.packtpub.com/submit-errata`, selecting your book, clicking on the **Errata Submission Form** link, and entering the details of your errata. Once your errata are verified, your submission will be accepted and the errata will be uploaded to our website or added to any list of existing errata under the Errata section of that title.

To view the previously submitted errata, go to `https://www.packtpub.com/books/content/support` and enter the name of the book in the search field. The required information will appear under the **Errata** section.

Piracy

Piracy of copyrighted material on the Internet is an ongoing problem across all media. At Packt, we take the protection of our copyright and licenses very seriously. If you come across any illegal copies of our works in any form on the Internet, please provide us with the location address or website name immediately so that we can pursue a remedy.

Please contact us at `copyright@packtpub.com` with a link to the suspected pirated material.

We appreciate your help in protecting our authors and our ability to bring you valuable content.

Questions

If you have a problem with any aspect of this book, you can contact us at `questions@packtpub.com`, and we will do our best to address the problem.

1
OpenDaylight Fundamentals

OpenDaylight is a collaborative platform supported by leaders in the networking industry and hosted by the Linux foundation. The goal of the platform is to enable the adoption of **software-defined networking (SDN)** and create a solid base for **network functions virtualization (NFV)**.

In this chapter, we will cover the following recipes:

- Connecting OpenFlow switches
- Mounting a NETCONF device
- Browsing data models with YANGUI
- Basic distributed switching
- Bonding links using LACP
- Changing user authentication
- OpenDaylight clustering

Introduction

OpenDaylight is an open source project aiming to be a common tool across the networking industry - for enterprises, service providers, and manufacturers. It provides a highly available, multi-protocol infrastructure geared at building and managing software-defined networking deployments. Based on a Model Driven Service Abstraction Layer, the platform is extensible and allows users to create applications to communicate with a wide variety of south-bound protocols and hardware.

In other words, OpenDaylight is a framework used to solve networking-related use cases in both software-defined networking and network function virtualization domains.

To download the OpenDaylight software, select the Beryllium-SR4 release available at this link:

`https://www.opendaylight.org/downloads`

Download the ZIP or the tarball, and once extracted, get into that folder through the command line, and you are ready to play with the recipes.

The recipes in this chapter will present fundamental use cases that one can solve using OpenDaylight.

A common and widely used network emulator, Mininet, is going to be required to perform various recipes within this book.

Prior to any recipe, as a requirement, you will need a running version of Mininet. To achieve this, please follow the steps explained in the Mininet documentation:

`http://mininet.org/download/`

 For REST APIs access, user: `admin` and password: `admin`.

Connecting OpenFlow switches

OpenFlow is a vendor-neutral, standard communications interface defined to enable the interaction between the control and forwarding channels of an SDN architecture. The OpenFlowPlugin project intends to support implementations of the OpenFlow specification as it evolves. It currently supports OpenFlow versions 1.0 and 1.3.2. In addition, to support the core OpenFlow specification, OpenDaylight Beryllium also includes preliminary support for the table type patterns and OF-CONFIG specifications.

The OpenFlow southbound plugin currently provides the following components:

- Flow management
- Group management
- Meter management
- Statistics polling

Let's connect an OpenFlow switch to OpenDaylight.

Getting ready

This recipe requires an OpenFlow switch. If you don't have any, you can use a Mininet-VM with OvS installed. You can download Mininet-VM from the following website:

`https://github.com/mininet/mininet/wiki/Mininet-VM-Images`

Any version should work.

The following recipe will be presented using a Mininet-VM with OvS 2.0.2.

How to do it...

Perform the following steps:

1. Start the OpenDaylight distribution using the `karaf` script. Using this script will give you access to the Karaf CLI:

   ```
   $ ./bin/karaf
   ```

2. Install the user-facing feature responsible for pulling in all dependencies needed to connect an OpenFlow switch:

   ```
   opendaylight-user@root>feature:install odl-openflowplugin-all
   ```

   It might take a minute or so to complete the installation.

3. Connect an OpenFlow switch to OpenDaylight.

   As mentioned in the *Getting ready* section, we will use Mininet-VM as our OpenFlow switch as this VM runs an instance of OpenVSwitch:

   - Log in to Mininet-VM using:
     - **Username**: `mininet`
     - **Password**: `mininet`

   - Let's create a bridge:

     ```
     mininet@mininet-vm:~$ sudo ovs-vsctl add-br br0
     ```

- Now let's connect OpenDaylight as the controller of `br0`:

```
mininet@mininet-vm:~$ sudo ovs-vsctl set-controller br0 tcp:
${CONTROLLER_IP}:6633
```

- Let's look at our topology:

```
mininet@mininet-vm:~$ sudo ovs-vsctl show
0b8ed0aa-67ac-4405-af13-70249a7e8a96
    Bridge "br0"
      Controller "tcp: ${CONTROLLER_IP}:6633"
        is_connected: true
      Port "br0"
        Interface "br0"
          type: internal
    ovs_version: "2.0.2"
```

`${CONTROLLER_IP}` is the IP address of the host running OpenDaylight.

We're establishing a TCP connection. For a more secure connection, we could use TLS protocol; however, this will not be included in this book as this is beyond the scope of the book.

4. Have a look at the created OpenFlow node.

Once the OpenFlow switch is connected, send the following request to get information regarding the switch:

- Type: GET

- Headers:

  Authorization: Basic YWRtaW46YWRtaW4=

- URL:
  `http://localhost:8181/restconf/operational/opendaylight-inventory:nodes/`

This will list all the nodes under the `opendaylight-inventory` subtree of MD-SAL that stores OpenFlow switch information. As we connected our first switch, we should have only one node there. It will contain all the information that the OpenFlow switch has, including its tables, its ports, flow statistics, and so on.

How it works...

Once the feature is installed, OpenDaylight is listening to connections on port 6633 and 6640. Setting up the controller on the OpenFlow-capable switch will immediately trigger a callback on OpenDaylight. It will create the communication pipeline between the switch and OpenDaylight so they can communicate in a scalable and non-blocking way.

Mounting a NETCONF device

The OpenDaylight component responsible for connecting remote NETCONF devices is called the NETCONF southbound plugin, aka the netconf-connector. Creating an instance of the netconf-connector will connect a NETCONF device. The NETCONF device will be seen as a mount point in the MD-SAL, exposing the device configuration and operational data store and its capabilities. These mount points allow applications and remote users (over RESTCONF) to interact with the mounted devices.

The netconf-connector currently supports RFC-6241, RFC-5277, and RFC-6022.

The following recipe will explain how to connect a NETCONF device to OpenDaylight.

Getting ready

This recipe requires a NETCONF device. If you don't have any, you can use the NETCONF test tool provided by OpenDaylight. It can be downloaded from the OpenDaylight Nexus repository:

```
https://nexus.opendaylight.org/content/repositories/opendaylight.release/org/op
endaylight/netconf/netconf-testtool/1.0.4-Beryllium-SR4/netconf-testtool-1.0.4-
Beryllium-SR4-executable.jar
```

How to do it...

Perform the following steps:

1. Start the OpenDaylight Karaf distribution using the karaf script. Using this script will give you access to the Karaf CLI:

   ```
   $ ./bin/karaf
   ```

2. Install the user-facing feature responsible for pulling in all dependencies needed to connect a NETCONF device:

```
opendaylight-user@root>feature:install odl-netconf-topology
odl-restconf
```

It might take a minute or so to complete the installation.

3. Start your NETCONF device.

If you want to use the NETCONF test tool, it is time to simulate a NETCONF device using the following command:

```
$ java -jar netconf-testtool-1.0.1-Beryllium-SR4-
executable.jar --device-count 1
```

This will simulate one device that will be bound to port `17830`.

4. Configure a new `netconf-connector`.

Send the following request using RESTCONF:

- Type: `PUT`

- URL:
  `http://localhost:8181/restconf/config/network-topology:netwo`
  `rk-topology/topology/topology-netconf/node/new-netconf-`
  `device`

  By looking closer at the URL you will notice that the last part is `new-netconf-device`. This must match the `node-id` that we will define in the payload.

- Headers:

  Accept: `application/xml`

  Content-Type: `application/xml`

  Authorization: Basic `YWRtaW46YWRtaW4=`

- Payload:

```
<node xmlns="urn:TBD:params:xml:ns:yang:network-topology">
<node-id>new-netconf-device</node-id>
<host xmlns="urn:opendaylight:netconf-node-
topology">127.0.0.1</host>
<port xmlns="urn:opendaylight:netconf-node-
topology">17830</port>
<username xmlns="urn:opendaylight:netconf-node-
topology">admin</username>
<password xmlns="urn:opendaylight:netconf-node-
topology">admin</password>
<tcp-only xmlns="urn:opendaylight:netconf-node-
topology">false</tcp-only>
</node>
```

5. Let's have a closer look at this payload:

- `node-id`: Defines the name of the `netconf-connector`.

- `address`: Defines the IP address of the NETCONF device.

- `port`: Defines the port for the NETCONF session.

- `username`: Defines the username of the NETCONF session. This should be provided by the NETCONF device configuration.

- `password`: Defines the password of the NETCONF session. As for the `username`, this should be provided by the NETCONF device configuration.

- `tcp-only`: Defines whether or not the NETCONF session should use TCP or SSL. If set to `true` it will use TCP.

 This is the default configuration of the `netconf-connector`; it actually has more configurable elements that we will look at later.

Once you have completed the request, send it. This will spawn a new `netconf-connector` that connects to the NETCONF device at the provided IP address and port using the provided credentials.

6. Verify that the `netconf-connector` has correctly been pushed and get information about the connected NETCONF device.

First, you could look at the log to see if any errors occurred. If no error has occurred, you will see the following:

```
2016-05-07 11:37:42,470 | INFO  | sing-executor-11 |
NetconfDevice                 | 253 -
org.opendaylight.netconf.sal-netconf-connector -
1.3.0.Beryllium | RemoteDevice{new-netconf-device}: Netconf
connector initialized successfully
```

Once the new `netconf-connector` is created, some useful metadata is written into the MD-SAL's operational data store under the network-topology subtree. To retrieve this information, you should send the following request:

- Type: `GET`

- Headers:

  Authorization: Basic `YWRtaW46YWRtaW4=`

- URL:
  `http://localhost:8181/restconf/operational/network-topology:network-topology/topology/topology-netconf/node/new-netconf-device`

We're using `new-netconf-device` as the `node-id` because this is the name we assigned to the `netconf-connector` in a previous step.

This request will provide information about the connection status and device capabilities. The device capabilities are all the YANG models the NETCONF device is providing in its `hello-message` that was used to create the schema context.

7. More configuration for the `netconf-connector`.

As mentioned previously, the `netconf-connector` contains various configuration elements. Those fields are non-mandatory, with default values. If you do not wish to override any of these values, you shouldn't provide them:

- `schema-cache-directory`: This corresponds to the destination schema repository for YANG files downloaded from the NETCONF device. By default, those schemas are saved in the cache directory (`$ODL_ROOT/cache/schema`). Using this configuration will define where to save the downloaded schema related to the cache directory. For instance, if you assigned `new-schema-cache`, schemas related to this device would be located under `$ODL_ROOT/cache/new-schema-cache/`.

- `reconnect-on-changed-schema`: If set to `true`, the connector will auto disconnect/reconnect when schemas are changed in the remote device. The `netconf-connector` will subscribe to base NETCONF notifications and listen for netconf-capability-change notifications. The default value is `false`.

- `connection-timeout-millis`: Timeout in milliseconds after which the connection must be established. The default value is 20000 milliseconds.

- `default-request-timeout-millis`: Timeout for blocking operations within transactions. Once this timer is reached, if the request is not yet finished, it will be canceled. The default value is 60000 milliseconds.

- `max-connection-attempts`: Maximum number of connection attempts. Nonpositive or null values are interpreted as infinity. The default value is `0`, which means it will retry forever.

- `between-attempts-timeout-millis`: Initial timeout in milliseconds between connection attempts. This will be multiplied by the sleep-factor for every new attempt. The default value is 2000 milliseconds.

- `sleep-factor`: Back-off factor used to increase the delay between connection attempt(s). The default value is `1.5`.

- `keepalive-delay`: `netconf-connector` sends keep-alive RPCs while the session is idle to ensure session connectivity. This delay specifies the timeout between keep-alive RPCs in seconds. Providing a 0 value will disable this mechanism. The default value is 120 seconds.

Using this configuration, your payload would look like this:

```
<node xmlns="urn:TBD:params:xml:ns:yang:network-topology">
<node-id>new-netconf-device</node-id>
  <host xmlns="urn:opendaylight:netconf-node-
topology">127.0.0.1</host>
  <port xmlns="urn:opendaylight:netconf-node-
topology">17830</port>
  <username xmlns="urn:opendaylight:netconf-node-
topology">admin</username>
  <password xmlns="urn:opendaylight:netconf-node-
topology">admin</password>
  <tcp-only xmlns="urn:opendaylight:netconf-node-
topology">false</tcp-only>
<schema-cache-directory xmlns="urn:opendaylight:netconf-
node-topology">new_netconf_device_cache</schema-cache-
directory>
  <reconnect-on-changed-schema
xmlns="urn:opendaylight:netconf-node-
topology">false</reconnect-on-changed-schema>
  <connection-timeout-millis
xmlns="urn:opendaylight:netconf-node-
topology">20000</connection-timeout-millis>
  <default-request-timeout-millis
xmlns="urn:opendaylight:netconf-node-
topology">60000</default-request-timeout-millis>
  <max-connection-attempts xmlns="urn:opendaylight:netconf-
node-topology">0</max-connection-attempts>
  <between-attempts-timeout-millis
xmlns="urn:opendaylight:netconf-node-
topology">2000</between-attempts-timeout-millis>
  <sleep-factor xmlns="urn:opendaylight:netconf-node-
topology">1.5</sleep-factor>
  <keepalive-delay xmlns="urn:opendaylight:netconf-node-
topology">120</keepalive-delay>
</node>
```

How it works...

Once the request to connect a new NETCONF device is sent, OpenDaylight will set up the communication channel used for managing and interacting with the device. At first, the remote NETCONF device will send its `hello-message` defining all of the capabilities it has. Based on this, the `netconf-connector` will download all the YANG files provided by the device. All those YANG files will define the schema context of the device.

At the end of the process, some exposed capabilities might end up as unavailable, for two possible reasons:

1. The NETCONF device provided a capability in its `hello-message`, but hasn't provided the schema.
2. OpenDaylight failed to mount a given schema due to YANG violation(s).

OpenDaylight parses YANG models as per RFC 6020; if a schema is not respecting the RFC, it could end up as an unavailable-capability.

If you encounter one of these situations, looking at the logs will pinpoint the reason for such a failure.

There's more...

Once the NETCONF device is connected, all its capabilities are available through the mount point. View it as a pass-through directly to the NETCONF device.

GET data store

To see the data contained in the device data store, use the following request:

- Type: `GET`
- Headers:

    Authorization: Basic `YWRtaW46YWRtaW4=`

- URL:
  `http://localhost:8080/restconf/config/network-topology:network-topology/topology/topology-netconf/node/new-netconf-device/yang-ext:mount/`

Adding `yang-ext:mount/` to the URL will access the mount point created for `new-netconf-device`. This will show the configuration data store. If you want to see the operational one, replace `config` with `operational` in the URL.

If your device defines the YANG model, you can access its data using the following request:

- Type: `GET`
- Headers:

    Authorization: Basic `YWRtaW46YWRtaW4=`

- URL:
  ```
  http://localhost:8080/restconf/config/network-topology:network-
  topology/topology/topology-netconf/node/new-netconf-
  device/yang-ext:mount/<module>:<container>
  ```

The `<module>` represents a schema defining the `<container>`. The `<container>` can either be a list or a container. It is not possible to access a single leaf. You can access containers/lists within containers/lists. The last part of the URL would look like this:

```
.../ yang-ext:mount/<module>:<container>/<sub-container>
```

Invoking RPC

In order to invoke an RPC on the remote device, you should use the following request:

- Type: `POST`
- Headers:

    Accept: `application/xml`

    Content-Type: `application/xml`

    Authorization: Basic `YWRtaW46YWRtaW4=`

- URL:
  ```
  http://localhost:8080/restconf/config/network-topology:network-
  topology/topology/topology-netconf/node/new-netconf-
  device/yang-ext:mount/<module>:<operation>
  ```

This URL is accessing the mount point of `new-netconf-device`, and through this mount point we're accessing the `<module>` to call its `<operation>`. The `<module>` represents a schema defining the RPC and `<operation>` represents the RPC to call.

Deleting a netconf-connector

Removing a `netconf-connector` will drop the NETCONF session and all resources will be cleaned. To perform such an operation, use the following request:

- Type: `DELETE`
- Headers:

   Authorization: Basic `YWRtaW46YWRtaW4=`

- URL:
  `http://localhost:8181/restconf/config/network-topology:network-topology/topology/topology-netconf/node/new-netconf-device`

By looking closer at the URL, you can see that we are removing the netconf `node-idnew-netconf-device`.

Browsing data models with YANGUI

YANGUI is a user interface application through which one can navigate among all YANG models available in the OpenDaylight controller. Not only does it aggregate all data models, it also enables their usage. Using this interface, you can create, remove, update, and delete any part of the model-driven data store. It provides a nice, smooth user interface making it easier to browse through the model(s).

This recipe will guide you through those functionalities.

Getting ready

This recipe only requires the OpenDaylight controller and a web browser.

How to do it...

Perform the following steps:

1. Start your OpenDaylight distribution using the `karaf` script. Using this client will give you access to the Karaf CLI:

    ```
    $ ./bin/karaf
    ```

2. Install the user-facing feature responsible to pull in all dependencies needed to use YANGUI:

    ```
    opendaylight-user@root>feature:install odl-dlux-yangui
    ```

    It might take a minute or so to complete the installation.

3. Navigate to `http://localhost:8181/index.html#/yangui/index`:
    *   **Username**: `admin`
    *   **Password**: `admin`

    Once logged in, all modules will be loaded until you see this message at the bottom of the screen:

    Loading completed successfully

    You should see the **API** tab listing all YANG models in the following format:

    `<module-name> rev.<revision-date>`

    For instance:

    *   `cluster-admin rev.2015-10-13`
    *   `config rev.2013-04-05`
    *   `credential-store rev.2015-02-26`

    By default, there isn't much you can do with the provided YANG models. So let's connect an OpenFlow switch to better understand how to use this YANGUI. To do so, please refer to the first recipe, *Connecting OpenFlow switches*, step 2.

    Once done, refresh your web page to load newly added modules.

4. Look for `opendaylight-inventory rev.2013-08-19` and select the **operational** tab, as nothing will yet be in the config data store. Then click on nodes and you'll see a request bar at the bottom of the page with multiple options.

You can either copy the request to the clipboard to use it in your browser, send it, show a preview of it, or define a custom API request.

For now, we will only send the request.

You should see **Request sent successfully** and under this message should be the retrieved data. As we only have one switch connected, there is only one node. All the switch operational information is now printed on your screen.

 You could do the same request by specifying the `node-id` in the request. To do that you will need to expand nodes and click on `node {id}`, which will enable a more fine-grained search.

How it works...

OpenDaylight has a model-driven architecture, which means that all of its components are modeled using YANG. While installing features, OpenDaylight loads YANG models, making them available within the MD-SAL data store.

YANGUI is a representation of this data store. Each schema represents a subtree based on the name of the module and its revision-date. YANGUI aggregates and parses all those models. It also acts as a REST client; through its web interface we can execute functions such as `GET`, `POST`, `PUT`, and `DELETE`.

There's more...

The example shown previously can be improved upon, as there was no user YANG model loaded. For instance, if you mount a NETCONF device containing its own YANG model, you could interact with it through YANGUI.

You would use the config data store to push/update some data, and you would see the operational data store updated accordingly. In addition, accessing your data would be much easier than having to define the exact URL, as mentioned in the *Mounting a NETCONF device* recipe.

See also

- Using API doc as a REST API client

Basic distributed switching

The basic distributed switching in OpenDaylight is provided by the L2Switch project, proving layer 2 switch functionality. This project is built on top of the OpenFlowPlugin project, as it uses its capabilities to connect and interact with an OpenFlow switch.

The L2Switch project has the following features/components:

- Packet handler: Decodes the incoming packets, and dispatches them appropriately. It defines a packet lifecycle in three stages:
    1. Decode
    2. Modify
    3. Transmit
- Loop remover: Detects loops in the network and removes them.
- Arp handler: Handles ARP packets provided by the packet handler.
- Address tracker: Gathers MAC and IP addresses from network entities.
- Host tracker: Tracks hosts' locations in the network.
- L2Switch main: Installs flows on the switches present in the network.

Getting ready

This recipe requires an OpenFlow switch. If you don't have any, you can use a Mininet-VM with OvS installed.

You can download Mininet-VM from their website `https://github.com/mininet/mininet/wiki/Mininet-VM-Images`. All versions should work.

This recipe will be presented using a Mininet-VM with OvS 2.0.2.

How to do it...

Perform the following steps:

1. Start your OpenDaylight distribution using the `karaf` script. Using this script will give you access to the Karaf CLI:

   ```
   $ ./bin/karaf
   ```

2. Install the user-facing feature responsible for pulling in all dependencies needed to enable basic distributed switching:

   ```
   opendaylight-user@root>feature:install odl-l2switch-switch-ui
   ```

   It might take a few minutes to complete the installation.

3. Creating a network using Mininet:

   - Log in to Mininet-VM using:
       - **Username**: mininet
       - **Password**: mininet
   - Clean current Mininet state:

   If you're using the same instance as before, you want to clear its state. We previously created one bridge, br0, so let's delete it:

   ```
   mininet@mininet-vm:~$ sudo ovs-vsctl del-br br0
   ```

   - Create the topology:

   In order to do so, use the following command:

   ```
   mininet@mininet-vm:~$ sudo mn --
   controller=remote,ip=${CONTROLLER_IP}--topo=linear,3 --switch
   ovsk,protocols=OpenFlow13
   ```

Using this command will create a virtual network provisioned with three switches that will connect to the controller specified by ${CONTROLLER_IP}. The previous command will also set up links between switches and hosts.

We will end up with three OpenFlow nodes in the `opendaylight-inventory`:

- Type: `GET`
- Headers:

    Authorization: Basic `YWRtaW46YWRtaW4=`

- URL:
    `http://localhost:8080/restconf/operational/opendaylight-invento ry:nodes`

This request will return the following:

```
        --[cut]-
    {
      "id": "openflow:1",
        --[cut]-
    },
    {
      "id": "openflow:2",
        --[cut]-
    },
    {
      "id": "openflow:3",
        --[cut]-
```

4. Generate network traffic using `mininet`.

    Between two hosts using `ping`:

    mininet> h1 ping h2

    The preceding command will cause host1 (h1) to ping host2 (h2), and we can see that host1 is able to reach h2.

    Between all hosts:

    mininet> pingall

    The `pingall` command will make all hosts ping all other hosts.

5. Checking address observations.

    This is done thanks to the address tracker that observes address tuples on a switch's port (`node-connector`).

This information will be present in the OpenFlow node connector and can be retrieved using the following request (for `openflow:2`, which is the switch 2):

- Type: `GET`
- Headers:

    Authorization: Basic `YWRtaW46YWRtaW4=`

- URL:
  ```
  http://localhost:8080/restconf/operational/opendaylight-invento
  ry:nodes/node/openflow:1/node-connector/openflow:2:1
  ```

This request will return the following:

```
{
  "nodes": {
    "node": [
      {
        "id": "openflow:2",
        "node-connector": [
          {
            "id": "openflow:2:1",
            --[cut]--
            "address-tracker:addresses": [
              {
                "id": 0,
                "first-seen": 1462650320161,
                "mac": "7a:e4:ba:4d:bc:35",
                "last-seen": 1462650320161,
                "ip": "10.0.0.2"
              }
            ]
          }
        },
        --[cut]--
```

This result means the host with the mac address `7a:e4:ba:4d:bc:35` has sent a packet to switch 2 and that port 1 of switch 2 handled the incoming packet.

6. Checking the host address and attachment point to the node/switch:

- Type: `GET`
- Headers:

    Authorization: Basic `YWRtaW46YWRtaW4=`

- URL:
  ```
  http://localhost:8080/restconf/operational/network-topology:net
  work-topology/topology/flow:1/
  ```

This will return the following:

```
                --[cut]--
<node>
    <node-id>host:c2:5f:c0:14:f3:1d</node-id>
    <termination-point>
        <tp-id>host:c2:5f:c0:14:f3:1d</tp-id>
    </termination-point>
    <attachment-points>
        <tp-id>openflow:3:1</tp-id>
        <corresponding-
tp>host:c2:5f:c0:14:f3:1d</corresponding-tp>
        <active>true</active>
    </attachment-points>
    <addresses>
        <id>2</id>
        <mac>c2:5f:c0:14:f3:1d</mac>
        <last-seen>1462650434613</last-seen>
        <ip>10.0.0.3</ip>
        <first-seen>1462650434613</first-seen>
    </addresses>
    <id>c2:5f:c0:14:f3:1d</id>
</node>
                --[cut]--
```

`address` contains information about the mapping between the MAC address and the IP address, and `attachment-points` defines the mapping between the MAC address and the switch port.

7. Checking the spanning tree protocol status for each link.

   The spanning tree protocol status can be either forwarding, meaning packets are flowing on an active link, or discarding, indicating packets are not sent as the link is inactive.

   To check the link status, send this request:

   - Type: GET
   - Headers:

     Authorization: Basic YWRtaW46YWRtaW4=

- URL:
  ```
  http://localhost:8181/restconf/operational/opendaylight-invento
  ry:nodes/node/openflow:2/node-connector/openflow:2:2
  ```

This will return the following:

```
{
  "node-connector": [
    {
      "id": "openflow:2:2",
                --[cut]--
      "stp-status-aware-node-connector:status": "forwarding",
      "opendaylight-port-statistics:flow-capable-node-
connector-statistics": {}
    }
  ]
}
```

In this case, all packets coming in port 2 of switch 2 will be forwarded on the established link.

8. Checking created links.

   In order to check the links created, we are going to send the same request as the one sent at step 6, but we will focus on a different part of the response:

- Type: GET
- Headers:

  Authorization: **Basic** YWRtaW46YWRtaW4=

- URL:
  ```
  http://localhost:8080/restconf/operational/network-topology:net
  work-topology/topology/flow:1/
  ```

The different part this time is the following:

```
                --[cut]--
<link>
    <link-id>host:7a:e4:ba:4d:bc:35/openflow:2:1</link-id>
    <source>
        <source-tp>host:7a:e4:ba:4d:bc:35</source-tp>
        <source-node>host:7a:e4:ba:4d:bc:35</source-node>
    </source>
    <destination>
```

```
            <dest-node>openflow:2</dest-node>
            <dest-tp>openflow:2:1</dest-tp>
        </destination>
    </link>
    <link>
        <link-id>openflow:3:1/host:c2:5f:c0:14:f3:1d</link-id>
        <source>
            <source-tp>openflow:3:1</source-tp>
            <source-node>openflow:3</source-node>
        </source>
        <destination>
            <dest-node>host:c2:5f:c0:14:f3:1d</dest-node>
            <dest-tp>host:c2:5f:c0:14:f3:1d</dest-tp>
        </destination>
    </link>
            --[cut]--
```

It represents links that were established while setting the topology earlier. It also provides the source, destination node, and termination point.

How it works...

It leverages the OpenFlowPlugin project providing the basic communication channel between OpenFlow capable switches and OpenDaylight. The layer 2 discovery is handled by an ARP listener/responder. Using it, OpenDaylight is able to learn and track network entity addresses. Finally, using graph algorithms, it is able to detect the shortest path and remove loops within the network.

There's more...

It is possible to change or increase basic configuration of the L2Switch component to perform more accurate operations.

Configuring L2Switch

We have presented L2Switch usage with the default configuration.

To change the configuration, here are the steps to follow:

1. Execute the two first points mentioned previously.
2. Stop OpenDaylight:

   opendaylight-user@root>logout

3. Navigate to $ODL_ROOT/etc/opendaylight/karaf/.
4. Open the configuration file you want to modify.
5. Perform your modification.

 Do not play with the configuration files and their values, and be very careful and change only what is needed based on the link provided at the beginning of this tip, or else you could break functionality.

6. Save the file and re-execute the steps mentioned in the How to do it section.

   The new configuration should now be applied.

Bonding links using LACP

The **Link Aggregation Control Protocol (LACP)** project within OpenDaylight implements the LACP.

It will be used to auto-discover and aggregate links between the known OpenDaylight network and external equipment such as LACP capable endpoints or switches. Using LACP will increase the resilience of the link(s) and will aggregate the bandwidth.

LACP protocol was first released as an IEEE Ethernet specification 802.3ad, but later moved to Bridging and Management Group as an 802.1AX specification.

The LACP module will listen for LACP control packets that are generated from legacy switches (non-OpenFlow enabled).

Getting ready

This recipe requires an OpenFlow switch. If you don't have any, you can use a Mininet-VM with OvS installed.

You can download Mininet-VM from their website:

```
https://github.com/mininet/mininet/wiki/Mininet-VM-Images
```

OvS users:

You must use a version of OvS superior or equal to 2.1 so it can handle group tables. If you previously downloaded a Mininet-VM, you could create a new VM using its disk, and then update the OvS version within Mininet. Perform the update within `mininet`; you'll have to run the following commands:

```
$ cd /home/mininet/mininet/util
$ ./install.sh -V 2.3.1
```

This script will try updating your packages, but this operation can fail. If it does, run the command yourself then re-execute the script:

```
$ sudo apt-get update --fix-missing
```

Then rerun the install script. After a couple of minutes, the new version of OvS should be installed:

```
mininet@mininet-vm:~$ sudo ovs-vsctl show 1077578e-
f495-46a1-a96b-441223e7cc22 ovs_version: "2.3.1"
```

This recipe will be presented using a Mininet-VM with OvS 2.3.1.

In order to use LACP, you have to ensure that legacy (non-OpenFlow) switches are configured with the LACP mode active with a long timeout to allow the LACP plugin to respond to its messages.

The sample code for this recipe is available at:

```
https://github.com/jgoodyear/OpenDaylightCookbook/tree/master/chapter1/chapter1
-recipe5
```

How to do it...

Perform the following steps:

1. Start your OpenDaylight distribution using the `karaf` script. Using this script will give you access to the Karaf CLI:

   $ ./bin/karaf

2. Install the user-facing feature responsible for pulling in all dependencies needed to enable LACP functionality:

   opendaylight-user@root>feature:install odl-lacp-ui

   It might take a few minutes to complete the installation.

3. Creating a network using Mininet:

   - Log in to Mininet-VM using:
       - **Username**: `mininet`
       - **Password**: `mininet`
   - Create the topology:

   In order to do so, use the following command:

   mininet@mininet-vm:~$ sudo mn -- controller=remote, ip=${CONTROLLER_IP} --topo=linear, 1 --switch ovsk, protocols=OpenFlow13

   This command will create a virtual network containing one switch, connected to `${CONTROLLER_IP}`.

   We will end up with one OpenFlow node in the `opendaylight-inventory`:

   - Type: `GET`
   - Headers:

       Authorization: Basic `YWRtaW46YWRtaW4=`

   - URL:
     `http://localhost:8080/restconf/operational/opendaylight-inventory:nodes`

This request will return the following:

```
        --[cut]-
{
  "id": "openflow:1",
        --[cut]--
}
```

4. Open a new terminal to access your Mininet instance and verify that the flow entry handling LACP packets is installed:

```
mininet@mininet-vm:~$ sudo ovs-ofctl -O OpenFlow13 dump-flows
s1
OFPST_FLOW reply (OF1.3) (xid=0x2):
cookie=0x3000000000000003, duration=185.98s, table=0,
n_packets=0, n_bytes=0,
priority=5,dl_dst=01:80:c2:00:00:02,dl_type=0x8809
actions=CONTROLLER:65535
```

The flow is using ether type `0x8809`, which is the one defined for LACP.

5. From the Mininet CLI, let's add a new link between switch1 (`s1`) and host1 (`h1`), and then aggregate the two links. The Mininet CLI is where you ended up after creating the topology in step 3:

```
mininet> py net.addLink(s1, net.get('h1'))
<mininet.link.Link object at 0x7fe1fa0f17d0>
mininet> py s1.attach('s1-eth2')
```

6. Configure host1 (`h1`) to act as your legacy switch. To do that, we will create a bond interface with mode type set to LACP. In order to do so, we need to create a new file under /etc/mobprobe.d in your Mininet instance.

Use the terminal window opened at step 4 to access this directory and create a file bonding.conf with this content:

```
alias bond0 bonding
options bonding mode=4
```

`mode=4` refers to LACP, and by default the timeout is set to be long.

7. Using the Mininet CLI, let's create and configure the bond interface and add both physical interfaces of host, `h1-eth0`, and `h1-eth`, as members of the bound interface. Then set the interface up:

```
mininet> py net.get('h1').cmd('modprobe bonding')
mininet> py net.get('h1').cmd('ip link add bond0 type bond')
mininet> py net.get('h1').cmd('ip link set bond0 address
${MAC_ADDRESS}')
mininet> py net.get('h1').cmd('ip link set h1-eth0 down')
mininet> py net.get('h1').cmd('ip link set h1-eth0 master
bond0')
mininet> py net.get('h1').cmd('ip link set h1-eth1 down')
mininet> py net.get('h1').cmd('ip link set h1-eth1 master
bond0')
mininet> py net.get('h1').cmd('ip link set bond0 up')
```

Make sure to change `${MAC_ADDRESS}` with an appropriate MAC address.

Once the created `bond0` interface is up, `host1` will send LACP packets to switch1. OpenDaylight LACP's module will create the link aggregation group on the switch1 (`s1`).

To visualize the bound interface, you can use the following command:

```
mininet> py net.get('h1').cmd('cat /proc/net/bonding/bond0')
```

8. Finally, let's look at the switch1 table; there should be a new entry within the group table with `type=select`:

```
mininet@mininet-vm:~$ sudo ovs-ofctl -O Openflow13 dump-groups
s1
OFPST_GROUP_DESC reply (OF1.3) (xid=0x2):
group_id=41238,type=select,bucket=weight:0,actions=output:1,buc
ket=weight:0,actions=output:2
group_id=48742,type=all,bucket=weight:0,actions=drop
```

Let's focus on the first entry: the flow type is select, which means that the packets are processed by a single bucket in the group as well as have two buckets assigned with the same weight. Each bucket represents a given port on the switch, port 1 (`s1-eth1`) and 2 (`s1-eth2`) respectively, in this example.

9. To apply link aggregation group on switches, flows should define the `group_id` of the established group table entry, which in our case is `group_id=41238`. The flow presented here is for the ARP Ethernet frame (`dl_type = 0x0806`):

```
sudo ovs-ofctl -O Openflow13 add-flow s1
dl_type=0x0806,dl_src=SRC_MAC,dl_dst=DST_MAC,actions=group:6016
9
```

How it works...

It leverages the OpenFlowPlugin project providing the basic communication channel between OpenFlow capable switches and OpenDaylight. The LCAP project implements the Link Aggregation Control Protocol as a service in MD-SAL. Using the packet processing service, it will receive and process LACP packets. Based on a periodic state machine, it will define whether or not to maintain an aggregation.

Changing user authentication

OpenDaylight's security is, in part, provided by the AAA project, which implements mechanisms to bring:

- **Authentication**: Used to authenticate the users
- **Authorization**: Used to authorize access to resources for a given user
- **Accounting**: Used to record user's access to resources

By default, when you install any features, AAA authentication will be installed. It provides two users by default:

- User `admin` with password `admin`
- User `user` with password `user`

Getting ready

This recipe does not require anything more than OpenDaylight itself.

The sample code for this recipe is available at:

```
https://github.com/jgoodyear/OpenDaylightCookbook/tree/master/chapter1/chapter1
-recipe7
```

How to do it...

Perform the following steps:

1. Start your OpenDaylight distribution using the `karaf` script. Using this script will give you access to the Karaf CLI:

   $ ./bin/karaf

2. Install the user-facing feature, responsible for pulling in all dependencies needed to enable user authentication:

   opendaylight-user@root>feature:install odl-aaa-authn

   It might take a few minutes to complete the installation.

3. To retrieve the list of existing users, send the following request:

- Type: GET
- Headers:

   Authorization: Basic YWRtaW46YWRtaW4=

- URL: http://localhost:8181/auth/v1/users

```
{
  "users": [
    {
      "userid": "admin@sdn",
      "name": "admin",
      "description": "admin user",
      "enabled": true,
      "email": "",
      "password": "**********",
      "salt": "**********",
      "domainid": "sdn"
    },
    {
      "userid": "user@sdn",
      "name": "user",
      "description": "user user",
      "enabled": true,
      "email": "",
      "password": "**********",
      "salt": "**********",
      "domainid": "sdn"
```

```
            }
        ]
    }
```

4. Update the configuration of a user.

   First, you need the `userid` that can be retrieved using the previous request. For this tutorial, we will use `userid=user@sdn`.

   To update the password for this user, do the following request:

   - Type: `PUT`
   - Headers:

     Authorization: Basic `YWRtaW46YWRtaW4=`

     This is the basic `admin/admin` authorization. We will not modify this one.

   - Payload:

     ```
     {
        "userid": "user@sdn",
        "name": "user",
        "description": "user user",
        "enabled": true,
        "email": "",
        "password": "newpassword",
        "domainid": "sdn"
     }
     ```

   - URL: `http://localhost:8181/auth/v1/users/user@sdn`

   Once sent, you will receive the acknowledged payload.

5. Try your new user's password. Open your browser and go here `http://localhost:8181/auth/v1/users`, you should be asked for credentials. Use:
   - **Username**: `user`
   - **Password**: `newpassword`

   You should now be logged in with the new, updated password for the user.

How it works...

The AAA project supports **role-based access control** (**RBAC**) based on the Apache Shiro permissions system. It defines a REST application used to interact with the h2 database. Each table has its own REST endpoint that can be used using a REST client to modify the h2 database content, such as the user information.

OpenDaylight clustering

The objective of OpenDaylight clustering is to have a set of nodes providing a fault-tolerant, decentralized, peer-to-peer membership with no single point of failure. From a networking perspective, clustering is when you have a group of compute nodes working together to achieve a common function or objective.

Getting ready

This recipe will require three distinct VMs that will be spawned using Vagrant 1.7.4 `https://www.vagrantup.com/downloads.html`.

The Vagranfile for the VM is available at `https://github.com/adetalhouet/cluster-nodes`.

How to do it...

Perform the following steps:

1. Create three VMs.

   The mentioned repository in the *Getting ready* section is providing a Vagrantfile spawning VMs with the following network characteristics:

   * Adapter 1: `NAT`
   * Adapter 2: Bridge `en0: Wi-Fi` (AirPort)
   * Static IP address: `192.168.50.15X` (X being the number of the node)
   * Adapter type: `paravirtualized`

These are the steps to follow:

```
$ git clone https://github.com/adetalhouet/cluster-nodes.git
$ cd cluster-nodes
$ export NUM_OF_NODES=3
$ vagrant up
```

After a few minutes, to make sure the VMs are correctly running, execute the following command in the cluster-nodes folder:

```
$ vagrant status
Current machine states:
node-1                          running (virtualbox)
node-2                          running (virtualbox)
node-3                          running (virtualbox)
```

This environment represents multiple VMs. The VMs are all listed preceding with their current state. For more information about a specific VM, run `vagrant status NAME`.

The credentials of the VMs are:

- **User**: `vagrant`
- **Password**: `vagrant`

We now have three VMs available at those IP addresses:

- `192.168.50.151`
- `192.168.50.152`
- `192.168.50.153`

2. Prepare the cluster deployment.

In order to deploy the cluster, we will use the cluster-deployer script provided by OpenDaylight:

```
$ git clone
https://git.opendaylight.org/gerrit/integration/test.git
$ cd test/tools/clustering/cluster-deployer/
```

You will need the following information:

- Your VMs/containers IP addresses:

`192.168.50.151, 192.168.50.152, 192.168.50.153`

- Their credentials (must be the same for all the VMs/containers):

`vagrant/vagrant`

- The path to the distribution to deploy:

`$ODL_ROOT`

- The cluster's configuration files located under the `templates/multi-node-test` repository:

```
$ cd templates/multi-node-test/
$ ls -1
akka.conf.template
jolokia.xml.template
module-shards.conf.template
modules.conf.template
org.apache.karaf.features.cfg.template
org.apache.karaf.management.cfg.template
```

3. Deploy the cluster.

   We are currently located in the `cluster-deployer` folder:

   ```
   $ pwd
   test/tools/clustering/cluster-deployer
   ```

   We need to create a `temp` folder, so the deployment script can put some temporary files in there:

   ```
   $ mkdir temp
   ```

   Your tree architecture should look like this:

   ```
   $ tree
   .
   ├── cluster-nodes
   ├── distribution-karaf-0.4.0-Beryllium.zip
   └── test
       └── tools
           └── clustering
   ```

```
└── cluster-deployer
    ├── deploy.py
    ├── kill_controller.sh
    ├── remote_host.py
    ├── remote_host.pyc
    ├── restart.py
    ├── temp
    └── templates
        └── multi-node-test
```

Now let's deploy the cluster using this command:

```
$ python deploy.py --clean --
distribution=../../../../distribution-karaf-0.4.0-Beryllium.zip
--rootdir=/home/vagrant --
hosts=192.168.50.151,192.168.50.152,192.168.50.153 --
user=vagrant --password=vagrant --template=multi-node-test
```

If the process went fine, you should see similar logs while deploying:

```
https://github.com/jgoodyear/OpenDaylightCookbook/tree/master/chapte
r1/chapter1-recipe8
```

4. Verify the deployment.

Let's use Jolokia to read the cluster's nodes data store:

Let's request on node 1, located under 192.168.50.151, its config data store for the network-topology shard:

- Type: GET
- Headers:

    Authorization: Basic YWRtaW46YWRtaW4=

- URL:
  ```
  http://192.168.50.151:8181/jolokia/read/org.opendaylight.contro
  ller:Category=Shards,name=member-1-shard-topology-
  config,type=DistributedConfigDatastore
  ```

    ```
    {
        "request": {
            "mbean":
    "org.opendaylight.controller:Category=Shards,name=member-1-
    shard-topology-config,type=DistributedConfigDatastore",
            "type": "read"
        },
    ```

```
        "status": 200,
        "timestamp": 1462739174,
        "value": {
            --[cut]--
            "FollowerInfo": [
                {
                    "active": true,
                    "id": "member-2-shard-topology-config",
                    "matchIndex": -1,
                    "nextIndex": 0,
                    "timeSinceLastActivity": "00:00:00.066"
                },
                {
                    "active": true,
                    "id": "member-3-shard-topology-config",
                    "matchIndex": -1,
                    "nextIndex": 0,
                    "timeSinceLastActivity": "00:00:00.067"
                }
            ],
            --[cut]--
            "Leader": "member-1-shard-topology-config",
            "PeerAddresses": "member-2-shard-topology-config:
akka.tcp://opendaylight-cluster-
data@192.168.50.152:2550/user/shardmanager-config/member-2-
shard-topology-config, member-3-shard-topology-config:
akka.tcp://opendaylight-cluster-
data@192.168.50.153:2550/user/shardmanager-config/member-3-
shard-topology-config",
            "RaftState": "Leader",
            --[cut]--
            "ShardName": "member-1-shard-topology-config",
            "VotedFor": "member-1-shard-topology-config",
            --[cut]--
    }
```

The result presents a lot of interesting information such as the leader of the requested shard, which can be seen under `Leader`. We can also see the current state (under `active`) of followers for this particular shard, represented by its `id`. Finally, it provides the addresses of the peers. Addresses can be found in the AKKA domain, as AKKA is the tool used to enable a node's wiring within the cluster.

By requesting the same shard on another peer, you would see similar information. For instance, for node 2 located under `192.168.50.152`:

- Type: `GET`
- Headers:

  Authorization: Basic `YWRtaW46YWRtaW4=`

- URL:
  `http://192.168.50.152:8181/jolokia/read/org.opendaylight.contro`
  `ller:Category=Shards,name=member-2-shard-topology-`
  `config,type=DistributedConfigDatastore`

 Make sure to update the digit after `member-` in the shard name, as this should match the node you're requesting for:

```
{
    "request": {
        "mbean":
"org.opendaylight.controller:Category=Shards,name=member-2-
shard-topology-config,type=DistributedConfigDatastore",
        "type": "read"
    },
    "status": 200,
    "timestamp": 1462739791,
    "value": {
        --[cut]--
        "Leader": "member-1-shard-topology-config",
        "PeerAddresses": "member-1-shard-topology-config:
akka.tcp://opendaylight-cluster-
data@192.168.50.151:2550/user/shardmanager-config/member-1-
shard-topology-config, member-3-shard-topology-config:
akka.tcp://opendaylight-cluster-
data@192.168.50.153:2550/user/shardmanager-config/member-3-
shard-topology-config",
        "RaftState": "Follower",
        --[cut]--
        "ShardName": "member-2-shard-topology-config",
        "VotedFor": "member-1-shard-topology-config",
        --[cut]--
    }
}
```

We can see the peers for this shard as well as that this node is voted node 1 - to be elected the shard leader.

How it works...

OpenDaylight clustering heavily relies on AKKA technology to provide the building blocks for the clustering components, especially for operations on remote shards. The main reason for using AKKA is because it suits the existing design of MD-SAL, as it is already based on the actor model.

OpenDaylight clustering components include:

- `ClusteringConfiguration`: The `ClusteringConfiguration` defines information about the members of the cluster, and what data they contain.
- `ClusteringService`: The `ClusteringService` reads the cluster configuration, resolves the member's name to its IP address/hostname and maintains the registration of the components that are interested in being notified of member status changes.
- `DistributedDataStore`: The `DistributedDataStore` is responsible for the implementation of the DOMStore, which replaces the `InMemoryDataStore`. It creates the local shard actors in accordance with the cluster configuration and creates the listener wrapper actors when a consumer registers a listener.
- `Shard`: `Shard` is a processor that contains some of the data in the system. A `shard` is an actor, communicating via messages. Those are very similar to the operations on the DOMStore interface. When a shard receives a message, it will log the event in a journal, which could then be used as a method to recover the state of the data store. This one would be maintained in an `InMemoryDataStore` object.

See also

- The AKKA clustering framework
- `http://doc.akka.io/docs/akka/snapshot/common/cluster.html`

2
Virtual Customer Edge

In this chapter, we will cover the following recipes:

- Leveraging UNI manager for E2E WAN links
- Linking multiple networks across MPLS VPN
- Using USC secure channels to work with devices
- Using machine-to-machine protocol for Internet of Things
- Controlling the cable modem termination system

Introduction

Virtual Customer Edge is the capability of connecting network entity endpoints to each other and integrating them within the network by allowing some access policy rules. It is also to virtualize those endpoints and/or to bring the functionality closer to the core of a platform. By using **virtual customer premises equipment** (**vCPE**), one can dynamically add and/or run new services as needed at the edge.

 REST API access is using user: `admin`, and password: `admin`.

Leveraging UNI manager for E2E WAN links

The UNI manager project enables the configuration and the provisioning of connectivity services for both physical and virtual elements, particularly carrier Ethernet services, as defined by the **Metro Ethernet Forum** (**MEF**). It supports the creation of links between two virtual switches by creating a **Generic Routing Encapsulation** (**GRE**) tunnel between the two endpoints.

Getting ready

This recipe requires two virtual switches. If you don't have any, you can use a Mininet-VM with OvS installed. You can download Mininet-VM from `https://github.com/mininet/mininet/wiki/Mininet-VM-Images`. Any version should work.

The following recipe uses a Mininet-VM with OvS 2.3.1 and a Mininet-VM with OvS 2.4.0.

How to do it...

Perform the following steps:

1. Start the OpenDaylight distribution using the `karaf` script. Using this script will give you access to the Karaf CLI:

   ```
   $ ./bin/karaf
   ```

2. Install the user-facing feature responsible for pulling in all dependencies needed to connect an OpenFlow switch:

   ```
   opendaylight-user@root>feature:install odl-unimgr-ui
   ```

   It might take a minute or so to complete the installation.

3. Connect the OvS instance to OpenDaylight in either passive or active mode:

   - Log in to Mininet-VM using these credentials:
       - **Username**: `mininet`
       - **Password**: `mininet`

- Connect both OvS using active mode:

  ```
  $ sudo ovs-vsctl set-manager tcp:${CONTROLLER_IP}:6640
  ```

  Here, `${CONTROLLER_IP}` is the IP address of the host running OpenDaylight.

- Our virtual switch is now connected to OpenDaylight:

  ```
  mininet@mininet-vm:~$ sudo ovs-vsctl show
  0b8ed0aa-67ac-4405-af13-70249a7e8a96
      Manager "tcp:192.168.0.115:6640"
          is_connected: true
      ovs_version: "2.4.0"
  ```

4. Create the first **User Network Interface** (**UNI**):

   You will need the device's IP address and MAC address. To get those from the Mininet-VM, you can use the `ifconfig` command.

   The UNI creation is a REST call made against the controller; make sure to replace `${DEVICE_IP}` and `${DEVICE_IP}` with the appropriate information. The request has the following configuration:

- Type: `PUT`
- Headers:

   Authorization: Basic `YWRtaW46YWRtaW4=`

- URL:
  `http://localhost:8181/restconf/config/network-topology:network-topology/topology/unimgr:uni/node/uni:%2F%2F${DEVICE_IP}`
- Payload:

  ```json
  {
    "network-topology:node": [
    {
      "node-id": "uni://${DEVICE_IP}",
      "speed":
      {
        "speed-10M": 1
      },
      "uni:mac-layer": "IEEE 802.3-2005",
      "uni:physical-medium": "UNI TypeFull Duplex 2 Physical
      Interface",
      "uni:mtu-size": 0,
      "uni:type": "",
  ```

```
        "uni:mac-address": "${DEVICE_MAC_ADDRESS}",
        "uni:ip-address": "${DEVICE_IP}",
        "uni:mode": "Full Duplex"
      }
    ]
  }
```

You should expect the status code **200 OK**.

5. Repeat the same operation in the previous step for the second device.

    This UNI creation will result in having a create `ovsbr0` bridge on the virtual switch, of the type internal.

6. Create the **Ethernet Virtual Connection (EVC)**:

    As of now, the EVC creation is layer 3-based, thus you will need IP addresses of the two endpoints of the link (the two UNIs created in the previous step).

    You will have to define an `${EVC_ID}` as an integer. Make sure to replace `${DEVICE_1_IP}` and `${DEVICE_1_IP}` with the appropriate information.

    The request to create the EVC is as follows:

    - Type: `PUT`
    - Headers:

        Authorization: Basic `YWRtaW46YWRtaW4=`

    - URL:
      `http://localhost:8181/restconf/config/network-topology:network-topology/topology/unimgr:evc/link/evc:%2F%2F${EVC_ID}`
    - Payload:

```
{
  "link":[
    {
      "link-id":"evc://${EVC_ID}",
      "source":{
        "source-node":"/network
        -topology/topology/node/uni://${DEVICE_1_IP}"
      },
      "destination":{
        "dest-node":"/network
        -topology/topology/node/uni://${DEVICE_2_IP}"
      },
```

```json
      "cl-unimgr-mef:uni-source":[
          {
            "order":"0",
            "ip-address":"${DEVICE_1_IP}"
          }
      ],
      "cl-unimgr-mef:uni-dest":[
          {
            "order":"0",
            "ip-address":"${DEVICE_2_IP}"
          }
      ],
      "cl-unimgr-mef:cos-id":"string",
      "cl-unimgr-mef:ingress-bw":{
        "speed-10G":{
        }
      },
      "cl-unimgr-mef:egress-bw":{
        "speed-10G":{
          }
        }
      }
    ]
  }
```

You should expect the status code **200 OK**.

7. Let's look at the resulting topology on our switches:

- First device:

```
mininet@mininet-vm:~$ sudo ovs-vsctl show
1077578e-f495-46a1-a96b-441223e7cc22
    Manager "tcp:192.168.0.115:6640"
        is_connected: true
    Bridge "ovsbr0"
        Port "eth1"
            Interface "eth1"
        Port "gre1"
            Interface "gre1"
                type: gre
                options: {remote_ip="192.168.0.118"}
        Port "ovsbr0"
            Interface "ovsbr0"
                type: internal
    ovs_version: "2.3.1"
```

- Second device:

```
mininet@mininet-vm:~$ sudo ovs-vsctl show
0b8ed0aa-67ac-4405-af13-70249a7e8a96
    Manager "tcp:192.168.0.115:6640"
        is_connected: true
    Bridge "ovsbr0"
        Port "ovsbr0"
            Interface "ovsbr0"
                type: internal
        Port "eth1"
            Interface "eth1"
        Port "gre1"
            Interface "gre1"
                type: gre
                options: {remote_ip="192.168.0.117"}
    ovs_version: "2.4.0"
```

Under the `ovsbr0` bridge that was created, we can see the `gre1` port being the endpoint of the created GRE tunnel, with the `remote_ip` specified.

The `eth1` port is intended to be the device port.

8. Test the created end-to-end link.

Pick the Mininet-VM you want and ping the other one.

How it works...

UNI manager is leveraging the OVSDB project that uses the OpenFlowPlugin project to enable communication with OpenFlow-based switches. OVSDB provides the **Open VSwitch (OvS)** Database that lets you create ports, interface, and configure quality of service. Once the `odl-unimgr-ui` feature is installed, a listener will listen for connections on port `6640`. When a connection comes in, it will create the communication pipeline using the `OpenFlowJava` library and initialize the OvS database. Creating a UNI results in the association of an OVSDB node with the UNI definition. It creates a bridge and an internal port for internal communication. Then, when creating an EVC, it will create two new ports under the previously created bridge, one for tunneling (using GRE) and one to connect a device.

Linking multiple networks across MPLS VPN

To complete this recipe, we will be using the Network Intent Composition and VpnService projects.

The scope of the usecase is to enable a MPLS VPN connection across customer sites in a single MPLS domain. Within the domain, MPLS Label is used to isolate traffic between the sites.

The **Provider Edge routers** (**PE**) and the **Provider routers** (**P**) are managed by OpenDaylight.

In order to create end-to-end VPN connectivity across customer sites, OpenDaylight shall provision MPLS intents to respective PEs and Ps that form the shortest route between the two sites.

Additionally, by adding constraint attributes to intents for protection and failover mechanisms, we can ensure end-to-end connectivity between endpoints to reduce the risk of connectivity failure due to a single link or port down event on a forwarding device:

- **Protection constraint**: This requires end-to-end connectivity to be protected by providing redundant paths

- **Failover constraint**: This specifies the type of failover implementation
  - `slow-reroute`: Uses disjoint path calculation algorithms such as Suurballe to provide alternative end-to-end routes
  - `fast-reroute`: Uses failure detection features in hardware forwarding devices through OF group table features (future work)

When no constraint is requested by the user, we default to offering end-to-end routes using the Dijkstra shortest path.

Getting ready

This recipe requires one virtual switch. If you don't have any, you can use a Mininet-VM with OvS installed. You can download Mininet-VM from `https://github.com/mininet/mininet/wiki/Mininet-VM-Images`. Any version should work.

The following recipe will be presented using a Mininet-VM with OvS 2.3.1.

How to do it...

Perform the following steps:

1. Start your OpenDaylight distribution using the `karaf` script. Using this client will give you access to the Karaf CLI:

   ```
   $ ./bin/karaf
   ```

2. Install the user facing feature responsible for pulling in all dependencies needed to use the YANG UI:

   ```
   opendaylight-user@root>feature:install odl-vpnservice-intent
   ```

   It might take a minute or so to complete the installation.

3. Create the topology in the Mininet-VM:

   - Log in to Mininet-VM using these credentials:
     - **Username**: mininet
     - **Password**: mininet
   - Create the custom topology.

   The topology's script resides at the following location:

   ```
   $ wget -O shortest_path.py
   https://gist.githubusercontent.com/adetalhouet/shortest_path.py
   $ sudo mn --controller=remote,ip=${CONTROLLER_IP} --custom
   ~/shortest_path.py --topo shortest_path --switch
   ovsk,protocols=OpenFlow13
   ```

   Here, `${CONTROLLER_IP}` is the IP address of the host running OpenDaylight.

   The topology looks like the following diagram, where **openflow:1** and **openflow:3** are the PE switches and openflow: 42/43/44 are the P switches. There are two disjoint routes between the PE switches:

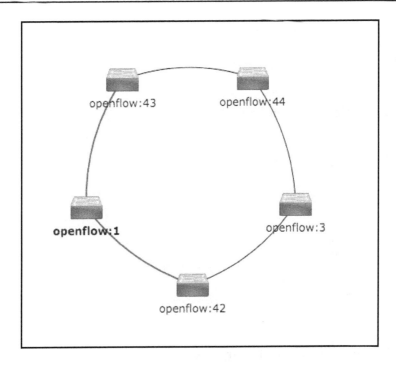

4. Create a VPN with the desired constraints (`slow-reroute` or `fast-reroute`). We will use `slow-reroute` in this example:

- Type: `POST`
- Headers:

     Authorization: Basic `YWRtaW46YWRtaW4=`

- URL: `http://localhost:8181/restconf/operations/vpnintent:vpns/`
- Payload:

```
{
  "vpn-intents": [
  {
  "vpn-name": "VPN #1"
  "path-protection": "true",
  "failover-type": "slow-reroute"
  }
]
}
```

5. Add the first member to our VPN:

- Type: POST
- Headers:

Authorization: Basic YWRtaW46YWRtaW4=

- URL:
`http://localhost:8181/restconf/operations/vpnintent:add-vpn-endpoint`
- Payload:

```json
{
  "input": {
  "vpn-name": "VPN #1",
  "site-name": "site1",
  "ip-prefix": "10.0.0.1/32",
  "switch-port-id": "openflow:1:1"
  }
}
```

6. Add the second member to our VPN:

- Type: POST
- Headers:

Authorization: Basic YWRtaW46YWRtaW4=

- URL:
`http://localhost:8181/restconf/operations/vpnintent:add-vpn-endpoint`
- Payload:

```json
{
  "input": {
  "vpn-name": "VPN #1",
  "site-name": "site2",
  "ip-prefix": "10.0.0.3/32",
  "switch-port-id": "openflow:3:1"
  }
}
```

7. Look at the current configuration in the OpenDaylight datastore:

- Type: `GET`
- Headers:

    Authorization: Basic `YWRtaW46YWRtaW4=`

- URL: `http://localhost:8181/restconf/config/vpnintent:vpns/`

    Result:

    ```
    <vpns xmlns="urn:opendaylight:params:xml:ns:yang:vpnintent">
        <vpn-intents>
            <vpn-name>VPN #1</vpn-name>
            <failover-type>fast-reroute</failover-type>
            <path-protection>true</path-protection>
            <endpoint>
                <site-name>site1</site-name>
                <ip-prefix>10.0.0.1/32</ip-prefix>
                <switch-port-id>openflow:1:1</switch-port-id>
            </endpoint>
            <endpoint>
                <site-name>site3</site-name>
                <ip-prefix>10.0.0.3/32</ip-prefix>
                <switch-port-id>openflow:3:1</switch-port-id>
            </endpoint>
        </vpn-intents>
    </vpns>
    ```

8. Look at the flows installed in the OvS instance:

    ```
    mininet@mininet-vm:~$ sudo ovs-ofctl -O OpenFlow13 dump-flows
    s1
    OFPST_FLOW reply (OF1.3) (xid=0x2):cookie=0x2,
    duration=96.839s, table=0, n_packets=0, n_bytes=0,
    priority=10000,arp actions=CONTROLLER:65535,NORMAL cookie=0x2,
    duration=96.827s, table=0, n_packets=20, n_bytes=1700,
    priority=9500,dl_type=0x88cc actions=CONTROLLER:65535
    cookie=0x0, duration=7.739s, table=0, n_packets=0, n_bytes=0,
    priority=9000,ip,nw_src=10.0.0.1,nw_dst=10.0.0.3
    actions=push_mpls:0x8847,set_field:494630->mpls_label,output:2
    cookie=0x0, duration=7.724s, table=0, n_packets=0, n_bytes=0,
    priority=9000,mpls,mpls_label=337082,mpls_bos=1
    actions=pop_mpls:0x0800,output:1

    mininet@mininet-vm:~$ sudo ovs-ofctl -O OpenFlow13 dump-flows
    s2a
    ```

```
OFPST_FLOW reply (OF1.3) (xid=0x2):cookie=0x3,
duration=95.968s, table=0, n_packets=0, n_bytes=0,
priority=10000,arp actions=CONTROLLER:65535,NORMAL cookie=0x3,
duration=89.545s, table=0, n_packets=37, n_bytes=3145,
priority=9500,dl_type=0x88cc actions=CONTROLLER:65535
cookie=0x0, duration=7.747s, table=0, n_packets=0, n_bytes=0,
priority=9000,mpls,mpls_label=494630,mpls_bos=1
actions=output:3 cookie=0x0, duration=7.736s, table=0,
n_packets=0, n_bytes=0,
priority=9000,mpls,mpls_label=337082,mpls_bos=1
actions=output:2

mininet@mininet-vm:~$ sudo ovs-ofctl -O OpenFlow13 dump-flows
s3
OFPST_FLOW reply (OF1.3) (xid=0x2): cookie=0x1,
duration=97.781s, table=0, n_packets=0, n_bytes=0,
priority=10000,arp actions=CONTROLLER:65535,NORMAL cookie=0x1,
duration=97.778s, table=0, n_packets=20, n_bytes=1700,
priority=9500,dl_type=0x88cc actions=CONTROLLER:65535
cookie=0x0, duration=7.747s, table=0, n_packets=0, n_bytes=0,
priority=9000,mpls,mpls_label=494630,mpls_bos=1
actions=pop_mpls:0x0800,output:1 cookie=0x0, duration=7.746s,
table=0, n_packets=0, n_bytes=0,
priority=9000,ip,nw_src=10.0.0.3,nw_dst=10.0.0.1
actions=push_mpls:0x8847,set_field:337082->mpls_label,output:2
```

The shortest path, s1-s2a-s3, is chosen.

9. Let's test path failover by removing switch `s2a`:

```
mininet@mininet-vm:~$  sudo ovs-vsctl del-br s2a
```

```
mininet@mininet-vm:~$ sudo ovs-ofctl -O OpenFlow13 dump-flows
s1
OFPST_FLOW reply (OF1.3) (xid=0x2):cookie=0x2,
duration=96.839s, table=0, n_packets=0, n_bytes=0,
priority=10000,arp actions=CONTROLLER:65535,NORMAL cookie=0x2,
duration=96.827s, table=0, n_packets=20, n_bytes=1700,
priority=9500,dl_type=0x88cc actions=CONTROLLER:65535
cookie=0x0, duration=7.739s, table=0, n_packets=0, n_bytes=0,
priority=9000,ip,nw_src=10.0.0.1,nw_dst=10.0.0.3
actions=push_mpls:0x8847,set_field:494630->mpls_label,output:2
cookie=0x0, duration=7.724s, table=0, n_packets=0, n_bytes=0,
priority=9000,mpls,mpls_label=337082,mpls_bos=1
```

```
actions=pop_mpls:0x0800,output:1

mininet@mininet-vm:~$ sudo ovs-ofctl -O OpenFlow13 dump-flows
s2a
ovs-ofctl: s2a is not a bridge or a socket

mininet@mininet-vm:~$ sudo ovs-ofctl -O OpenFlow13 dump-flows
s2b
OFPST_FLOW reply (OF1.3) (xid=0x2):cookie=0x3,
duration=95.968s, table=0, n_packets=0, n_bytes=0,
priority=10000,arp actions=CONTROLLER:65535,NORMAL cookie=0x3,
duration=89.545s, table=0, n_packets=37, n_bytes=3145,
priority=9500,dl_type=0x88cc actions=CONTROLLER:65535
cookie=0x0, duration=7.747s, table=0, n_packets=0, n_bytes=0,
priority=9000,mpls,mpls_label=494630,mpls_bos=1
actions=output:3 cookie=0x0, duration=7.736s, table=0,
n_packets=0, n_bytes=0,
priority=9000,mpls,mpls_label=337082,mpls_bos=1
actions=output:2

mininet@mininet-vm:~$ sudo ovs-ofctl -O OpenFlow13 dump-flows
s2c
OFPST_FLOW reply (OF1.3) (xid=0x2):cookie=0x3,
duration=95.968s, table=0, n_packets=0, n_bytes=0,
priority=10000,arp actions=CONTROLLER:65535,NORMAL cookie=0x3,
duration=89.545s, table=0, n_packets=37, n_bytes=3145,
priority=9500,dl_type=0x88cc actions=CONTROLLER:65535
cookie=0x0, duration=7.747s, table=0, n_packets=0, n_bytes=0,
priority=9000,mpls,mpls_label=494630,mpls_bos=1
actions=output:3 cookie=0x0, duration=7.736s, table=0,
n_packets=0, n_bytes=0,
priority=9000,mpls,mpls_label=337082,mpls_bos=1
actions=output:2

mininet@mininet-vm:~$ sudo ovs-ofctl -O OpenFlow13 dump-flows
s3
OFPST_FLOW reply (OF1.3) (xid=0x2): cookie=0x1,
duration=97.781s, table=0, n_packets=0, n_bytes=0,
priority=10000,arp actions=CONTROLLER:65535,NORMAL cookie=0x1,
duration=97.778s, table=0, n_packets=20, n_bytes=1700,
priority=9500,dl_type=0x88cc actions=CONTROLLER:65535
cookie=0x0, duration=7.747s, table=0, n_packets=0, n_bytes=0,
priority=9000,mpls,mpls_label=494630,mpls_bos=1
actions=pop_mpls:0x0800,output:1 cookie=0x0, duration=7.746s,
table=0, n_packets=0, n_bytes=0,
priority=9000,ip,nw_src=10.0.0.3,nw_dst=10.0.0.1
actions=push_mpls:0x8847,set_field:337082->mpls_label,output:2
```

The forward flows are now pushed to switches s2b and s2c.

How it works...

The VPN service project is used to provide a REST layer to create VPNs, perform MPLS label management, and to maintain the overall MPLS VPN state information.

VPN rules themselves will be realized via intents by requesting the proper isolation between the endpoint types using MPLS-capable intents. Thus, the VPN service has a project dependency on **Network Intent Composition** (**NIC**).

NIC is used to manage new MPLS-based endpoints that will have the required level of information required to establish the connectivity between the CE equipment when creating a VPN with a MPLS intent.

The endpoints will have to have the required MPLS information, but via the endpoint type's information and will map to the label.

Using USC secure channels to work with devices

The **unified secure channel** (**USC**) is an OpenDaylight project geared to enable secured and performant communication channels between the SDN controller and network elements within wide area networks. Lately, we have seen a growth in the type of elements being part of an enterprise network, cloud infrastructure, IoT devices, and network devices (NETCONF, OpenFlow, and so on). USC provides centralized management of communication channels, allowing the establishment and removal of those pipelines. Finally, it provides statistics regarding the written and read bytes through a given channel.

The project architecture contains the USC plugin responsible for the communication between the controller and the network elements, supporting the TLS and DTLS protocols. It also maintains the live connections through inbound and outbound channels. The USC manager provides high availability, clustering, security, and monitoring of the channel itself. The USC UI allows you to visualize the current, established channels along with some information, and the USC agent, supposed to run in the network elements, is a proxy used to maintain the live connection by allowing inbound and outbound channels to communicate with the controller.

Getting ready

This recipe requires the USC agent and a VM on which we will run the USC agent. Also, in order to showcase USC functionality, we will use the echo server that will respond to the messages sent to the USC agent.

The USC project and the USC agent share certificates in order to provide a secure location. Those certificates will be loaded under `${ODL_ROOT}/etc/usc/certificates`. Present certificates are the certificate authority, the private key, and the client certificate.

The USC agent, the echo server, and the certificates can be found here:

```
https://github.com/jgoodyear/OpenDaylightCookbook/tree/master/chapter3/chapter3
-recipe4
```

How to do it...

Perform the following steps:

1. Start the OpenDaylight Karaf distribution using the `karaf` script. Using this script will give you access to the Karaf CLI:

   ```
   $ ./bin/karaf
   ```

2. Install the user facing feature responsible for pulling in all dependencies needed to connect an NETCONF device:

   ```
   opendaylight-user@root>feature:install odl-usc-channel-ui
   ```

   It might take a minute or so to complete the installation.

3. Start the USC agent and the echo server using a TCP session.

   Open two terminal windows accessing this VM, then start the USC agent:

   ```
   $ java -jar UscAgent.jar -t true
   ```

   Start the echo server:

   ```
   $ java -jar EchoServer.jar -t true -p 2007
   ```

4. Create the channel using the following request. You will need the IP address of your VM, ${VM_IP_ADDRESS}:

- Type: POST
- Headers:

     Authorization: Basic YWRtaW46YWRtaW4=

- URL:
  ```
  http://localhost:8181/restconf/operations/usc-channel:add-channel
  ```
- Payload:

   ```
   {
     "input":{
        "channel":{
          "hostname":"${VM_IP_ADDRESS}",
          "port":2007,
          "remote":false,
          "tcp":true
        }
     }
   }
   ```

   If the request went fine, you will receive the following output:

   ```
   {
     "output": {
       "result": "Succeed to connect
   device(${VM_IP_ADDRESS}:2007)!"
     }
   }
   ```

5. View the created channel using either a REST call, or using the OpenDaylight DLUX component:

   1. **REST CALL**: All the information written by the USC plugin is located under the usc topology, so we're reading the content contained in this topology:

- Type: POST
- Headers:

    Authorization: Basic YWRtaW46YWRtaW4=

- URL: `http://localhost:8181/restconf/operations/usc-channel:view-channel`
- Payload:

```
{
    "input":{
        "topology-id":"usc"
    }
}
```

This will return, among other information, a payload containing channel information such as its ID, composed of the hostname running OpenDaylight (inocybe.local), the VM IP address (192.168.2.26), and the type of protocol used to established the session (TLS). It also contains data regarding the session; this is the first created session, and we have zero written or read bytes:

```
"channel": [
    {
        "channel-id": "Controller:inocybe.local
        -Device:192.168.2.26-type:TLS",
        "channel-type": "TLS",
--[cut]--
        "session": [
            {
                "session-id": "1",
                "bytes-in": 0,
                "bytes-out": 0,
                "termination-point": {
                    "termination-point-id": "2007"
                },
            }
        ],
        "destination": {
```

```
                "dest-node": "192.168.2.26"
            }
        --[cut]--
        }
    ]
```

2. Navigate to `http://localhost:8181/index.html`:

Log in using `admin/admin`. On the right, click the **USC** tab:

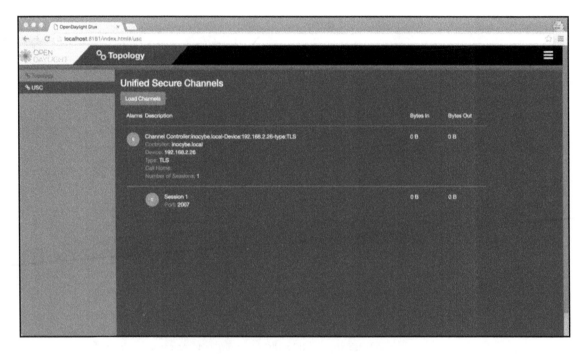

6. Send a message through the channel. For this you will require the IP address of the VM running the USC agent, the port behind which the echo server is running, whether or not you're using TCP, and the message content:

- Type: `POST`
- Headers:

Authorization: Basic `YWRtaW46YWRtaW4=`

- URL:
  `http://localhost:8181/restconf/operations/usc-channel:send-mess`
  `age`
- Payload:

```
{
   "input":{
       "channel":{
           "hostname":"192.168.2.26",
           "port":"2007",
           "tcp":"true",
           "content":"This is a test message."
       }
    }
}
```

This request should return a message saying it worked. The return message here is going to be similar to the one sent, as we're using an echo server. Using your own device, you could define the return statement, and you could react as desired when receiving the message:

```
{
   "output": {
       "result": "Succeed to send request to
device(192.168.2.26:2007),content is This is a test message."
    }
}
```

7. Look at the channel information again; we will now see the number of input and output bytes had increased. Use the same process as defined in step 5.

   Here is the output for current session 1 for the channel. You can see the number of bytes has increased. It shows the bytes per session and for the whole channel:

```
"channel": [
       {
           "channel-id": "Controller:inocybe.local
           -Device:192.168.2.26-type:TLS",
           "source": {
             "source-node": "inocybe.local"
           },
           "sessions": 1,
           "channel-type": "TLS",
           "call-home": "",
           "channel-alarms": 0,
           "session": [
             {
```

```
            "session-id": "1",
            "bytes-in": 23,
            "termination-point": {
              "termination-point-id": "2007"
            },
            "session-alarms": 0,
            "bytes-out": 23
          }
        ],
        "destination": {
          "dest-node": "192.168.2.26"
        },
        "bytes-in": 23,
        "bytes-out": 23
      }
    ]
```

8. Remove the `session`, cleaning up all the statistics:

- Type: POST
- Headers:

    Authorization: Basic YWRtaW46YWRtaW4=

- URL:
  http://localhost:8181/restconf/operations/usc-channel:remove-ch
  annel
- Payload:

```
{
  "input":{
      "channel":{
          "hostname":"192.168.2.26",
          "port":"2007",
          "tcp":"true"
      }
    }
}
```

This request will respond with a positive message saying the channel was successfully removed:

```
{
  "output": {
    "result": "Succeed to remove device(192.168.2.26:2007)!"
  }
}
```

You can send the request seen at point 5; you will see the channel is still present, but the session was removed.

How it works...

Using Netty, an asynchronous event-driven network application framework, to establish the channel pipeline when you create a channel, the USC plugin will first establish a session between the host and the remote device. Then it will create the inbound and outbound channel within the session to enable two-way communication. The creation of the session is done by using the certificates provided by OpenDaylight and the USC agent; they must be the same, or the connection will fail to establish.

In this example, we used an echo server that was acting as the callback for a sent message, sending its content back.

There's more...

You could create multiple sessions for the same channel. To do so, in step 3, open another terminal console for the VM and start the echo server a second time, but on a different port:

1. `$ java -jar EchoServer.jar -t true -p 2008`.
2. Create a channel specifying this port using step 4.
3. Send the request to see the channel. See the request sent at step 5.

The response will this time contain two sessions:

```
--[cut]--
            "session": [
              {
                "session-id": "2",
                "bytes-in": 0,
                "termination-point": {
                  "termination-point-id": "2008"
```

```
        },
        "session-alarms": 0,
        "bytes-out": 0
      },
      {
        "session-id": "1",
        "bytes-in": 0,
        "termination-point": {
          "termination-point-id": "2007"
        },
        "session-alarms": 0,
        "bytes-out": 0
      }
    ]
--[cut]--
```

You can have as many sessions as you wish per channel. This means you can have a number of devices running on the same host and you can connect to each one of them using the same secured channel.

Using machine-to-machine protocol for Internet of Things

The **IoT Data Management** (**IoTDM**) project implements a subset of oneM2M protocol. Its purpose is to provide a common machine-to-machine layer that can be embedded with various kinds of devices and software. It follows the latest oneM2M specifications as closely as possible, publicly available at the following website:

```
http://www.onem2m.org/technical/published-documents
```

The OpenDaylight IoTDM project offers data-centric middleware acting as a oneM2M broker. It also enables authorized applications to access and get data uploaded by any device. The reason behind the data-centric architecture is to provide a single version of a global data space for applications of interest, optimizing network traffic, and application processing along with the addition and/or removal of devices from the IoT domain.

The IoTDM project is capable of interacting with data producers such as sensors, IoT management systems, and data consumers. It supports **Constrained Application Protocol** (**CoAP**), **MQ Telemetry Transport** (**MQTT**), and HTTP southbound protocols. The project allows create, retrieve, update, delete, and notify operations on a given set of resources, such as CSEBase, AE, container, content instance, subscription, access control policy, and node. More resources will be supported as the project evolves.

Getting ready

This recipe requires OpenDaylight to program the IoTDM services, and a REST client. It is recommended to download and use Postman, `https://www.getpostman.com`, as it's a handy tool, letting you import collections of defined REST APIs along with their payload.

This is the Postman collection we will be using in this recipe:

`https://www.getpostman.com/collections/f2a7e723ee6da44715e9`

How to do it...

Perform the following steps:

1. Start your OpenDaylight distribution using the `karaf` script. Using this script will give you access to the Karaf CLI:

   $ ./bin/karaf

2. Install the user facing feature responsible for pulling in all dependencies needed to enable LACP functionalities:

   opendaylight-user@root>feature:install odl-iotdm-onem2m

   It might take a few minutes to complete the installation.

3. Start your PostMan client and import the collection linked earlier and then follow these steps:
   1. At the top of the Postman window, click **Import**.
   2. From the pop up, select **Import From Link**.
   3. Paste `https://www.getpostman.com/collections/f2a7e723ee6da44715e9`.

4. Click **Import**. You should see a message saying the collection was imported, and it will now be available from the sidebar:

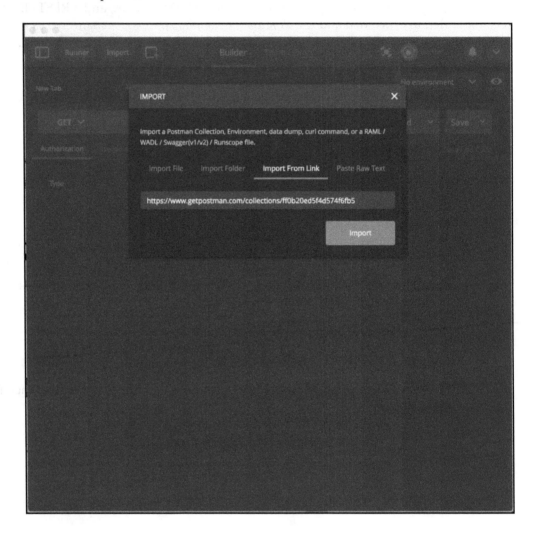

5. Click the top-right button, **Show/Hide** sidebar.
6. Click on the **Basic IOTDM CRUD Test** folder. You now have all the REST APIs to test the application:

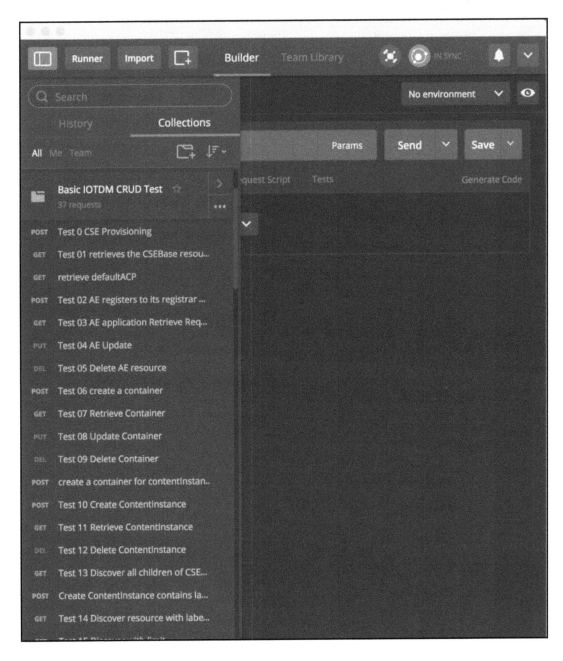

4. Provision a **Common Services Entity (CSE)** named InCSE1:

- Type: POST
- Headers:

  Authorization: Basic YWRtaW46YWRtaW4=

- URL: http:// localhost:8181/restconf/operations/onem2m:onem2m-cse-provisioning
- Payload:

```
{
    "input":{
      "onem2m-primitive":[
          {
            "name":"CSE_ID",
            "value":"InCSE1"
          },
          {
            "name":"CSE_TYPE",
            "value":"IN-CSE"
          }
      ]
    }
}
```

5. The **Application Entity (AE)** registers to its registrar CSE.

   X-M2M-Origin represents the composer of the request and X-M2M-RI is the Request Identifier parameter:

- Type: POST
- Headers:

  Content-Type: application/vnd.onem2m-res+json;ty=2

  X-M2M-Origin: Test_AE_ID

  X-M2M-RI: 12345

- URL: http:// localhost:8282/InCSE1

- Payload:

```
{
  "m2m:ae":{
      "api":"testAppId",          /*Application ID*/
      "apn":"testAppName",        /*Application name*/
      "rn":"TestAE",              /*Resource name*/
      "or":"http://ontology/ref", /*On topology reference*/
      "rr":true                   /*Request reachability*/
  }
}
```

6. The AE is requested to send a create request to create a container named `TestContainer`:

- Type: POST
- Headers:

  Content-Type: `application/vnd.onem2m-res+json;ty=3`

  X-M2M-Origin: `//iotsandbox.cisco.com:10000`

  X-M2M-RI: `12345`

- URL: `http://localhost:8282/InCSE1`
- Payload:

```
{
  "m2m:cnt":{
      "rn":"TestContainer"        /*Resource name*/
  }
}
```

7. Create a content instance named `Cin2` in `TestContainer`:

- Type: POST
- Headers:

  Content-Type: `application/vnd.onem2m-res+json;ty=4`

  X-M2M-Origin: `//iotsandbox.cisco.com:10000`

  X-M2M-RI: `12345`

- URL: `http://localhost:8282/InCSE1/TestContainer`
- Payload:

```
{
  "cin":{
      "con":"CCDS",                    /*Content/*
      "rn":"Cin1"                       /*Resource name*/
    }
}
```

8. Get all the children under the CSE `InCSE1` created in step 4:

- Type: `GET`
- Headers:

    Content-Type: `application/vnd.onem2m-res+json`

    X-M2M-Origin: `//iotsandbox.cisco.com:10000`

    X-M2M-RI: `12345`

- URL: `http://localhost:8282/InCSE1?fu=1`

This will retrieve all information about the CSE, and its enclosing children, the AE, the container, and the content instance. It also has default access control policies.

9. Get a given number of children located under CSE `InCSE1`:

- Type: `GET`
- Headers:

    Content-Type: `application/vnd.onem2m-res+json`

    X-M2M-Origin: `//iotsandbox.cisco.com:10000`

    X-M2M-RI: `12345`

- URL: `http://localhost:8282/InCSE1?fu=1&lim=2`

The limit in this request is set to 2. See the `lim` parameter in the URL. You can increase or decrease this number to retrieve the desired number of elements.

10. Create a subscription to get notified of changes happening in a given container located in the CSE `InCSE1`:

- Type: `POST`
- Headers:

  Content-Type: `application/vnd.onem2m-res+json;ty=23`

  X-M2M-Origin: `//iotsandbox.cisco.com:10000`

  X-M2M-RI: `12345`

- URL: `http://localhost:8282/InCSE1/TestContainer`

How it works...

The IoTDM project provides and implements RPCs, enabling the interaction with a subset of oneM2M resources. An RPC is a remote procedure call intended to be processed in a synchronized way and providing less latency than a REST call. For each RPC, its associated implementation corresponds to a callback that will define the expected behavior. The IoTDM project defines the oneM2M resources as models, thus providing a tree using the MD-SAL architecture provided by OpenDaylight. When a resource is modified, a notifier will issue a oneM2M notification to the subscribers. This process uses a publish-subscribe type of mechanism. Finally, the IoTDM project implements three southbound protocols, the **constrained application protocol (CoAP - RFC-7252)**, the MQTT, and the HTTP protocol, the one used in the recipe.

Controlling the cable modem termination system

OpenDaylight's **PacketCable Multimedia (PCMM)** project is an interface that lets you control and manage service flow for **cable modem termination system (CMTS)** network elements. The service flow enables a **dynamic quality of service (DQoS)** between a CMTS and a **cable modem (CM)** using the **Data Over Cable Service Interface Specification (DOCSIS)** standard. The project is composed of a policy server allocating network resources per subscriber and application, an application manager specifying QoS requirements per-application to the policy server, a CMTS enforcing the policies based on bandwidth capacity, and a CM connecting to the client's network (cable system).

Getting ready

This recipe will only require a CTMS device. If you don't have one, you can use the CMTS emulator provided by the PCCM project.

We will be using this emulator within this recipe. For those who don't need it, please go directly to step 4 given in the next section.

We previously introduced the Postman tool and Postman collection. For this recipe, we will also use a Postman collection, `https://www.getpostman.com/collections/e58cca444488dd90753b`, that provides all the required APIs. This collection requires a Postman environment, which can be fetched from `https://github.com/jgoodyear/OpenDaylightCookbook/blob/master/chapter3/chapter3 -recipe6/PCMM_Sample_Local.postman_environment`. A Postman environment lets you set up default values. Copy and paste the raw data into the import section. Then on the top-right, there is a drop-down box where you can select the environment. Choose the PCMM sample local. By clicking on the right button (the one that looks like an eye) you will see the content of that environment:

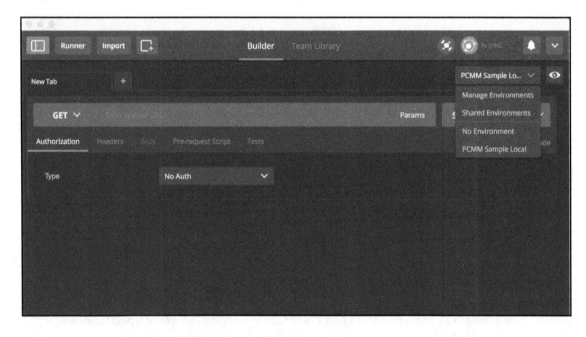

How to do it...

Perform the following steps:

1. Get the `packetcable-emulator` JAR here:
   `https://nexus.opendaylight.org/content/repositories/opendaylight.relea se/org/opendaylight/packetcable/packetcable-emulator/1.4.2-Boron-SR2/packetcable-emulator-1.4.2-Boron-SR2.jar`

   If you want to look into the source code and build the emulator yourself, use the following command to clone the source code repository and assemble the JAR:

   ```
   $ git clone --branch release/boron-sr2
   https://git.opendaylight.org/gerrit/packetcable
   $ cd packetcable/packetcable-emulator/
   $ mvn assembly:assembly
   ```

   In the target folder will be the JARs. The one of interest ends with `-jar-with-dependencies.jar`.

2. Create a configuration file in the YAML format containing the following values:

   - The CMTS communication port number:

     ```
     port: 3918
     ```

   - The maximum number of classifiers per gate this CMTS supports:

     ```
     numberOfSupportedClassifiers: 4
     ```

   - Configuration for the service class names:

     ```
     serviceClassNames:
       - direction: UPSTREAM
         names:
           - extrm_up
           - foo_up
       - direction: DOWNSTREAM
         names:
           - extrm_dn
           - foo_dn
     ```

- Cable modem information:

```
cmStatuses:
  - host: 10.32.110.180
    status: true
  - host: 10.32.110.179
    status: true
```

3. Start the emulator using the JAR and the configuration file as follows:

```
$ java -cp packetcable-emulator-1.4.2-Boron-SR2-jar-with-
dependencies.jar org.pcmm.rcd.impl.CMTS {path to yaml}
22:00:02.966 [main] INFO  org.pcmm.concurrent.IWorkerPool -
Pool size :32
22:00:02.984 [main] INFO  org.pcmm.rcd.impl.AbstractPCMMServer
- Server started and listening on port :3918
```

4. Start your OpenDaylight distribution using the `karaf` script. Using this script will give you access to the Karaf CLI:

```
$ ./bin/karaf
```

5. Install the user-facing feature responsible for pulling in all dependencies needed to enable user authentication:

```
opendaylight-user@root>feature:install odl-packetcable-policy-
server
```

It might take a few minutes to complete the installation.

6. Before setting any PCMM gates, we need to establish a persistent connection between OpenDaylight and a CTMS/**Converged Cable Access Platform (CCAP)** (add a `CCAP 1` request from the Postman collection).

We're going to connect to one of the simulated devices configured and started previously (you could use your own device here). The request will require the IP address and the port of the device, along with the downstream and upstream service class name.

 If you're using the emulator, you need to use the IP address of the host running it.

Finally, you will have to define the `${ID}` for the new entry in both the URL and the payload (the `${ID}` is a string):

- Type: `PUT`
- Headers:

    Authorization: Basic `YWRtaW46YWRtaW4=`

- URL:
  `http://localhost:8181/restconf/config/packetcable:ccaps/ccap/${ID}`
- Payload:

```
{
    "ccap": [{
        "ccapId": "${ID}",
        "amId": {
            "am-tag": "0xcada",
            "am-type": "1"
        },
        "connection": {
            "ipAddress": "10.32.110.180",
            "port": "3918"
        },
        "subscriber-subnets": [
            "10.32.110.1/24"
        ],
        "downstream-scns": [
            "extrm_dn"
        ],
        "upstream-scns": [
            "extrm_up"
        ]
    }]
}
```

If the connection to a CCAP succeeded, the HTTP request will return `200 OK`. You will see a lot of activity in the command line where you started the emulator. The first message is the new connection:

```
[pool-2-thread-1] INFO  org.pcmm.rcd.impl.AbstractPCMMServer -
Accepted a new connection from :192.168.2.11:49682
```

Once the connection is established, a keep-alive mechanism is in place to ensure the connection is still up.

7. Verify the status of the connection we just created (operational -Get All CCAPs).

For this request, we're going to use the operational datastore, providing operational data. It reflects current state of the device:

- Type: GET
- Headers:

  Authorization: Basic YWRtaW46YWRtaW4=

- URL:
  http://localhost:8181/restconf/operational/packetcable:ccaps/cc ap/${ID}

This request returns the connection information for the device with ${ID}=1. Our device is currently connected:

```
{
  "ccap": [
    {
      "ccapId": "1",
      "connection": {
        "connected": true
      }
    }
  ]
}
```

8. Let's create a gate now. To do so, we will submit the following request:

   Gate w/ classifier

   We will use the first cable modem defined in the configuration file for our gate. You will have to define three variables for this request: the ${APPLICATION_CLASSIFIER}, the ${SUBSCRIBER_ID} and the ${GATE_ID}:

   - Type: PUT
   - Headers:

     Authorization: Basic YWRtaW46YWRtaW4=

- URL:

```
http://localhost:8181//restconf/config/packetcable:qos/apps/app
/${APPLICATION_CLASSIFIER}/subscribers/subscriber/${SUBSCRIBER_
ID}/gates/gate/${GATE_ID}/
```

- Payload:

```
{
"gate":
  {
  "gateId": "${APPLICATION_CLASSIFIER}",
  "classifiers":
    {
    "classifier-container":
      [
      {
      "classifier-id": "1",
      "classifier":
        {
        "srcIp": "10.10.10.0",
        "dstIp": "10.32.110.178",
        "protocol": "0",
        "srcPort": "1234",
        "dstPort": "4321",
        "tos-byte": "0xa0",
        "tos-mask": "0xe0"
        }
      }
      ]
    },
    "gate-spec":
      {
      "dscp-tos-overwrite": "0xa0",
      "dscp-tos-mask": "0xff"
      },
      "traffic-profile":
        {
        "service-class-name": "extrm_up"
        }
    }
  }
```

If the request went well, it will return 200 OK and you will see some activity in the terminal console, saying the gate was successfully processed:

```
[Thread-0] INFO  org.pcmm.rcd.impl.CmtsPepReqStateMan -
Returning SUCCESS for gate request [extrm_up] direction
[Upstream] for host - 10.32.110.180
```

How it works...

The project is using a DOCSIS abstraction layer to manage both DOCSIS itself and PCMM specific attributes, and stores/changes default QoS values applied by the service flow. This component is also responsible for adding or removing CTMS equipment. It provides northbound REST APIs specific to DOCSIS. The southbound component allows communication with CMTS, using the **Common Open Policy Service (COPS)** protocol. It fulfills the PCMM/COPS/PDP functionality defined here:

http://www.cablelabs.com

 When creating the gate, you have the choice between three different types of classifier: the standard type (as used in this example), the extended type, and the IPv6 type.

3
Dynamic Interconnects

In this chapter, we will cover the following recipes:

- Using the SNMP plugin with OpenDaylight
- Managing an Ethernet switch in an SDN Environment
- Automating legacy devices
- Remote configuration for OpenFlow switches
- Dynamically updating the network device YANG model
- Securing network bootstrapping infrastructures
- Providing virtual private cloud services for enterprises
- Managing SXP-capable devices using OpenDaylight
- Using OpenDaylight as an SDN controller server

Introduction

In this chapter, our recipes will focus on establishing dynamic connections between network devices within the SDN Environment. As there are different network management and configuration protocols such as SNMP and OpConf, OpenDaylight has implemented the southbound API of different protocols to be able to manage a vast range of network devices.

Using the SNMP plugin with OpenDaylight

Simple Network Management Protocol (**SNMP**) is widely used to configure and collect information from network devices. The SNMP plugin allows network applications to communicate with network devices that use SNMP.

Getting ready

In this recipe, you will learn how OpenDaylight connects to a network device using the SNMP protocol to retrieve device data. To step through this recipe, you will need a new OpenDaylight Beryllium distribution and SNMP simulator, and you will need to download the recipe folder from this book's GitHub repository.

How to do it...

Perform the following steps:

1. Start the OpenDaylight distribution using the `karaf` script. Using this client will give you access to the Karaf CLI:

```
$ cd distribution-karaf-0.4.1-Beryllium-SR1/
$ ./bin/karaf


_____ _____ .__ .__ .__ __
\_____  \ _____ \ _____ ___  ___ \_____  \ _____ ___.___.| | |__| ____
 |  |__/ |_
/  |  \\____  \_/ __ \ / \ |  |  \\_ \< |  ||  |  |  |/ __\|  | \ \_\
/  |  \  |_> >  ___/|  |  \|  ` \/ __ \\___  ||  |_|  /  /_/ >  Y \  |
_____/  __/ \___  >__| /_____  (____  / ____||____/__\___
 /|____| /__|
\/|__| \/ \/ \/ \/\/ /_____/ \/
Hit '<tab>' for a list of available commands
and '[cmd] --help' for help on a specific command.
Hit '<ctrl-d>' or type 'system:shutdown' or 'logout' to    shut
down OpenDaylight.
opendaylight-user@root>
```

2. Install the SNMP-plugin southbound API features using the following commands:

```
opendaylight-user@root> feature:install odl-snmp-plugin
opendaylight-user@root> feature:install odl-restconf-all
opendaylight-user@root> feature:install odl-dlux-all
```

You can check OF-Config installed features in Karaf CLI using the following command:

```
opendaylight-user@root> feature:list -i | grep snmp
```

You should see something the following this in your Karaf CLI:

3. If you are not able to connect to a real switch that has SNMP support, you will need to install the SNMP simulator. Open a new console and run the following command:

```
$ easy_install snmpsim
```

For more info about the free SNMP simulator, check the website `http://snmpsim.sourceforge.net/download.html`.

4. There are two options to use the SNMP simulator:

You can run the SNMP agent locally in your machine or you can use the public SNMP simulator provided by `http://snmpsim.sourceforge.net/public-snmp-simulator.html`.

Use the following command to run the local SNMP simulator:

```
$ snmpsimd.py –agent-udpv4-endpoint=127.0.0.1:1161
```

Then you will need to open a new console and run the SNMP agent:

$snmpwalk -On -v2c -c public localhost:1161 1.3.6

To use the SNMP agent at http://snmpsim.sourceforge.net/public-snmp-simulator.html use the following command:

$snmprec.py --agent-udpv4-endpoint=demo.snmplabs.com

You should see all the SNMP OID and its values:

```
SNMP version 2c, Community name: public
Querying UDP/IPv4 agent at 195.218.195.228:161
Agent response timeout: 3.00 secs, retries: 3
Sending initial GETBULK request for 1.3.6 (stop at <end-of-mib>)....
1.3.6.1.2.1.1.1.0|4x|53756e4f53207a6575732e736e6d706c6162732e636f6d20342e312e335f5531203120073756e346d
1.3.6.1.2.1.1.2.0|6|1.3.6.1.4.1.20408
1.3.6.1.2.1.1.3.0|67|150288885
1.3.6.1.2.1.1.4.0|4x|534e4d50204c61626f7261746f726965732c20696e666f40736e6d706c6162732e636f6d
1.3.6.1.2.1.1.5.0|4x|7a6575732e736e6d706c6162732e636f6d
1.3.6.1.2.1.1.6.0|4x|4d6f73636f772c20527573736961
1.3.6.1.2.1.1.7.0|2|72
1.3.6.1.2.1.1.8.0|67|150288886
1.3.6.1.2.1.1.9.1.2.1|6|1.3.6.1.4.1.20408.1.1
1.3.6.1.2.1.1.9.1.3.1|4x|4e6577207379737465642064657363726970696f6e
1.3.6.1.2.1.1.9.1.4.1|67|12
1.3.6.1.2.1.2.2.1.1.1|2|1
1.3.6.1.2.1.2.2.1.1.2|2|2
1.3.6.1.2.1.2.2.1.2.1|4|eth0
1.3.6.1.2.1.2.2.1.2.2|4|eth1
1.3.6.1.2.1.2.2.1.3.1|2|6
1.3.6.1.2.1.2.2.1.3.2|2|6
1.3.6.1.2.1.2.2.1.4.1|2|1500
1.3.6.1.2.1.2.2.1.4.2|2|1500
1.3.6.1.2.1.2.2.1.5.1|66|100000000
1.3.6.1.2.1.2.2.1.5.2|66|100000000
1.3.6.1.2.1.2.2.1.6.1|4x|00127962f940
1.3.6.1.2.1.2.2.1.6.2|4x|00127962f941
1.3.6.1.2.1.2.2.1.7.1|2|1
```

5. Now you can use OpenDaylight's YANGUI visualizer to retrieve SNMP agent information. Open your browser and go to the following URL `http://localhost:8181/index.html#/yangui`.

   The default username and password are `admin`, `admin`. Then select the **Yang UI** panel from the main page and scroll down the YANG model panel until you can see the **snmp rev.2014-09-22** model:

As you can see, in the preceding screenshot there are four RPC calls that we can use to retrieve the SNMP switch information; **get-interface**, **snmp-set**, **snmp-get**, and **get-node-properties**.

6. In the recipe folder `chapter4-recipe1`, the `SNMP-Plugin.postman_collection.json` file contains the definition of the previous RPC calls configured to connect to `http://snmpsim.sourceforge.net/public-snmp-simulator.html`. Use PostMan or any REST API client to import the `postman_collection.json` file. You should see the following payloads; **get interfaces**, **get node properties**, and **set snmp** as the following screenshot shows. As we are connecting to a simulated SNMP device, use the get interfaces payload to retrieve the device data:

Managing an Ethernet switch in an SDN Environment

OpenDaylight uses the SNMP4SDN plugin to manage Ethernet switches in the SDN Environments. The SNMP4SDN plugin will let you configure the forwarding tables and ACL of the Ethernet switches by using the SNMP plugin.

Getting ready

This recipe requires an OpenDaylight Beryllium distribution and you will need to download the recipe folder from this book's GitHub repository. In this recipe, you will learn how OpenDaylight can be used to install flow configurations in Ethernet switches and to manage different Ethernet switches provided by different vendors.

How to do it...

Perform the following steps:

1. Start the OpenDaylight distribution using the `karaf` script. Using this client will give you access to the Karaf CLI:

```
$ cd distribution-karaf-0.4.1-Beryllium-SR1/
$ ./bin/karaf

_____                        .__ .__ .__ __ __
\_____  \   _____   ____   ____ _____   _____ __.__.| | |_____| _____
 |  |___/ |_          /  |  \
/ |  \\___  \./  _ \/  /\   | |  \\_  \<  |  || | | |/ __\|  |  \ _\\
/ |  \  |_> > ___/|  |  \|    `  \/  __ \\___  || |_| / /_/  > Y \  |
_____  /  __/ \___  >__| /_____  (____  / ____||____/_____
      /|__| /__|
\/|__| \/ \/ \/ \/\/ /_____/ \/
Hit '<tab>' for a list of available commands
and '[cmd] --help' for help on a specific command.
Hit '<ctrl-d>' or type 'system:shutdown' or 'logout' to    shut
down OpenDaylight.
opendaylight-user@root>
```

2. Install the SNMP4SDN plugin features using the following command:

```
opendaylight-user@root> feature:install odl-snmp4sdn-all
```

You can check OF-Config installed features in Karaf CLI using the following command:

```
opendaylight-user@root> feature:list -i | grep snmp4sdn
```

You should see something like this in your Karaf CLI:

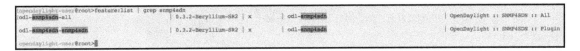

3. OpenDaylight needs to have basic information about the available Ethernet switches in the SDN network. An example switch information list exists in `snmp4sdn_swdb.csv` in the recipe folder:

```
Mac-Address,IP-Address,SNMP_Community,UserName,Password,Model
90:94:e4:23:13:e0,192.168.0.32,private,admin,password,D-
Link_DGS3650
90:94:e4:23:0b:00,192.168.0.33,private,admin,password,D-
Link_DGS3650
90:94:e4:23:0b:20,192.168.0.34,private,admin,password,D-
Link_DGS3650
```

4. You will need to copy the `snmp4sdn_swdb.csv` file to the OpenDaylight distribution directory under the `etc` folder.

5. Now we will let OpenDaylight load the switch list. In OpenDaylight Karaf CLI run the following command:

```
$ snmp4sdn:ReadDB etc/snmp4sdn_swdb.csv
```

```
opendaylight-user@root>snmp4sdn:ReadDB etc/snmp4sdn_swdb.csv
MAC_address (sid)                        IP_address     SNMP_community  CLI_username   CLI_password   Model_name
======================================================================================================================
00:00:90:94:e4:23:13:e0 (158969157063648 )  192.168.0.32   private         admin          password       D-Link_DGS3650
00:00:90:94:e4:23:0b:00 (158969157061376 )  192.168.0.33   private         admin          password       D-Link_DGS3650
00:00:90:94:e4:23:0b:20 (158969157061408 )  192.168.0.34   private         admin          password       D-Link_DGS3650
```

If you want to print the switch list you can run the following command in the Karaf CLI:

```
$ snmp4sdn:PrintDB
```

6. You can manually let OpenDaylight discover the network topology by running the following command in the Karaf CLI:

```
$ snmp4sdn:TopoDiscover
```

7. If your network has many switches and many edges, you can run different commands to distinguish between switch and edge discovery. For switch discovery, run the following command in the Karaf CLI:

```
$ snmp4sdn:TopoDiscoverSwitches
```

And for edge discovery, run the following command:

```
$ snmp4sdn:TopoDiscoverEdges
```

There's more...

SNMP4SDN has support for configuring and managing the Ethernet switches through the REST API. Flow configurations in Ethernet switches are installed based on the forwarding table, ACL, and VLAN table. Now we will show you how to use the REST APIs to configure Ethernet switches and manage different Ethernet switches provided by different vendors.

Configuring the Ethernet switch using the REST API

The forwarding table is the most important configuration for an Ethernet switch. In the recipe folder there is the SNMP4SDN.postman_collection.json file, which contains the REST calls that we can use to configure an Ethernet switch forwarding tables and other configurations. You can use PostMan as the REST API client to import the JSON file.

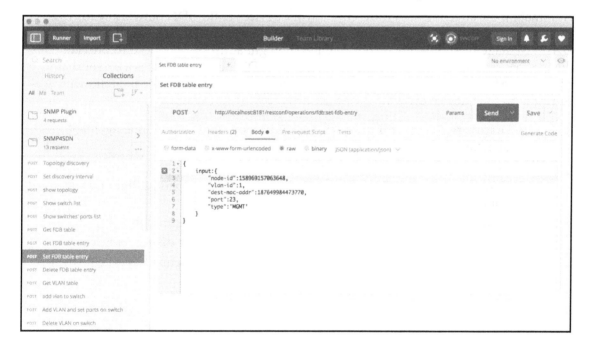

Multivendor support

As the SDN network might have different Ethernet switches provided by different vendors, there will be different configurations between switches. For example, adding VLAN and setting the ports is supported via SNMP standard MIB. However, there are Ethernet switches that require adding VLAN first and then they allow setting the ports. For that reason SNMP4SDN allows the network administrator to define the switch vendor configuration in the `snmp4sdn_VendorSpecificSwitchConfig.xml` file to the work with all Ethernet switches in the network. There is a good example of the `snmp4sdn_VendorSpecificSwitchConfig.xml` file in the recipe folder.

Automating legacy devices

Automating the attachment of different network devices to the SDN network requires a predefined specification for each device in OpenDaylight. The **Device Identification and Driver Management** (DIDM) project in OpenDaylight addresses the need to provide device-specific functionality. For each device in the SDN network there is a driver that contains the basic specification. The DIDM provides the ability to define the following functions in each device driver:

- **Discovery**: Discover if the device exists in the OpenDaylight management domain
- **Identification**: Identify the device type
- **Driver registration**: Register the device driver to the OpenDaylight management domain
- **Synchronization**: Collect device information and configuration
- **Features data model**: Data model should be defined for device features
- **RPC for features**: Remote procedures calls should be defined to execute device features

Getting ready

In this recipe, you will learn how to use OpenDaylight to detect OpenVSwitch nodes that connect to it using the DIDM functionality. This recipe requires a new refresh OpenDaylight distribution and Ubuntu 14.04 VM has OpenVSwitch 2.4. You can use the Vagrant file that exists in the recipe folder. You will need Vagrant to be installed on your machine to use the Vagrant file. You can check the Vagrant website to download and install it: `https://www.vagrantup.com/`. Finally, you can use PostMan or any REST API client to execute the OpenDaylight REST API RPCs.

How to do it...

Perform the following steps:

1. Start the OpenDaylight distribution using the `karaf` script. Using this client will give you access to the Karaf CLI:

```
$ cd distribution-karaf-0.4.1-Beryllium-SR1/
$ ./bin/karaf

_____ _____   .__ .__ .__  _ __
_____ \ _____   _____ _____   _____ \ ____  __.__.| | |_| ____
 |  |___/  |_
/  |  \_____ \/ _ \ / \ |  |  \\__  \<  | || |  |  | / ___\|  |  \ _\
/  |  \ |_> > ___/| |  \| ` \/ __ \\__  || |_| / /_/ > Y \ |
_____/ __/ \__ >__| /_____  (____  / ____||____/__\_\__
/|___| /__|
\/|__| \/ \/ \/ \/\/ /_____/ \/
Hit '<tab>' for a list of available commands
and '[cmd] --help' for help on a specific command.
Hit '<ctrl-d>' or type 'system:shutdown' or 'logout' to   shut
down OpenDaylight.
opendaylight-user@root>
```

2. Install the DIDM features using the following command:

```
opendaylight-user@root> feature:install odl-didm-ovs-all
opendaylight-user@root> feature:install odl-dlux-all
```

You can check OF-Config installed features in Karaf CLI using the following command:

```
opendaylight-user@root> feature:list | grep didm
```

You should see something like the following in your Karaf CLI:

As you can see, there is another driver for other network devices such as the HP device. However, for our demo we will use the OVS driver to work with the OVS devices.

3. Next, you will need to change the network interface name in the Vagrant file to match your machine network interface:

```
$ vi Vagrantfile
```

Go to line 46 and change the en0 to match your machine network interface, then save the file.

Now start the VM using:

```
$ vagrant up
```

It will take around five minutes to start the VM and install the required software.

4. We will need to create bridge br1 in the VM to allow OpenDaylight to connect to the OvS. You can ssh to the VM using the following command:

```
$ vagrant ssh
```

Then run the following command to check that OvS is running fine:

```
vagrant@vagrant-ubuntu-trusty-64:~$ sudo ovs-vsctl show
```

Now we will create a br1 and set the br1 controller to OpenDaylight:

```
vagrant@vagrant-ubuntu-trusty-64:~$ sudo ovs-vsctl add-br br1
vagrant@vagrant-ubuntu-trusty-64:~$ sudo ovs-vsctl set-
controller br1 tcp:<IP-Address>:6633
```

5. Now we will need to import the `DIDM.postman_collection.json` file in the recipe folder to retrieve the driver info.

After importing the `DIDM.postman_collection.json`, you will find two REST calls: **Get Mininet Type** and **Get Network**:

See also

The main purpose of the DIDM project is to let you define a new driver for your SDN network devices and adjust their functionality. Check the developer guide of the DIDM project for more: `https://wiki.opendaylight.org/view/DIDM:Developer_Guide`.

Remote configuration for OpenFlow switches

Configuring an OpenFlow switch by an SDN controller becomes easier by using the **OpenFlow Config protocol** (**OF-Config**). OF-Config is a southbound plugin for OpenDaylight to allow remote configuration of OpenFlow datapaths.

Getting ready

In this recipe, you will learn how to use OpenDaylight to remotely configure OpenVSwitch as it is an OpenFlow switch base. This recipe requires a new refresh OpenDaylight distribution and Ubuntu 14.04 VM has OpenVSwitch 2.3, libnetconf, and OF-Config supporting for OvS. You can download the Vagrant file that has all the requirements from `https://github.com/serngawy/of-config`. You will need Vagrant to be installed in your machine to use the Vagrant file. To download and install Vagrant, check out the Vagrant website: `https://www.vagrantup.com/` . Finally, you can use PostMan or any REST API client to execute the OpenDaylight REST API RPCs.

How to do it...

Perform the following steps:

1. Start the OpenDaylight distribution using the `karaf` script. Using this client will give you access to the Karaf CLI:

```
$ cd distribution-karaf-0.4.1-Beryllium-SR1/
$ ./bin/karaf

_____ _____  .__  .__  .__  __
_____ \ \_____  \ ____  ____  _____ \ _____ __.__.| | |__| ____
 |    |  \ /   |   \\_/ _ \ /  \  |    |  \\__  \\<  |  |  |  |/  ___\
 |    ` \ |_> > ___/|  |  \|  `   \/ _  \\___   ||  |_|  / /_/  > Y  \  |
_____ / __/ \__  >__| /_____  (____ / ____||____/____/
 /|___| /__|
\/|__| \/ \/ \/ \/\/ /_____/ \/
Hit '<tab>' for a list of available commands
and '[cmd] --help' for help on a specific command.
Hit '<ctrl-d>' or type 'system:shutdown' or 'logout' to    shut
down OpenDaylight.
opendaylight-user@root>
```

2. Install the OF-Config southbound API features using the following command:

```
opendaylight-user@root> feature:install odl-of-config-all
```

You can check OF-Config installed features in Karaf CLI using the following command:

```
opendaylight-user@root> feature:list -i | grep of-config
```

You should see something like this in your Karaf CLI:

```
opendaylight-user@root>feature:list -i | grep of-config
odl-of-config-all                     | 1.0.1-Beryllium-SR1 | x     | odl-of-config-1.0.1-Beryllium-SR1            | OpenDaylight :: of-config :: ALL
odl-of-config-southbound-api          | 1.0.1-Beryllium-SR1 | x     | odl-of-config-southbound-1.0.1-Beryllium-SR1 | OpenDaylight :: of-config:: southbound :: api
odl-of-config-southbound-ofconfigmodels | 1.0.1-Beryllium-SR1 | x   | odl-of-config-southbound-1.0.1-Beryllium-SR1 | OpenDaylight :: of-config:: southbound :: ofconfi
g
odl-of-config-southbound-all          | 1.0.1-Beryllium-SR1 | x     | odl-of-config-southbound-1.0.1-Beryllium-SR1 | OpenDaylight :: of-config:: southbound
odl-of-config-southbound-rest         | 1.0.1-Beryllium-SR1 | x     | odl-of-config-southbound-1.0.1-Beryllium-SR1 | OpenDaylight :: of-config:: southbound :: REST
```

3. Now you will need to clone the OF-Config repository from GitHub using the following command. Open a new console and type the following:

```
$ git clone https://github.com/serngawy/of-config.git
$ cd of-config/
```

4. You will need to change the network interface name in the Vagrant file to match your machine network interface:

```
$ vi Vagrantfile
```

Go to line 65 and change the en0 to match your machine network interface and save the file.

Now start the VM using:

```
$ vagrant up
```

It will take around five minutes to start the VM and install the required software.

5. We will need to run the OvS OF-Config server inside the VM. You can `ssh` to the VM using the following command:

```
$ vagrant ssh
```

Then run the following command to start the OFC-Server:

```
vagrant@vagrant-ubuntu-trusty-64:~$ sudo ofc-server -v 3 -f
```

6. Now we need to establish a connection between the OpenDaylight distribution and the OFC-server component that is running on the VM. Inside the `of-config` directory there is an `OF-CONFIG.postman_collection` file; we will use it to send a REST call to the OpenDaylight distribution.

Open the PostMan application and import `OF-CONFIG.postman_collection` and you will find three REST calls: **Connection Establishment, Modify controller connection**, and **Get Network**:

7. Use the **Connection Establishment** payload to connect OpenDaylight to OvS. Don't forget to change the `VM-Ip-Address` in the payload to match the VM IP address. You should receive status code 204.

8. Check the network topology using the **Get Network** payload. You should be able to see the VM IP address and the available capabilities:

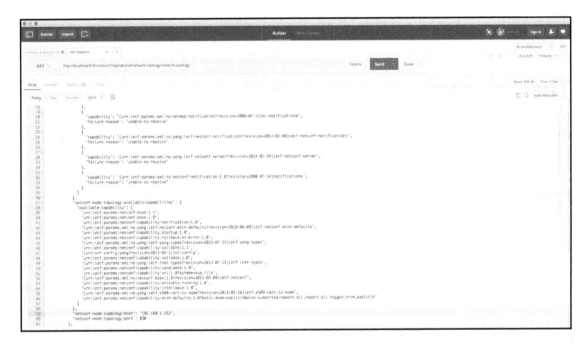

How it works...

OpenDaylight uses the OF-Config southbound plugin to define the OpenFlow switch as an abstraction logical switch. The OF-Config protocol will allow OpenDaylight to configure the essential artifacts of the OpenFlow logical switch so that OpenDaylight can communicate and control the switch via the OpenFlow protocol. The essential artifacts that OF-Config provides are as follows:

- `sync-conf-ocs`: Synchronizes the configuration with the OpenFlow-capable switch
- `modify-controller-connection`: Modifies the configuration of the controller connection in the OpenFlow logic switch
- `create-tls`: Creates a TLS tunnel for the OpenFlow logic switch and controller, and configures authentication certificates
- `opt-flowtable`: Operates the flow table of the OpenFlow logic switch

- `config-tunnel`: Configures tunnels in the OpenFlow logic switch
- `config-port`: Configures ports and queues in the OpenFlow capable switch
- `config-ols-basic`: Configures some basic items in the OpenFlow logic switch, such as `dpid` and `lost-connection-behavior`

There's more...

As an example of how to use these essential artifacts in the PostMan collection there is a payload for modifying the controller connection. However, you can use the OpenDaylight `apidoc` explorer to check all of them
`http://localhost:8181/apidoc/explorer/index.html`:

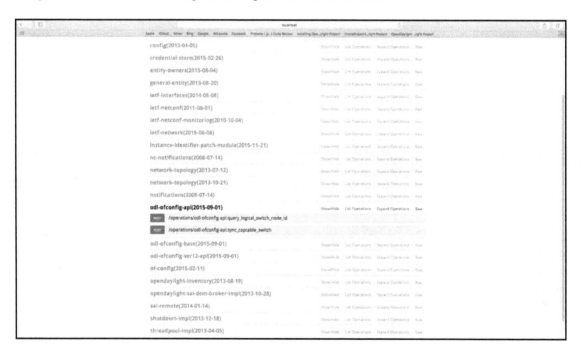

Dynamically updating the network device YANG model

Updating the YANG models of a network device, which use the netconf protocol, requires OpenDaylight to make a continuous set of fetching requests to the device. The iterative fetching requests of the data (device YANG models) from the network devices in large-scale networks will impose a load on the network. The YANG PubSub project allows OpenDaylight to request only the updated parts of the YANG models from the network device. In this recipe, we will show you how to use OpenDaylight to register a continuous fetching request with a netconf network device to push updates of the YANG model.

Getting ready

This recipe requires an OpenDaylight Beryllium distribution, the OpenDaylight netconf test tool or a network device with netconf functionality, and YANG push capability, for example, a Cisco IOS-XR device. Also you will need a REST API client and finally you will need to download the recipe folder from this book's GitHub repository.

How to do it...

Perform the following steps:

1. Start the OpenDaylight distribution using the `karaf` script. Using this client will give you access to the Karaf CLI:

```
$ cd distribution-karaf-0.4.1-Beryllium-SR1/
$ ./bin/karaf


_____ _____  .__ .__ .__  _ _
\_____  \ _____ \_____  _ \_____  \ _____  __.__.| | |_| ___
 |  |___/ |_
/  |  \\___  \_/ _ \ / \ | | \\__ \< | || | | | |/ __\| | \ _\
/  |  \ |_> > ___/| | \|` \/ _ \\__  || |_| / /_/ > Y \ |
_____ / __/ \__ >__| /_____  (___ / ___||___/__\__
/|___| /__|
\/|__| \/ \/ \/ \/\/ /____/ \/
Hit '<tab>' for a list of available commands
and '[cmd] --help' for help on a specific command.
Hit '<ctrl-d>' or type 'system:shutdown' or 'logout' to    shut
down OpenDaylight.
opendaylight-user@root>
```

2. Install the YANG Push features using the following command:

```
opendaylight-user@root> feature:install odl-yangpush-ui
```

You can check out YANG Push installed features in the Karaf CLI using the following command:

```
opendaylight-user@root> feature:list -i | grep yangpush
```

You should see something like this in your Karaf CLI:

```
opendaylight-user@root>feature:list -i | grep yangpush
odl-yangpush-api        | 1.0.2-Beryllium-SR2 | x    | odl-yangpush-1.0.2-Beryllium-SR2    | OpenDaylight :: yangpush :: api
odl-yangpush            | 1.0.2-Beryllium-SR2 | x    | odl-yangpush-1.0.2-Beryllium-SR2    | OpenDaylight :: yangpush
odl-yangpush-rest       | 1.0.2-Beryllium-SR2 | x    | odl-yangpush-1.0.2-Beryllium-SR2    | OpenDaylight :: yangpush :: REST
odl-yangpush-ui         | 1.0.2-Beryllium-SR2 | x    | odl-yangpush-1.0.2-Beryllium-SR2    | OpenDaylight :: yangpush :: UI
```

3. We are going to download the OpenDaylight netconf test tool. Go to the recipe directory and use the following commands to download the test tool:

```
$ cd chapter4/chapter4-recipe5/
$ wget https://nexus.opendaylight.org/content/repositories
/opendaylight.release/org/opendaylight/netconf/netconf-
testtool/1.0.2-Beryllium-SR2/netconf-testtool-1.0.2-Beryllium-
SR2-executable.jar
```

4. Now start the netconf test tool using the following command:

```
$ java -Xmx1G -XX:MaxPermSize=256M -jar netconf-testtool-
1.0.2-Beryllium-SR2-executable.jar --debug true --schemas-dir
schema/
```

You should be able to see the following message:

[main] INFO NetconfDeviceSimulator - All simulated devices started successfully from port 17830 to 17830

5. Check that the simulated devices are running fine by executing the following command:

```
$ ssh admin@localhost -p 17830 -s netconf
```

The simulated device accepts any password; if it asks for a password you can press *Enter* to continue. You should then see the hello message.

6. Now we will use PostMan as a REST API client to add the simulated netconf device to the OpenDaylight data store and register a continuous push update request to make OpenDaylight able to fetch the updated YANG models. In the recipe folder import the `yang-push.postman_collection.json` file to PostMan. You should see the following payloads; **Post YangPush Device**, **Get Netconf devices**, and **Post RPC Push Updates**:

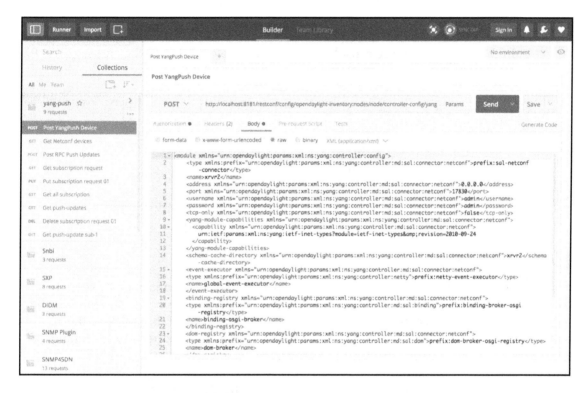

7. We will use the first REST API payload, **Post YangPush Device**, to register the device in the OpenDaylight data store. As you can see from the payload row data the device name is xrvr2, so you can use the second REST API payload **Get Netconf device** to check if the device successfully registered and connected.

8. Now we will use **Post RPC Push Updates** payload to register a continuous fetch request to receive the updated YANG models from the simulated device. The response of the request should be as follows:

```
{
  "output": {
  "subscription-id": "sub-2"
  }
}
```

In the simulated device console you should be able to see the RPC message output:

```
19:09:30.220 [nioEventLoopGroup-2-3] DEBUG o.o.p.f.AbstractProtocolSession - Message was received: <rpc xmlns="urn:
ietf:params:xml:ns:netconf:base:1.0" message-id="m-0">
<create-subscription xmlns="urn:ietf:params:xml:ns:netconf:notification:1.0">
<stream>push-update</stream>
<filter type="subtree">
<interface-configurations xmlns="http://cisco.com/ns/yang/Cisco-IOS-XR-ifmgr-cfg"/>
</filter>
<period xmlns="urn:opendaylight:params:xml:ns:yang:yangpush">60</period>
<subscription-id xmlns="urn:opendaylight:params:xml:ns:yang:yangpush">sub-2</subscription-id>
</create-subscription>
</rpc>
```

How it works...

The push update request that we registered in OpenDaylight will continuously send a fetching update request to the simulated netconf device every 60 seconds. We simulate the YANG Push capabilities in the netconf test tool by adding `yang-push` models to the simulator schema directory. Under the `schema` folder in the recipe directory the following files exist: `ietf-datastore-push@2015-10-15.yang`, `yangpush@2015-01-05.yang`, and `notifications@2008-07-14.yang`.The `itef-datastore-push.yang` model contains the definitions of the subscriptions and filters that OpenDaylight can register to the device and also has the definition of the RPC calls that have been sent by OpenDaylight. When the netconf device's data has been updated, only the updated data will be sent to OpenDaylight through the continuous fetching update request that we registered.

Securing network bootstrapping infrastructures

In a scaled SDN network, certificate-based authentication and key distribution are a challenge. The OpenDaylight SNBI project provides a zero-touch approach to securely establishing communication between the network device and OpenDaylight as an SDN controller. Any network device that leverages the IEEE 802.1AR - 2009 standard for secure device identification can securely bootstrap the communication with OpenDaylight. OpenDaylight and network devices will automatically discover each other and then get the IP address assigned to each other, exchange key certificates, and finally establish secure IP connectivity.

Getting ready

For this recipe, you need three Ubuntu 14.04 hosts, OpenDaylight distribution, docker, an snbi/beryllium docker image, PostMan as a REST API client, and Vagrant if you use the predefined Vagrant file in our recipe folder. In this recipe, you will learn how to use OpenDaylight to establish a secure bootstrap communication with two simulated network devices that have implemented the secure device identification stander.

How to do it...

Perform the following steps:

1. If you already have the pre-request installed you can skip this step and start directly from step 4. If you do, use the predefined Vagrant file to establish the environment. First you need to install Vagrant if it is not already installed. Then you need to go to the `SnbiVMs` directory in the recipe folder:

   ```
   $ cd chapter4-recipe6/SnbiVMs/
   ```

   You will need to change the network interface name in the Vagrant file to match your machine network interface:

   ```
   $ vi Vagrantfile
   ```

   Change the `en0` to match your machine network interface and save the file. Then you need to start the VM installation:

   ```
   $ vagrant up
   ```

The installation should take between 15-20 minutes, so it is a good time to get a coffee.

2. After the installation is done, you should have three VMs running: `SnbiODL`, `Snbi01`, and `Snbi02`:

    ```
    $ vagrant status
    ```

    You should see the currently running VMs:

    ```
    Mohameds-MacBook-Pro:SnbiODL-VM mohamedel-serngawy$ vagrant status
    Current machine states:

    snbiODL-vm                    running (virtualbox)
    snbi1-vm                      running (virtualbox)
    snbi2-vm                      running (virtualbox)
    ```

3. Now open four consoles, log in to each VM using the `vagrant ssh` command, and specify the VM name:

    ```
    $ vagrant ssh snbiODL-vm
    $ vagrant ssh snbi1-vm
    $ vagrant ssh snbi2-vm
    ```

    In the fourth console log in to `snbiODL-vm` as we will need to keep this on for the OpenDaylight Karaf console.

4. Start the OpenDaylight distribution using the `karaf` script. Using this client will give you access to the Karaf CLI:

    ```
    $ cd distribution-karaf-0.4.1-Beryllium-SR1/
    $ ./bin/karaf
    ```

    ```
    _____ _____        .__  .__  .__  __
    \_____  \_____ \   ____ |  | |  | |__|/  |_  _____ __
     |  |__/ |_  \ \/ _ \ /   \ / \ |  | \  \_   \   /\ / / /_/ > Y \ |
    ...
    Hit '<tab>' for a list of available commands
    and '[cmd] --help' for help on a specific command.
    Hit '<ctrl-d>' or type 'system:shutdown' or 'logout' to    shut
    down OpenDaylight.
    opendaylight-user@root>
    ```

5. Install the SNBI features using the following command:

```
opendaylight-user@root> feature:install odl-snbi-all
```

You can check OF-Config installed features in Karaf CLI using the following command:

```
opendaylight-user@root> feature:list -i | grep snbi
```

You should see something like this in your Karaf CLI:

```
opendaylight-user@root>feature:list -i | grep snbi
odl-snbi-all              | 1.2.2-Beryllium-SR2 | x    | odl-snbi-1.2.2-Beryllium-SR2    | OpenDaylight :: snbi :: All
odl-snbi-southplugin      | 1.2.2-Beryllium-SR2 | x    | odl-snbi-1.2.2-Beryllium-SR2    | OpenDaylight :: SNBI :: SouthPlugin
odl-snbi-shellplugin      | 1.2.2-Beryllium-SR2 | x    | odl-snbi-1.2.2-Beryllium-SR2    | OpenDaylight :: SNBI :: ShellPlugin
odl-snbi-dlux             | 1.2.2-Beryllium-SR2 | x    | odl-snbi-1.2.2-Beryllium-SR2    | OpenDaylight :: SNBI :: Dlux
```

6. Now we need to create the required network topology to simulate our recipe; the `Snbi1-vm` and `snbi2-vm` networks connect to the `snbiODL-vm` through a direct link.

   Use the following commands to create a network interface in each VM:

```
$ sudo ip6tables -A INPUT -j DROP -p udp --destination-port
4936 -i eth0
```

Then check the iptables:

```
$ sudo ip6tables --list
```

You should see something like this:

```
vagrant@snbi-vm:~$ sudo ip6tables --list
Chain INPUT (policy ACCEPT)
target     prot opt source               destination
DROP       udp      anywhere             anywhere             udp dpt:4936

Chain FORWARD (policy ACCEPT)
target     prot opt source               destination

Chain OUTPUT (policy ACCEPT)
target     prot opt source               destination
```

7. Now create a link to the network interface using the following commands:

```
$ sudo ip link add snbi-ra type dummy
$ sudo ip addr add fd08::aaaa:bbbb:1/128 dev snbi-ra
$ sudo ifconfig snbi-ra up
```

You can check the `snbi-ra` interface information by using the following command:

```
$ ifconfig
```

```
snbi-ra   Link encap:Ethernet  HWaddr 0e:22:f7:22:cf:0b
          inet6 addr: fd08::aaaa:bbbb:1/128 Scope:Global
          inet6 addr: fe80::c22:f7ff:fe22:cf0b/64 Scope:Link
          UP BROADCAST RUNNING NOARP  MTU:1500  Metric:1
          RX packets:0 errors:0 dropped:0 overruns:0 frame:0
          TX packets:3 errors:0 dropped:0 overruns:0 carrier:0
          collisions:0 txqueuelen:1000
          RX bytes:0 (0.0 B)  TX bytes:210 (210.0 B)
```

8. Now open PostMan and import the `Snbi.postman_collection.json` file from the recipe folder. You will find three REST API requests: **Add domain list**, **Get domain list**, and **Del domain list**:

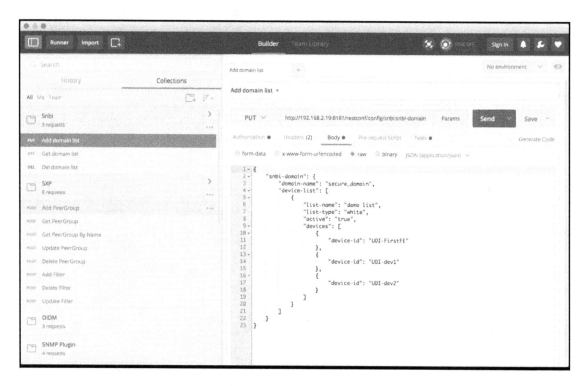

Use the **Add domain list** request to send the white domain list to OpenDaylight.

9. In the Karaf CLI execute the start secure domain command to put OpenDaylight in active discover mode:

```
opendaylight-user@root> snbi:start secure_domain
```

```
[opendaylight-user@root>snbi:start secure_domain
Starting SNBI for domain:secure_domain
```

10. We will start the `snbi/beryllium` docker image in `snbiODL-vm` first and then we'll start the `snbi/beryllium` docker image in the other VMs, `snbi1-vm` and `snbi2-vm`. Use the following commands to start the `snbi/beryllium` docker image in all VMs:

- For `snbiODL-vm`:

```
$ sudo docker run -v /etc/timezone:/etc/timezone:ro --net=host
--privileged=true --rm -t -i -e SNBI_UDI=UDI-FirstFE -e
SNBI_REGISTRAR=fd08::aaaa:bbbb:1 snbi/beryllium:latest
/bin/bash
```

- For `snbi1-vm`:

```
$ sudo docker run -v /etc/timezone:/etc/timezone:ro --net=host
--privileged=true --rm -t -i -e SNBI_UDI=UDI-dev1 -e
SNBI_REGISTRAR=fd08::aaaa:bbbb:1 snbi/beryllium:latest
/bin/bash
```

- For `snbi2-vm`:

```
$ sudo docker run -v /etc/timezone:/etc/timezone:ro --net=host
--privileged=true --rm -t -i -e SNBI_UDI=UDI-dev2 -e
SNBI_REGISTRAR=fd08::aaaa:bbbb:1 snbi/beryllium:latest
/bin/bash
```

Now in the container CLI execute the following command to check the device information:

```
snbi.d> show snbi device
```

```
.snbi.d >   ure   show snbi device

            Device UDI             - UDI-FirstFE
            Device ID              - 0e22.f722.cf0b-1
            Domain ID              - secure_domain
            Domain Certificate     - (sub:) /name=0e22.f722.cf0b-1/CN=0e22.f722.cf0b-1/OU=secure_domain/serialNumber=UDI-FirstFE
            Certificate Serial Number - 01556990E671
            Device Address         - fd02:a8f9:890b:0:e22:f722:cf0b:1
            Domain Cert is Valid
```

11. Now go back to the Karaf CLI; you should be able to see the `snbi/beryllium` containers certificate and key information in the logs. Execute the following command:

```
opendaylight-user@root> log:tail
```

12. Verify the routes in each host using the following command:

```
$ ip -6 route show
```

```
fd02:a8f9:890b:0:e22:f722:cf0b:1 dev snbi-fe   proto kernel   metric 256
fd02:a8f9:890b:0:e22:f722:cf0b:3 via fe80::e9f:33f9:83b:2 dev snbi_tun_2   metric 1024
fd08::aaaa:bbbb:1 dev snbi-ra   proto kernel   metric 256
unreachable fd00::/8 dev lo   metric 1024   error -113
fe80::/64 dev eth0   proto kernel   metric 256
fe80::/64 dev eth1   proto kernel   metric 256
fe80::/64 dev snbi-ra   proto kernel   metric 256
fe80::/64 dev snbi-fe   proto kernel   metric 256
fe80::/64 dev snbi_tun_2   proto kernel   metric 256
fe80::/64 dev snbi_tun_3   proto kernel   metric 256
```

You should see in each `snbi-vm` the routes to the two other `snbi-vm`.

13. Now verify the secure connectivity between them by using the ping command:

```
snbiODL-vm > $ ping6 fd02:a8f9:890b:0:e22:f722:cf0b:1
```

```
PING fd02:a8f9:890b:0:e22:f722:cf0b:1(fd02:a8f9:890b:0:e22:f722:cf0b:1) 56 data bytes
64 bytes from fd02:a8f9:890b:0:e22:f722:cf0b:1: icmp_seq=1 ttl=64 time=0.071 ms
64 bytes from fd02:a8f9:890b:0:e22:f722:cf0b:1: icmp_seq=2 ttl=64 time=0.037 ms
64 bytes from fd02:a8f9:890b:0:e22:f722:cf0b:1: icmp_seq=3 ttl=64 time=0.037 ms
64 bytes from fd02:a8f9:890b:0:e22:f722:cf0b:1: icmp_seq=4 ttl=64 time=0.040 ms
64 bytes from fd02:a8f9:890b:0:e22:f722:cf0b:1: icmp_seq=5 ttl=64 time=0.040 ms
64 bytes from fd02:a8f9:890b:0:e22:f722:cf0b:1: icmp_seq=6 ttl=64 time=0.041 ms
64 bytes from fd02:a8f9:890b:0:e22:f722:cf0b:1: icmp_seq=7 ttl=64 time=0.040 ms
```

How it works...

In the `snabiODL-vm`, OpenDaylight, and the snapi-agent that is running in the snabi container, establish a SSL connection to secure their communication. This is considered as a secure IP communication as OpenDaylight and the snbi-agent are running in the same host. At the same time all the snapi-agents that run on `snabiODL-vm`, `snabi1-vm`, and `snabi2-vm` are discovering each other using their own discovery protocol. The snabi-agents will establish secure SSL connections among themselves, which also can be considered as a secure IP communication between the snabi-agents. Now to realize the benefits from using OpenDaylight's snbi project and snbi-agent, any other network service that runs on one of the snabi-agent hosts can use the secure SSL connection that the snabi-agent been established to start a secure IP communication with OpenDaylight.

Providing virtual private cloud services for enterprises

With the rise of the SDN Environment, the network becomes more complicated and hard to manage. The OpenDaylight Nemo project provides the Intent northbound interface to simplify use of the network. The main idea behind the Intent northbound interface is to let the network operator express how the network topology should be configured instead of thinking how to implement the new network topology configuration. In this recipe, we will use the OpenDaylight Nemo project to provide a secure **virtual private cloud** (**VPC**) service to an enterprise site. The scenario of our recipe is that a network operator wants to allocate two zones: the **Data Management Zone** (**DMZ**) and the Interior Zone. The DMZ zone provides video/e-mail access from the internet and the Interior Zone provides compute and storage resources. A constrain in the network topology allows only one zone and it can only communicate with other zones that directly connect to it. Also the network operator provides **Bandwidth On Demand** (**BOD**) services for the connection between the enterprise site and the interior zone.

The following figure shows a high-level design for the network topology:

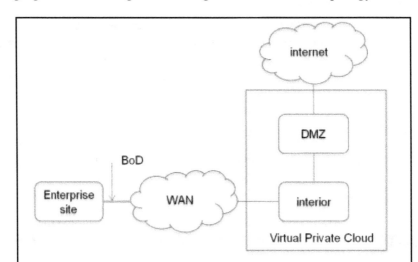

Getting ready

This recipe requires an Ubuntu 12.04 or higher Linux environment, OpenDaylight distribution, OfSoftSwitch 1.3 (`https://github.com/CPqD/ofsoftswitch13`), and the recipe folder. You can use the predefined Vagrant file in the recipe folder `chapter4-recipe7/NemoVM/` to easily get into the recipe work.

How to do it...

Perform the following steps:

1. If you already have the pre-request installed you can skip this step and start directly from step 3. Otherwise, you will use the predefined Vagrant file to establish the environment. First you need to install Vagrant if it is not already installed. Then you need to go to the `NemoVM` directory in the recipe folder:

```
$ cd chapter4-recipe7/NemoVM/
```

You will need to change the network interface name in the Vagrant file to match your machine network interface:

```
$ vi Vagrantfile
```

Go to line 59, change the en0 to match your machine network interface, and save the file. Then you need to start the VM installation:

```
$ vagrant up
```

The installation should take between 15-20 minutes, so it is a good time to get a coffee.

2. After the installation is done, you should be able to access NemoVM using the vagrant ssh command:

```
$ vagrant ssh
```

Now you need to download or copy the VPC folder chapter4-recipe7/VPC to NemoVM.

3. At NemoVM, start the OpenDaylight distribution using the karaf script. Using this client will give you access to the Karaf CLI:

```
$ cd distribution-karaf-0.4.1-Beryllium-SR1/
$ ./bin/karaf

_____ _____ .__ .__ .__ __
\_____  \ _____   ____  ____  _____   \ _____ ___.__.| | |__| _____
 |  |___/  |_
/   |  \\____  \_/ __ \/  \ |  |    \\__  \<   |  ||  |  ||/  ___\|  |  \  _\
/   |  \  |_> >  ___/| |  \| `  \/  __ \\___  || |_| / /_/ >  Y  \ |
_____  / __/ \___  >__| /_____  (____  / ___||____/__\___
/|___| /__|
\/|___| \/ \/ \/ \/\/ /_____/ \/
Hit '<tab>' for a list of available commands
and '[cmd] --help' for help on a specific command.
Hit '<ctrl-d>' or type 'system:shutdown' or 'logout' to   shut
down OpenDaylight.
opendaylight-user@root>
```

4. Install the Nemo required features using the following command:

```
opendaylight-user@root> feature:install odl-nemo-openflow-
render
opendaylight-user@root> feature:install odl-restconf-all
opendaylight-user@root> feature:install odl-nemo-engine-ui
```

You can check Nemo installed features in Karaf CLI using the following command:

```
opendaylight-user@root> feature:list -i | grep nemo
```

You should see something like this in your Karaf CLI:

```
opendaylight-user@root>feature:list -i | grep nemo
odl-nemo-api                 | 1.0.2-Beryllium-SR2 | x   | odl-nemo-1.0.2-Beryllium-SR2   | OpenDaylight :: NEMO :: API
odl-nemo-engine              | 1.0.2-Beryllium-SR2 | x   | odl-nemo-1.0.2-Beryllium-SR2   | OpenDaylight :: NEMO :: Engine
odl-nemo-engine-rest         | 1.0.2-Beryllium-SR2 | x   | odl-nemo-1.0.2-Beryllium-SR2   | OpenDaylight :: NEMO :: Engine :: REST
odl-nemo-openflow-renderer   | 1.0.2-Beryllium-SR2 | x   | odl-nemo-1.0.2-Beryllium-SR2   | OpenDaylight :: NEMO :: OpenFlow Renderer
odl-nemo-engine-ui           | 1.0.2-Beryllium-SR2 | x   | odl-nemo-1.0.2-Beryllium-SR2   | OpenDaylight :: NEMO :: Engine :: UI
```

5. Now you need to establish the network topology of our recipe. In the VPC folder you will find a detailed explanation and the commands to create the virtual network topology in the network-up.sh file. Execute the netowrk-up.sh script to create the network topology:

```
$ cd chapter4-recipe6/VPC
$ sudo ./network-up.sh
```

Now you need to check for network creation by checking the NemoVM network interfaces:

```
$ ifconfig
```

If you have any trouble creating the network you can use the network-down.sh script to remove all created networks and rerun the network-up script.

6. OpenDaylight needs to have the predefined Intent expression that will be applied on our network topology. In the VPC folder you will find a detailed explanation and the REST API calls to send basic Intent expressions information to OpenDaylight in the nemo-odl.py file. Execute nemo-odl.py using the following command:

```
$ python nemo-odl.py
```

You may need to install the Python requests library. Run the following command to install it and then execute `nemo-odl.py`:

`$ sudo easy_install -U requests`

7. As we explained at the beginning of the recipe, the network operator should be able to express the Intent policy of the network topology. You will find under the VCP folder a detailed explanation and the REST API calls to send the Intent policy information to OpenDaylight in the `bod-512.py` file. Execute `bod-512.py` by using the following command:

    $ python bod-512.py

8. Now you can open your browser and enter the following URL to access the Nemo UI:

    `http://:8181/index.html#/nemo`

    The default username and password for the OpenDaylight distribution is `admin`, `admin`:

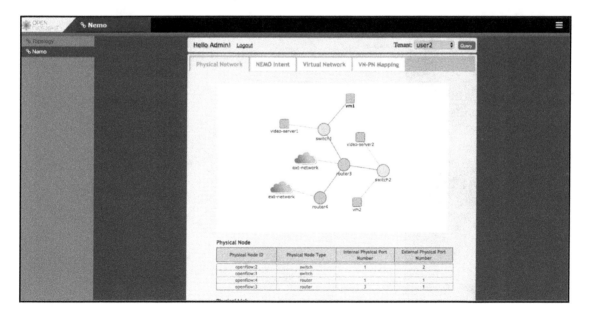

How it works...

Let's take a look at the virtual network topology we created using the `network-up.sh` script. We created four network interfaces to be presented as switches and six network links to be presented as hosts. The hosts are linked to the switches; all switches are controlled by the controller and flow rules have been pushed to the switches.

Then by executing the `nemo-odl.py` script, we defined the basic Intent expressions that OpenDaylight needs to map those expressions to the network topology. For detailed information about the Intent expressions you can check out the following URL from the openDaylight wiki website:

```
https://wiki.opendaylight.org/images/e/ee/Reference_manual.01.pdf
```

Finally, we executed the `bod-512.py` script to create our recipe network topology, as you can see in the Nemo UI webpage. We have created two switches, two routers, two ext-networks, and four hosts. Also, the network security constraints have been created and the network zone can only communicate with directly connected zones and BOD services with 512 Hz have been applied between the enterprise host and the Interior Zone. You can check the Nemo Intent tab on the Nemo UI to see the Intent expressions and the policy rules:

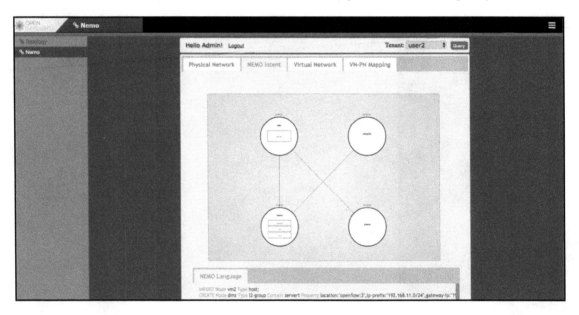

At the **Nemo Language** tab, you will see that our recipe Intent policy has been represented by Intent abstract expressions. By scrolling down, you should see the following line:

CREATE Connection c1 Type p2p Endnodes interior, enterprise Property bandwidth:"512";

Now to achieve the benefits from using the OpenDaylight Nemo project, the network operator wants to allow the BOD service between the enterprise side and the Interior zone to be 512 Hz at off-work times and 1 GHz at work times. To increase the BOD service bandwidth to 1 GHz you can execute the `bod-1024.py` script under the `VCP` folder. After you run the `bod-1024.py` script you should be able to see that the bandwidth connection has been increased to 1024 GHz in the **Nemo Language** tab:

CREATE Connection c1 Type p2p Endnodes interior, enterprise Property bandwidth:"1024";

For more information about the Nemo language you can check out the following URL from the OpenDaylight wiki website:

```
https://wiki.opendaylight.org/images/9/9e/Instruction_for_NEMO_editor.pdf
```

Managing SXP-capable devices using OpenDaylight

Source-Group Tag eXchange Protocol (**SXP**) is used in most Cisco devices to handle the binding between the IP address and the secure group tag. SXP consider the source groups as endpoints connecting to the network. Those source groups have common network policies applied and configured. The SXP project in OpenDaylight is used to handle the binding information between the IP address and the **Secure Group Tagging** (**SGT**) of each endpoint's connection.

Getting ready

This recipe requires an OpenDaylight Beryllium distribution and you will need to download the recipe folder from this book's GitHub repository. In this recipe, you will learn how OpenDaylight can be used to configure SXP network devices.

How to do it...

Perform the following steps:

1. Start the OpenDaylight distribution using the `karaf` script. Using this client will give you access to the Karaf CLI:

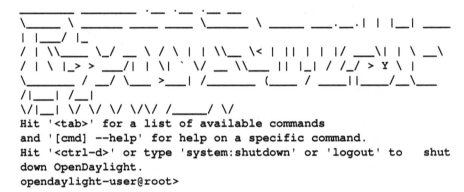

```
$ cd distribution-karaf-0.4.1-Beryllium-SR1/
$ ./bin/karaf
```

```
Hit '<tab>' for a list of available commands
and '[cmd] --help' for help on a specific command.
Hit '<ctrl-d>' or type 'system:shutdown' or 'logout' to    shut
down OpenDaylight.
opendaylight-user@root>
```

2. Install the SXP features using the following command in Karaf CLI:

```
opendaylight-user@root> feature:install odl-sxp-all
```

You can check SXP installed features in Karaf CLI using the following command:

```
opendaylight-user@root> feature:list -i | grep sxp
```

You should see something like this in your Karaf CLI:

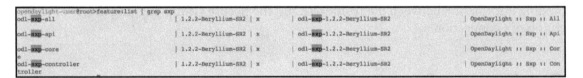

3. Now, after you have installed the SXP features, you need to check `22-sxp-controller-one- node.xml` in the OpenDaylight `distribution` directory, `etc/opendaylight/karaf/22-sxp- controller-one-node.xml`. The file contains the initial configuration and the predefined connections for the SXP nodes. The most important part to be configured based on your network configuration is the `sxp-controller` section:

```
<sxp-controller>
  <sxp-node>
<!--name></name-->
  <enabled>true</enabled>
  <node-id>127.0.0.1</node-id>
<!--source-ip></source-ip-->
  <tcp-port>64999</tcp-port>
  <version>version4</version>
<!--security>
  <password>cisco123</password>
</security-->
  <mapping-expanded>5</mapping-expanded>
  <description>ODL SXP Controller</description>
<!-- Binding format: prefix/length -->
  <master-database></master-database>
<!-- Timers setup: 0 to disable specific timer usability -->
  <timers>
<!-- Common -->
  <retry-open-time>5</retry-open-time>
<!-- Speaker -->
  <hold-time-min-acceptable>120</hold-time-min-acceptable>
  <keep-alive-time>30</keep-alive-time>
<!-- Listener -->
  <hold-time>90</hold-time>
  <hold-time-min>90</hold-time-min>
  <hold-time-max>180</hold-time-max>
  </timers>
  </sxp-node>
</sxp-controller>
```

Do not forget to restart OpenDaylight if you have changed that file.

4. You are ready now to start adding the secure groups and filters to OpenDaylight. We will need to use the REST API collection `SXP.postman_collection.json` in the recipe folder and import it to the PostMan application.

5. You will find in the SXP PostMan collection peer group these REST API calls: **Add PeerGroup**, **Get PeerGroup**, and so on. You'll also find the following filter REST API calls: **Add Filter**, **Delete Filter**, and so on. You might need to adjust their information based on your network configuration:

There's more...

For more network topology examples you can check the following `22-sxp-controller-one-node.xml` files:

- Multi Node SXP network topology:

  ```
  https://github.com/opendaylight/integration-test/tree/master/csit/su
  ites/sxp/topology
  ```

- Filter Node SXP network topology:

  ```
  https://github.com/opendaylight/integration-test/tree/master/csit/su
  ites/sxp/filtering
  ```

Using OpenDaylight as an SDN controller server

In a real SDN Environment, the possibility of using multiple SDN controllers to manage the network exists. SDN controllers such as **Ryu**, **Floodlight**, and **Pyretic** can use OpenDaylight as a controller server to communicate with the network devices. In fact, OpenDaylight will work as an SDN controller server and other SDN controllers will work as SDN controller clients. The OpenDaylight NetIDE project provides portability and cooperation in a single SDN network to achieve multi SDN controller client/server architectures. The main benefits from using the client/server SDN controller architecture is to let network applications that were written for other SDN controllers such as Ryu communicate with OpenDaylight. Also you can dispatch the SDN network management between different SDN controllers based on network needs with smooth integration. The following diagram shows an example of multi SDN controllers:

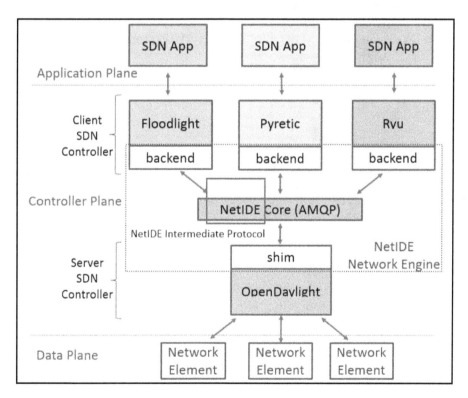

Getting ready

This recipe requires an Ubuntu 14.04 environment, OVS 2.3, Mininet, an OpenDaylight distribution, Ryu as another SDN controller, and the network Engine project from fp7 `https ://github.com/fp7-netide/Engine`. Also you need Vagrant if you use the predefined Vagrant file in the recipe folder. In this recipe, we will learn how a firewall network application runs on top of Ryu as an SDN controller client can communicate with OpenDaylight as an SDN controller server.

How to do it...

Perform the following steps:

1. If you already have the pre-request software installed you can skip this step and start directly from step 3. Otherwise, you will use the predefined Vagrant file to establish the environment. First you need to install Vagrant if it is not already installed. Then you need to go to the `NemoVM` directory in the recipe folder:

   ```
   $ cd chapter4-recipe8/NetIDEVM/
   ```

   You will need to change the network interface name in the Vagrant file to match your machine network interface:

   ```
   $ vi Vagrantfile
   ```

   Go to line 72, change the `en0` to match your machine network interface, and save the file. Then you need to start the VM installation:

   ```
   $ vagrant up
   ```

   The installation should take between 15-20 minutes, so it is a good time to get a coffee.

2. After the installation is done, you should be able to access the `NetIDEVM` using the `vagrant ssh` command:

   ```
   $ vagrant ssh
   ```

3. At Net IDEVM start the OpenDaylight distribution using the `karaf` script. Using `karaf` script will give you access to the Karaf CLI:

```
$ cd distribution-karaf-0.4.1-Beryllium-SR1/
$ ./bin/karaf
```

```
_____ _____ .__ .__ .__ __ __
_____ \ _____ ___ ___ _____ \ _____ ___.__.| | | |__| _____
 | | \/ |_
/ | \\___ \/ _ \ / \ | | \\_ \< | || | | |/ __\| | \ _\
/ | \ |_> > ___/| | \| ` \/ _ \\___ || |_| / /_/ > Y \ |
_____ / __/ \___ >___| /_____ ( ___ / ___||___/_/\___
 /|___| /__|
\/|___| \/ \/ \/ \/\/ /_____/ \/
Hit '<tab>' for a list of available commands
and '[cmd] --help' for help on a specific command.
Hit '<ctrl-d>' or type 'system:shutdown' or 'logout' to   shut
down OpenDaylight.
opendaylight-user@root>
```

4. Install the NetIDE features using the following command:

```
opendaylight-user@root> feature:install odl-netide-rest
```

You can check NetIDE installed features in Karaf CLI using the following command:

```
opendaylight-user@root> feature:list -i | grep netide
```

You should see something like this in your Karaf CLI:

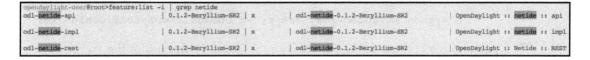

5. Now you will need to open a new console and go to the `ryu-backend` folder under the `Engine` directory:

```
$ cd Engine/ryu-backend/tests
```

Then you will create a simple network topology that consists of three hosts and three switches by using Mininet. Execute the following command to create the network topology:

```
$ sudo mn --custom netide-topo_13.py --topo mytopo -
controller=remote, ip=127.0.0.1, port=6644
```

 As the Engine project is in the active development phase, you might not find the netide-topo_13.py file under the test directory. You will need to copy the netide-topo.py file as netide-topo_13.py by using the following command:
```
$ sudo cp netide-topo.py ~/netide-topo_13.py
```

Then we will modify the OpenFlow protocol version from 1.0 to 1.3 using the following commands:

```
$ cd ~/
$ vi netide-topo_13.py
```

Now change all OpenFlow10 values to OpenFlow13 and save the file. Re-execute the Mininet command.

6. Open another console, and go to the ryu-backend folder in the Engine directory:

```
$ cd ~/Engine/ryu-backend/tests
```

Run the Engine proxy to manage communication between OpenDaylight and other SDN controllers:

```
$ python AdvancedProxyCore.py -c CompositionSpecification.xml
```

7. Open another console and go to the ryu-backend folder under the Engine directory:

```
$ cd ~/Engine/ryu-backend/
```

Start the Ryu controller and the fireware network application by using the following command:

```
$ ryu-manager --ofp-tcp-listen-port 7733 ryu-backend.py
tests/simple_switch_13.py tests/firewall_13.py
```

8. Now to verify that everything is working fine go back to the `mininet` console and ping all the hosts using the following command:

```
$ mininet> pingall
```

You should see that all hosts can reach each other.

How it works...

The network Engine works as a translator between the firewall (the network application) that runs with Ryu as the SDN controller client and OpenDaylight as the SDN controller server. In fact, the network Engine uses NetIDE as the intermediate protocol to handle communications between the client/server SDN controllers. The following diagram shows the internal design of the network Engine:

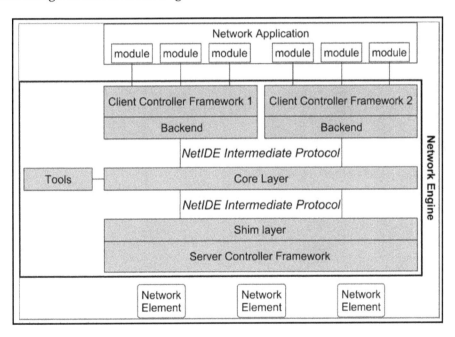

When the firewall module sends a request to the network to retrieve flow statistics, for example, the network Engine will justify and correctly drive the request between Ryu (the SDN controller client) and OpenDaylight (the SDN controller server). For more information about the network Engine and NetIDE protocol, you can check out the NetIDE project wiki at the OpenDaylight website:

```
https://wiki.opendaylight.org/view/NetIDE:Developer_Guide
```

See also

The OpenDaylight NetIDE project can work with other SDN controllers, such as Floodlight. You can check out the NetIDE system test wiki page for more information about how to integrate with Floodlight:

```
https://wiki.opendaylight.org/view/NetIDE:Beryllium:System_Test
```

4
Network Virtualization

In this chapter, we will cover the following recipes:

- Network virtualization with OpenFlow
- Integrating with OpenStack neutron
- OpenStack integration with OpenDaylight
- Edge-based virtual networks
- Service function chaining

Introduction

Network virtualization provides the ability to decouple network hardware resources from a virtual network to scale better and be supported in a virtual environment. Virtualization is the capacity to simulate a hardware platform in software using one hardware platform to support multiple **virtual machines** (**VMs**), which are manageable on demand. **Network function virtualization** (**NFV**) enables the shift toward network function as virtualized software.

Coupled with software defined networking, NFV's interaction can be highly increased and customized in order to provide fine-grained optimization for the cloud/data center. Dynamic provisioning and monitoring, scale-out infrastructure using on-demand network functions, better management and understanding of production topology, and many other functions are some of the benefits NFV and SDN are bringing to the telecommunications ecosystem. This offers cost-effective, scalable, and manageable solutions.

Within this chapter, we will see some usage of network virtualization provided by OpenDaylight.

REST API access is using user: `admin`, and password: `admin`.

While carrying out the recipes, REST requests could be required, for which you will be provided the operation, the headers, the payload, and the URL. To send those requests, use a `curl` command as follows:

```
curl -v --user "admin":"admin" -H "Accept: application/json" -H "Content-
type: application/josn" -k -X ${OPERATION}  -d '
${PAYLOAD}'
```

Network virtualization with OpenFlow

A company is conventionally divided into several departments, each having a well-defined purpose. The same goes for the network system and hardware residing within each of these departments. The purpose of the virtual network tenant project of OpenDaylight is to alleviate the physical network consideration, letting the software deal with it. **Virtual Tenant Network (VTN)** allows you to create network functions as virtual entities without having to consider the physical network, as it will automatically map the desired network capabilities on it once the configuration is done. Thus, you will better utilize resources and reduce the reconfiguration time of network services.

The project provides two main components:

- **VTN Manager**:
    - This is an internal OpenDaylight application that interacts with other modules, implementing components of the VTN model. Using REST APIs, you can create, delete, update, and remove (CRUD) VTN components as desired. Also, the VTN Manager implements the OpenStack L2 network function API.
- **VTN Coordinator**:
    - Provided as an external application, but delivered in the OpenDaylight release package, it allows REST APIs to interact with the VTN Manager component in order to define user configuration. It is part of the services and orchestration layer, supporting multi-controller orchestration and enabling virtual network tenant functionalities.

The purpose of this recipe is to provide a virtual layer 2 network in order to interconnect hosts using a virtual bridge using the VTN manager component.

Getting ready

This recipe will require one virtual switch. If you don't have one, you can use a Mininet-VM with OvS installed. You can download Mininet-VM from `https://github.com/mininet/mininet/wiki/Mininet-VM-Images`. Any version should work.

The following recipe will be presented using a Mininet-VM with OvS 2.3.1.

If you have Postman, get the Postman collection for this recipe:

`https://www.getpostman.com/collections/d49899eae85985d8e4ba`

How to do it...

Perform the following steps:

1. Now that you have downloaded all the required ingredients, and you have an environment to perform this recipe, let's create a virtual layer 2 network.
2. Start the OpenDaylight distribution using the `karaf` script. Using this script will give you access to the karaf CLI:

    ```
    $ ./bin/karaf
    ```

3. Install the user-facing feature responsible for pulling in all dependencies needed to connect an OpenFlow switch:

    ```
    opendaylight-user@root>feature:install odl-vtn-manager-neutron
    opendaylight-user@root>feature:install odl-vtn-manager-rest
    ```

It might take a minute or so to complete the installation.

VTN manager features are incompatible with other OpenStack-related features pulling in **neutron northbound** (**NN**), and aren't compatible with other flow programming features.

4. Connect the OvS instance to OpenDaylight in either passive or active mode:

- Login to Mininet-VM using the credentials:
    - **Username**: `mininet`
    - **Password**: `mininet`
- Connect to OvS using active mode:

```
$ sudo ovs-vsctl set-manager tcp:${CONTROLLER_IP}:6640
```

Here, `${CONTROLLER_IP}` is the IP address of the host running OpenDaylight.

Our virtual switch is now connected to OpenDaylight:

```
mininet@mininet-vm:~$ sudo ovs-vsctl show
0b8ed0aa-67ac-4405-af13-70249a7e8a96
    Manager "tcp:192.168.0.115:6640"
        is_connected: true
    ovs_version: "2.3.1"
```

5. Create a network topology containing three switches and four hosts within Mininet-VM using this command:

```
$ sudo mn --controller=remote,ip=${CONTROLLER_IP} --topo tree,2
```

You can see the topology using the following command:

```
mininet> net
```

Here is a visual representation:

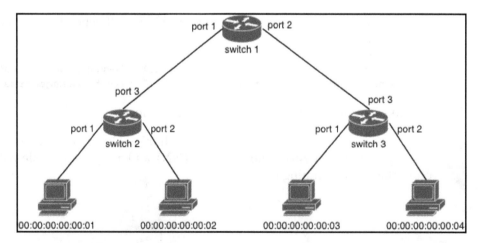

6. Try to ping `h1` from `h3`. It will fail because as is, switch 2 can't reach switch 3:

```
mininet> h1 ping h3
PING 10.0.0.3 (10.0.0.3) 56(84) bytes of data.
From 10.0.0.1 icmp_seq=1 Destination Host Unreachable
From 10.0.0.1 icmp_seq=2 Destination Host Unreachable
From 10.0.0.1 icmp_seq=3 Destination Host Unreachable
^C
--- 10.0.0.3 ping statistics ---
5 packets transmitted, 0 received, +3 errors, 100% packet loss,
time 4024ms
```

7. Add the required flows per switch to forward packets to the controller when there is a table-miss:

```
$ sudo ovs-ofctl add-flow s1
priority=0,actions=output:CONTROLLER
$ sudo ovs-ofctl add-flow s2
priority=0,actions=output:CONTROLLER
$ sudo ovs-ofctl add-flow s3
priority=0,actions=output:CONTROLLER
```

 This step is only required for the first release of Beryllium. For releases after Beryllium-SR, those flows are automatically added.

8. Create a Virtual Tenant named `vtn1` using the following request:

- Type: `POST`
- Headers:

   Authorization: Basic `YWRtaW46YWRtaW4=`

- URL: `http://localhost:8181/restconf/operations/vtn:update-vtn`
- Payload:

```
{
    "input":{
      "tenant-name":"vtn1"
    }
}
```

You should receive **200 OK** as the response.

9. Create a virtual bridge named `vBr1` within the tenant created previously:

- Type: `POST`
- Headers:

  Authorization: Basic `YWRtaW46YWRtaW4=`

- URL: `http://localhost:8181/restconf/operations/vtn:update-vtn`
- Payload:

```json
{
  "input":{
      "tenant-name":"vtn1",
      "bridge-name":"vbr1"
    }
}
```

You should receive **200 OK** as the response.

10. Create two interfaces within the virtual bridge, `if1` and `if2`:

- Type: `POST`
- Headers:

  Authorization: Basic `YWRtaW46YWRtaW4=`

- URL:
  `http://localhost:8181/restconf/operations/vtn-vinterface:update`
  `-vinterface`
- Payload:

```json
{
  "input":{
      "tenant-name":"vtn1",
      "bridge-name":"vbr1",
      "interface-name":"if1"
    }
}
```

You should receive **200 OK** as the response.

11. Repeat this request to create the second interface, but change interface-name to `if2`.

12. Create the mappings between the previously created interfaces and the actual port within the switch. The purpose is to create a bridge between `h1` and `h3`. Within OvS, `h1` is connected to port `s2-eth1` and `h3` is connected to port `s3-eth1`.

13. In order to perform the mapping, we also need the OpenFlow node within the OpenDaylight datastore related to the switch port. It can be retrieved by reading the OpenFlow node information (see `Chapter 1`, *OpenDaylight Fundamentals*, recipe 1, *Connecting OpenFlow switches*). In our case, `s2-eth1` is correlated to `openflow:2` and `s3-eth1` to `openflow:3`:

- Type: `POST`
- Headers:

    Authorization: Basic `YWRtaW46YWRtaW4=`

- URL:
  `http://localhost:8181/restconf/operations/vtn-port-map:set-port-map`
- Payload for host 1:

```
{
    "input":{
        "tenant-name":"vtn1",
        "bridge-name":"vbr1",
        "interface-name":"if1",
        "node":"openflow:2",
        "port-name":"s2-eth1"
    }
}
```

You should receive **200 OK** as the response.

14. Repeat the operation; make sure to replace the interface-name, node, and port-name with the values for host 3.

Host 1 should now be able to ping host 3 using the created virtual bridge:

```
mininet> h1 ping h3
PING 10.0.0.3 (10.0.0.3) 56(84) bytes of data.
64 bytes from 10.0.0.3: icmp_seq=1 ttl=64 time=47.4 ms
64 bytes from 10.0.0.3: icmp_seq=2 ttl=64 time=0.220 ms
64 bytes from 10.0.0.3: icmp_seq=3 ttl=64 time=0.055 ms
64 bytes from 10.0.0.3: icmp_seq=4 ttl=64 time=0.150 ms
^C
--- 10.0.0.3 ping statistics ---
4 packets transmitted, 4 received, 0% packet loss, time 3002ms
rtt min/avg/max/mdev = 0.055/11.968/47.450/20.485 ms
```

How it works...

When attaching the physical port to the virtual interface, the VTN project will push flow rules within the switches to enable communication using matches on the port, the VLAN, and the MAC address.

See flows within each switch (only switch 1 is shown, but similar flows are present in other switches) match packets tagged with VLAN 0x000 (and any priority):

```
mininet@mininet-vm:~$ sudo ovs-ofctl dump-flows s1 -OOpenFlow13
OFPST_FLOW reply (OF1.3) (xid=0x2): cookie=0x0, duration=123.379s, table=0,
n_packets=48, n_bytes=4080, priority=0 actions=CONTROLLER:65535
cookie=0x7f56000000000001, duration=118.249s, table=0, n_packets=4,
n_bytes=336, send_flow_rem
priority=10,in_port=2,vlan_tci=0x0000/0x1fff,dl_src=a6:33:4c:dd:fb:9f,dl_ds
t=92:bd:3b:89:75:6b actions=output:1 cookie=0x7f56000000000002,
duration=118.243s, table=0, n_packets=4, n_bytes=336, send_flow_rem
priority=10,in_port=1,vlan_tci=0x0000/0x1fff,dl_src=92:bd:3b:89:75:6b,dl_ds
t=a6:33:4c:dd:fb:9f actions=output:2
```

There's more...

- Retrieve the whole configuration using this request:
  - Type: `GET`
  - Headers:

    Authorization: Basic `YWRtaW46YWRtaW4=`

  - URL:
    `http://localhost:8181/restconf/operational/vtn:vtns/`
- Delete the whole configuration for the created tenant using this request:
  - Type: POST
  - Headers:

    Authorization: Basic `YWRtaW46YWRtaW4=`

  - URL:
    `http://localhost:8181/restconf/operations/vtn:remove-vtn`
  - Payload:

    ```
    {
        "input":{
          "tenant-name":"vtn1"
        }
    }
    ```

Integrating with OpenStack neutron

The OpenStack component networking-odl gates neutron APIs to OpenDaylight in a pass-through fashion. The neutron northbound project, within OpenDaylight, defines YANG models for each API that is defined in neutron. Those models, for the Beryllium release, can be found in the GitHub mirror of the project, `https://github.com/opendaylight/neutron/tree/stable/beryllium/model/src/main/yang`. Those two projects establish the bridge between the NFV platform and the software defined networking framework.

It is the duty of the modular layer 2 driver of OpenStack and the neutron northbound project of OpenDaylight to keep their own internal database in sync any time the data is shared across the two frameworks.

The neutron northbound project does not interact at all with the data. It provides it to the datastore when a neutron event occurs. Consumer services of neutron northbound will be able to register listeners on those models in order to react and program networking behavior based on events.

In this recipe, we will show how to create a network, a subnet, and a port using a dummy provider, so that nothing will happen after the creation. The purpose is to demonstrate how neutron APIs are integrated within OpenDaylight.

Getting ready

This recipe requires OpenDaylight and the feature file to add the dummy provider in order to test neutron northbound APIs without any consumer being registered (will be provided within the *How to do it...* steps).

 The recipe won't work in the Boron release, as the dummy provider was removed. It only works with Lithium and Beryllium releases.

How to do it...

Perform the following steps:

1. Now that you have downloaded all the required ingredients, and you have an environment to perform this recipe, let's see how OpenDaylight can mimic neutron events, before implementing an end-to-end integration.

2. Start the OpenDaylight karaf distribution using the `karaf` script. Using this script will give you access to the karaf CLI:

   ```
   $ ./bin/karaf
   ```

3. Install the user-facing feature responsible for pulling in all dependencies:

   ```
   opendaylight-user@root>feature:install odl-neutron-service
   ```

   It might take a minute or so to complete the installation.

4. Verify the deployment using the following command on the karaf CLI:

   `$ web:list`

```
opendaylight-user@root>web:list
ID  | State    | Web-State   | Level | Web-ContextPath      | Name
220 | Active   | Deployed    | 80    | /oauth2              | aaa-authn-sts (0.3.2.Beryllium-SR2)
226 | Active   | Failed      | 80    | /auth                | aaa-idmlight (0.3.2.Beryllium-SR2)
234 | Active   | Deployed    | 80    | /oauth2/federation   | aaa-authn-federation (0.3.2.Beryllium-SR2)
237 | Active   | Deployed    | 80    | /controller/nb/v2/neutron | org.opendaylight.neutron.northbound-api (0.6.2.Beryllium-SR2)
opendaylight-user@root>
```

You can see the **Web-State** of the **Web-ContextPath** that is
`/controller/nb/v2/neutron` is **Deployed**, which means the web server acting
as the neutron northbound within OpenDaylight is deployed and useable.

5. Add a feature repository bringing in the dummy provider in order to test the
   APIs.

   Download the appropriate feature file, depending on the version you are using:

   - **Beryllium-SR**:
     https://raw.githubusercontent.com/jgoodyear/OpenDaylightCookbook/maste
     r/chapter5/chapter5-recipe2/src/main/resources/features-neutron-
     test-0.6.0-Beryllium-features.xml

   - **Beryllium-SR1**:
     https://raw.githubusercontent.com/jgoodyear/OpenDaylightCookbook/maste
     r/chapter5/chapter5-recipe2/src/main/resources/features-neutron-
     test-0.6.1-Beryllium-SR1-features.xml

   - **Beryllium-SR2**:
     https://raw.githubusercontent.com/jgoodyear/OpenDaylightCookbook/maste
     r/chapter5/chapter5-recipe2/src/main/resources/features-neutron-
     test-0.6.2-Beryllium-SR2-features.xml

6. Then use this command to add the repositories within your running instance of
   OpenDaylight:

   ```
   $ feature:repo-add
   https://nexus.opendaylight.org/content/repositories/opendayligh
   t.release/org/opendaylight/neutron/features-neutron-test/0.6.0-
   Beryllium/features-neutron-test-0.6.0-Beryllium-features.xml
   ```

7. Once added, install the dummy provider feature:

   ```
   $ feature:install odl-neutron-dummyprovider-test
   ```

8. Add a network.

   To perform this operation, you need to send the following request, along with the payload.

9. The `tenant_id` corresponds to the UUID of the tenant that will own this network. We haven't created a tenant for that recipe, but in a real OpenStack deployment, you do so through OpenStack APIs.

10. The `segmentation_id` is an isolated segment on the physical network. The `network_type` attribute defines the segmentation model. For example, if the `network_type` is VLAN, this ID is a VLAN identifier. If `network_type` is `gre`, this ID is a `gre` key.

11. The ID is a generated UUID that will uniquely identify this network:

   - Type: `POST`
   - Headers:

         Authorization: Basic `YWRtaW46YWRtaW4=`

   - URL: `http://localhost:8080/controller/nb/v2/neutron/networks/`
   - Payload:

```
{
  "networks":[
      {
        "status":"ACTIVE",
        "subnets":[],
        "name":"network1",
        "admin_state_up":true,
        "tenant_id":"60cd4f6dbc5f499982a284e7b83b5be3",
        "provider:network_type":"local",
        "router:external":false,
        "shared":false,
        "id":"e9330b1f-a2ef-4160-a991-169e56ab17f5",
        "provider:segmentation_id":100
      }
  ]
}
```

   As we're using the dummy provider, the response will request `201` created.

12. Add a subnet within our network for the same tenant.

    The ID is a generated UUID that will uniquely identify this subnet:

- Type: POST
- Headers:

    Authorization: Basic YWRtaW46YWRtaW4=

- URL: http://localhost:8080/controller/nb/v2/neutron/subnets/
- Payload:

```json
{
  "subnet": {
    "name": "",
    "enable_dhcp": true,
    "network_id": "e9330b1f-a2ef-4160-a991-169e56ab17f5",
    "tenant_id": "4fd44f30292945e481c7b8a0c8908869",
    "dns_nameservers": [
    ],
    "allocation_pools": [
      {
        "start": "192.168.199.2",
        "end": "192.168.199.254"
      }
    ],
    "host_routes": [
    ],
    "ip_version": 4,
    "gateway_ip": "192.168.199.1",
    "cidr": "192.168.199.0/24",
    "id": "3b80198d-4f7b-4f77-9ef5-774d54e17126"
  }
}
```

13. Create a port within our subnet and for the same tenant.

    The id is a generated UUID that will uniquely identify this port:

- Type: POST
- Headers:

    Authorization: Basic YWRtaW46YWRtaW4=

- URL: `http://localhost:8080/controller/nb/v2/neutron/ports/`
- Payload:

```
{
  "port": {
    "status": "DOWN",
    "binding:host_id": "",
    "name": "port1",
    "allowed_address_pairs": [
    ],
    "admin_state_up": true,
    "network_id": "e9330b1f-a2ef-4160-a991-169e56ab17f5",
    "tenant_id": "4fd44f30292945e481c7b8a0c8908869",
    "binding:vif_details": {
    },
    "binding:vnic_type": "normal",
    "binding:vif_type": "unbound",
    "mac_address": "fa:16:3e:c9:cb:f0",
    "binding:profile": {
    },
    "fixed_ips": [
      {
        "subnet_id": "3b80198d-4f7b-4f77-9ef5-774d54e17126",
        "ip_address": "192.168.199.1"
      }
    ],
    "id": "65c0ee9f-d634-4522-8954-51021b570b0d"
  }
}
```

How it works...

Each of the requests we have sent are equivalent to a write in the OpenDaylight datastore, through the defined models mentioned at the beginning. The neutron northbound project supports many more operations than those three basic ones, but the purpose was to demonstrate how it works, along with the payload that matches the OpenStack neutron APIs.

OpenStack integration with OpenDaylight

Various projects within OpenDaylight integrate OpenStack, such as the VTN project presented in a previous recipe. Within this recipe, we will focus on a different project, the network virtualization project NetVirt.

NetVirt is a virtualization solution using the **Open vSwitch database project** (**OVSDB**) as a southbound provider for both open vSwitch and hardware VTEP switches. The NetVirt project also support service function chaining (which will be discussed in the next recipe).

In this recipe, we will demonstrate OpenStack integrated with OpenDaylight using DevStack.

Getting ready

This recipe requires at least two OpenStack nodes, one control node, and one compute node (you could have more than one compute node), and an OpenDaylight distribution. For your convenience, an OVA image, working with VirtualBox, has been set up to provide all you need to easily bring up the deployment. It contains OpenStack Liberty with OpenDaylight Beryllium. Download this image:

```
https://drive.google.com/file/d/0B8ihDx8wnbwjMU5nUmttUFRJOEU
```

The OVA image provides three nodes:

- OpenStack control and compute – devstack – OvS – CentOS7
- OpenStack compute – devstack – OvS – CentOS7
- Router for external access – CentOS6.5

> Running this recipe will require at least 8 GB to 16 GB of RAM if you were to run everything on the same host.

How to do it...

Perform the following steps:

1. Now that you have downloaded all the required ingredients, let's build our OpenStack environment and connect it to OpenDaylight so it can manage the underlying networking layer.
2. Open VirtualBox.

   If you don't have it, you can download it from here:

   ```
   https://www.virtualbox.org/wiki/Downloads
   ```

3. Import the OVA into VirtualBox, **File** | **Import Appliance**.

4. Select the previously downloaded appliance:

   `ovsdbtutorial15_2_liberty_be_external.ova`

5. After a few minutes, you will have three new nodes in VirtualBox, named odl31-control, odl32-compute, and router-node

6. Start the first two VMs and `ssh` into them using the terminal command line.

7. Log into the control node. The password is `odl`:

   $ ssh odl@192.168.50.31

8. Log into the compute node. The password is `odl`:

   $ ssh odl@192.168.50.32

9. In order to spin up and configure OpenStack efficiently, the integration is done using DevStack:

   `http://docs.openstack.org/developer/devstack/`

   DevStack provides tools enabling the installation of OpenStack key components from source, allowing the user to select the services to use.

   The configuration file of DevStack is `local.conf`.

10. Let's have a closer look at the DevStack configuration file:

    * The first lines are setting up the logging configuration, outputting the logs in a different direction than the source one for better manipulation:

      ```
      LOGFILE=/opt/stack/logs/stack.sh.log
      SCREEN_LOGDIR=/opt/stack/logs
      LOG_COLOR=False
      ```

    * As the images provided in the VMs contain all the required source code and tools in order to stack properly, we set those options to avoid any update of the source code:

      ```
      OFFLINE=True
      RECLONE=no
      VERBOSE=TRUE
      ```

- Disable all services so we can explicitly enable what we need:

  ```
  disable_all_services
  ```

- Enable core services: glance, keystone, nova, vnc, horizon:

  ```
  enable_service g-api g-reg key n-api n-crt n-obj n-cpu n-cond
  n-sch n-novnc n-xvnc n-cauth
  enable_service horizon
  ```

- Set OpenDaylight as the neutron backend engine rather than the OpenStack L2 agent:

  ```
  enable_service neutron q-dhcp q-meta q-svc odl-compute odl-
  neutron
  ```

- Set up host information. You'll need the IP address of the host running DevStack, in this case 192.168.254.31, and you will have to define the hostname, in this case odl31:

  ```
  HOST_IP=192.168.254.31
  HOST_NAME=odl31
  SERVICE_HOST_NAME=$HOST_NAME
  SERVICE_HOST=$HOST_IP
  Q_HOST=$SERVICE_HOST
  ```

- Enable the networking-odl plugin using its repository information.
- As we configured to be offline, DevStack will try to retrieve the networking-odl repository from the /opt/stack/networking-odl folder (this is where the source code is actually located):

  ```
  enable_plugin networking-odl
  http://git.openstack.org/openstack/networking-odl
  ```

- A few configurations regarding OpenDaylight have to be done within this file. The most important ones are the following:

  ```
  ODL_PORT=8080
  ODL_MGR_IP=192.168.2.11
  ODL_L3=True
  ODL_PROVIDER_MAPPINGS=br-ex:eth2
  ```

- This is where you can specify the OpenDaylight IP address, which port OpenDaylight listens to, whether or not L3 forwarding is enabled, and mappings configuration, in this case setting `br_ex` to be bounded behind `eth2`.
- If OpenDaylight is running on the same host as DevStack (control node), you will disable L3 forwarding as the two entities will be able to communicate well using L2. But if OpenDaylight is external to the DevStack setup, you should enable L3 in both the DevStack and OpenDaylight configuration (see the bullet point regarding OpenDaylight configuration).
- The remaining configuration bits in `local.conf` are mostly regarding OpenStack internals; we won't go through them.
- Learn more about the configuration file here:

  ```
  http://docs.openstack.org/developer/devstack/configuration.html#local-conf
  ```

11. On the control and compute node, edit the `local.conf` to add the IP address of the host running OpenDaylight:

    ```
    $ vi /opt/devstack/local.conf
    ```

12. Replace the value of `ODL_MGR_IP` with the IP address of the host running OpenDaylight.

13. Enable L3 forwarding within OpenDaylight:

    ```
    $ vi etc/custom.properties
    ```

14. Uncomment line 83 in order to have this enabled:

    ```
    ovsdb.l3.fwd.enabled=yes
    ```

15. Start the OpenDaylight karaf distribution using the `karaf` script. Using this script will give you access to the karaf CLI:

    ```
    $ ./bin/karaf
    ```

16. Install the user-facing feature responsible for pulling in all dependencies:

    opendaylight-user@root>feature:install odl-ovsdb-openstack

    It might take a minute or so to complete the installation.

17. Let's stack.

    On each node, execute the following commands:

    ```
    $ cd /opt/devstack
    $ ./stack.sh
    ```

    Once done, you should have the following output:

    ```
    This is your host IP address: 192.168.254.31
    This is your host IPv6 address: ::1
    Horizon is now available at http://192.168.254.31/dashboard
    Keystone is serving at http://192.168.254.31:5000/
    The default users are: admin and demo
    The password: admin
    ```

Instead of using `192.168.254.31` as the horizon IP address, you should use `192.168.50.31`. The reason for this is because the `192.168.254.0` subnet is an isolated network that is not reachable from the host, whereas the `192.168.50.0` subnet is reachable from the host.

Each node has an OvS instance running, and is configured with two bridges, an integration (`br-int`) and an external bridge (`br-ex`).

The `br-int`, for integration, is geared to connect the VMs, whereas `br-ex`, for external, will serves as a gateway to the outside world.

As we have enabled L3 forwarding, OpenDaylight will automatically configure patch ports to connect `br-int` with `br-ex` if trying to connect tenant VMs to an external subnet.

Here is the bridge topology:

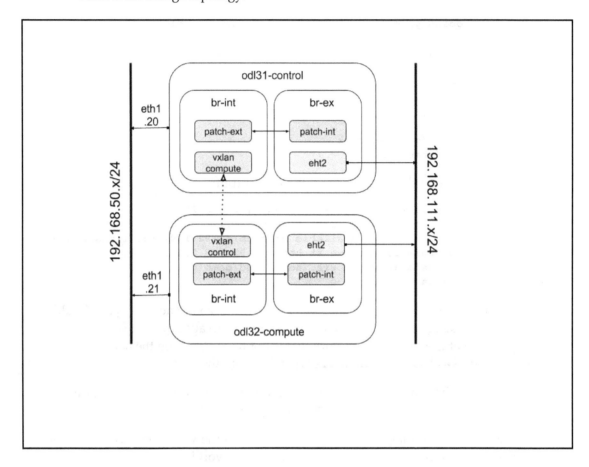

18. Look at the output of the topology using the following command:

```
[odl@odl31 devstack]$ sudo ovs-vsctl show
6b96af57-f05b-4663-9e1d-180c0c788a5b
    Manager "tcp:192.168.1.164:6640"
        is_connected: true
    Bridge br-ex
        Controller "tcp:192.168.1.164:6653"
            is_connected: true
        fail_mode: secure
        Port br-ex
            Interface br-ex
                type: internal
    Bridge br-int
        Controller "tcp:192.168.1.164:6653"
```

```
        is_connected: true
    fail_mode: secure
    Port br-int
        Interface br-int
            type: internal
ovs_version: "2.4.0"
```

19. Each bridge is set up with a set of flows in order to manage services. Here is the dump of the flows for each bridge:

```
[odl@odl32 stack]$ sudo ovs-ofctl dump-flows br-int -O
OpenFlow13
OFPST_FLOW reply (OF1.3) (xid=0x2):
 cookie=0x0, duration=2688.686s, table=0, n_packets=0,
n_bytes=0, dl_type=0x88cc actions=CONTROLLER:65535
 cookie=0x0, duration=2688.649s, table=0, n_packets=0,
n_bytes=0, priority=0 actions=goto_table:20
 cookie=0x0, duration=2688.649s, table=20, n_packets=0,
n_bytes=0, priority=0 actions=goto_table:30
 cookie=0x0, duration=2688.649s, table=30, n_packets=0,
n_bytes=0, priority=0 actions=goto_table:40
 cookie=0x0, duration=2688.649s, table=40, n_packets=0,
n_bytes=0, priority=0 actions=goto_table:50
 cookie=0x0, duration=2688.649s, table=50, n_packets=0,
n_bytes=0, priority=0 actions=goto_table:60
 cookie=0x0, duration=2688.649s, table=60, n_packets=0,
n_bytes=0, priority=0 actions=goto_table:70
 cookie=0x0, duration=2688.649s, table=70, n_packets=0,
n_bytes=0, priority=0 actions=goto_table:80
 cookie=0x0, duration=2688.649s, table=80, n_packets=0,
n_bytes=0, priority=0 actions=goto_table:90
 cookie=0x0, duration=2688.649s, table=90, n_packets=0,
n_bytes=0, priority=0 actions=goto_table:100
 cookie=0x0, duration=2688.649s, table=100, n_packets=0,
n_bytes=0, priority=0 actions=goto_table:110
 cookie=0x0, duration=2688.649s, table=110, n_packets=0,
n_bytes=0, priority=0 actions=drop
[odl@odl32 stack]$ sudo ovs-ofctl dump-flows br-ex -O
OpenFlow13
OFPST_FLOW reply (OF1.3) (xid=0x2):
 cookie=0x0, duration=2700.054s, table=0, n_packets=0,
n_bytes=0, dl_type=0x88cc actions=CONTROLLER:65535
 cookie=0x0, duration=2700.054s, table=0, n_packets=0,
n_bytes=0, priority=0 actions=NORMAL
```

20. The internal bridge, `br-int`, is set up to provide the following flow pipeline:

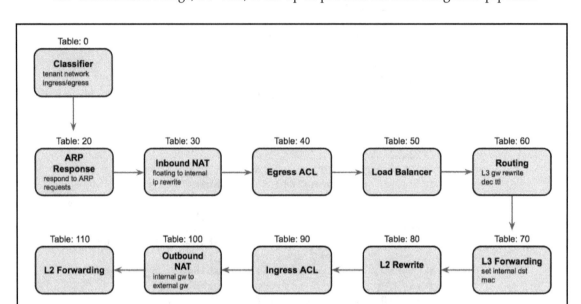

21. Looking closer at the interface configuration of your nodes, they share the same internal configuration, which is as follows:
    - `eth0`: VirtualBox NAT address, `10.0.2.15`. Management interface that can be used but requires adding VirtualBox port-forwarding to reach from host.
    - `eth1`: Internal interface for tenant traffic.
    - `eth2`: External interface for `floatingip`.
    - `eth3`: VirtualBox Bridged Adapter, `192.168.50.3{1,2}`. Management interface reachable from host.

How it works...

- As we're using an external instance of OpenDaylight, we had to enable L3 forwarding so that the two entities (OpenStack control node and OpenDaylight) are able to communicate with each other. Also, we have set up the interface behind which the external bridge is bounded (`eth2`) in the DevStack configuration.

- While stacking, the OvS instance contained in both the control and compute node is going to connect to OpenDaylight. Thanks to OpenFlowPlugin and the OpenFlowJava project, the NetVirt project is able to register a listener on such events, and thus react by adding the internal bridge (`br-int`) and the external bridge. The latter is added only if L3 forwarding is enabled.

- In order to add those bridges, NetVirt is communicating using the OVSDB southbound plugin that talks to OvS.

- Finally, within the bridge, the basic flow pipeline is pushed so they know how to react and where to follow packets based on their match actions.

Edge-based virtual networks

One of the various key features enabled using the OpenStack integration within OpenDaylight is the ability to create a **virtual extensible LAN** (**VXLAN**) between hosts and network entities thanks to network, subnet, and port configuration. Using security groups and security rules, you can easily define specifications for groups of ports, either the ingress and/or egress port, within a given namespace, and define rules within the group dictating the allowed behavior.

In this recipe, we will demonstrate network virtualization using VXLAN overlay, along with L3 and floating IP.

Getting ready

This recipe requires at least two OpenStack nodes, one control node and one compute node (you could have more than one compute node), and an OpenDaylight distribution. For your convenience, an OVA image, working with VirtualBox, has been set up to provide all you need to easily bring up the deployment. It contains OpenStack Liberty with OpenDaylight Beryllium. Download this image:

```
https://drive.google.com/file/d/0B8ihDx8wnbwjMU5nUmttUFRJOEU
```

The OVA image provides three nodes:

- OpenStack control and compute - devstack - OvS - CentOS7
- OpenStack compute - devstack - OvS - CentOS7
- Router for external access - CentOS6.5

How to do it...

Perform the following steps:

1. We have previously set up the basic environment enabling OpenStack's integration with OpenDaylight. Now it is time to use that environment to create a VXLAN.
2. Use the setup completed in the previous recipe. If you don't have it yet, please read and execute the previous recipe before moving forward.
3. Set up the neutron environment.

   Once you have the environment ready and stacked, let's start using neutron from the control node:

   ```
   $ source openrc admin admin
   ```

4. Set up a nano flavor with 64 MB memory, no disk space, and one VCPU. A flavor is a defined hardware configuration within a server:

   ```
   $ nova flavor-create m1.nano auto 64 0 1
   ```

5. The following script can be used to execute the same operation:

   ```
   /opt/tools/os_addnano.sh
   ```

6. Create an admin `keypair`:

   ```
   $ nova keypair-add --pub-key ~/.ssh/id_rsa.pub admin_key
   ```

7. The following script can be used to execute the same operation:

   ```
   /opt/tools/os_addadminkey.sh
   ```

8. Create an external flat network and subnet defined with the following allocation pool [192.168.56.9 – 192.168.56.14], gateway 192.168.56.1, and network 192.168.56.0/24:

```
$ neutron net-create ext-net --router:external --
provider:physical_network public --provider:network_type flat
$ neutron subnet-create --name ext-subnet --allocation-pool
start=192.168.56.9,end=192.168.56.14 --disable-dhcp --gateway
192.168.56.1 ext-net 192.168.56.0/24
```

9. Create an external router and add the external network created earlier as its gateway:

```
$ neutron router-create ext-rtr
$ neutron router-gateway-set ext-rtr ext-net
```

10. Create a VXLAN network and subnet:

```
$ neutron net-create vx-net --provider:network_type vxlan --
provider:segmentation_id 1500
$ neutron subnet-create vx-net 10.100.5.0/24 --name vx-subnet -
-dns-nameserver 8.8.8.8
```

11. Add the VXLAN subnet as an interface of the router created in step 5:

```
$ neutron router-interface-add ext-rtr vx-subnet
```

12. The following script can be used to execute operations 5, 6, and 7:

```
/opt/tools/os_addextnetrtr.sh
```

13. Let's create two VMs and attach them to the VXLAN:

```
$ nova boot --poll --flavor m1.nano --image $(nova image-list |
grep 'uec\s' | awk '{print $2}' | tail -1) --nic net-
id=$(neutron net-list | grep -w vx-net | awk '{print $2}')
vmvx1 --availability_zone=nova:odl31 --key_name admin_key
$ nova boot --poll --flavor m1.nano --image $(nova image-list |
grep 'uec\s' | awk '{print $2}' | tail -1) --nic net-
id=$(neutron net-list | grep -w vx-net | awk '{print $2}')
vmvx2 --availability_zone=nova:odl32 --key_name admin_key
$ nova get-vnc-console vmvx1 novnc
$ nova get-vnc-console vmvx2 novnc
```

14. The following script can be used to execute the same operation:

    /opt/tools/os_addvms.sh

15. Create `floatingip` for each VM so they can be reachable though the external network:

    ```
    for vm in vmvx1 vmvx2; do
        vm_id=$(nova list | grep $vm | awk '{print $2}')
        port_id=$(neutron port-list -c id -c fixed_ips -- --
    device_id $vm_id | grep subnet_id | awk '{print $2}')
        neutron floatingip-create --port_id $port_id ext-net
    done;
    ```

16. The following script can be used to execute the same operation:

    /opt/tools/os_addfloatingips.sh

17. You could also run all those commands using this script:

    /opt/tools/os_ doitall.sh

18. Here is the global output on the console once you run all those commands:

    https://github.com/jgoodyear/OpenDaylightCookbook/blob/master/chapte
    r5/chapter5-recipe4/src/main/resources/console-output.txt

19. Look at the created topology using the web UI interface. To do so, install the following feature in `karaf`:

    opendaylight-user@root>feature:install odl-ovsdb-ui

20. Navigate to the following URL. Make sure to change `${CONTROLLER_IP}` to the IP address of the host running OpenDaylight:

    http://${CONTROLLER_IP}:8181/index.html#/ovsdb/index

21. User is `admin`, password is `admin`.

22. You will be able to see the following view. By clicking on any component of the view, you will be provided information about it.

In the following view you can see the external and VXLAN network created, along with the two VMs contained in the VXLAN network:

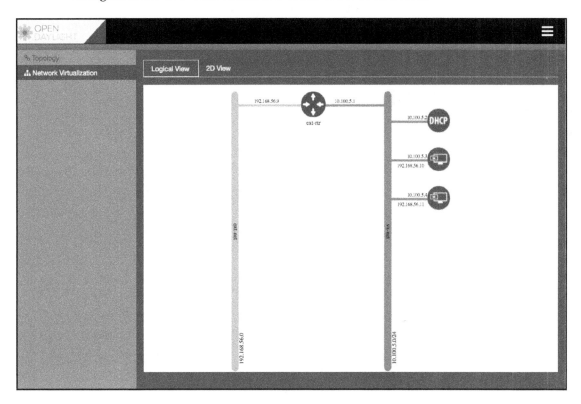

23. You can also see a similar topology using the OpenStack UI. Just browse to the following address:

    http://192.168.50.31/dashboard/project/network_topology/

    User is admin, password is admin.

24. Look at the data in OpenDaylight datastore:
    1. OVSDB Operational Datastore:
        - Type: POST
        - Headers:

            Authorization: Basic YWRtaW46YWRtaW4=

- URL:
  ```
  http://localhost:8080/restconf/operational/netw
  ork-topology:network-topology/
  ```

2. Neutron Datastore (in-sync with OpenStack):
  - Network:

    - Type: POST
    - Headers:

      Authorization: Basic YWRtaW46YWRtaW4=

    - URL:
      ```
      http://localhost:8080/controller/nb/
      v2/neutron/networks/
      ```

  - Subnet:

    - Type: POST
    - Headers:

      Authorization: Basic YWRtaW46YWRtaW4=

    - URL:
      ```
      http://localhost:8080/controller/nb/
      v2/neutron/subnets/
      ```

  - Ports:

    - Type: POST
    - Headers:

      Authorization: Basic YWRtaW46YWRtaW4=

    - URL:
      ```
      http://localhost:8080/controller/nb/
      v2/neutron/ports/
      ```

- Security Group:
    - Type: POST
    - Headers:

        Authorization: Basic `YWRtaW46YWRtaW4=`

    - URL:
      `http://localhost:8080/controller/nb/v2/neutron/security-groups/`
- Security Rules:
    - Type: POST
    - Headers:

        Authorization: Basic `YWRtaW46YWRtaW4=`

    - URL:
      `http://localhost:8080/controller/nb/v2/neutron/security-group-rules/`

25. Look at the OvS topology for both the control and the compute. We can see the VXLAN tunnel is well established.

26. This is what you should expect for the control node:

    ```
    https://github.com/jgoodyear/OpenDaylightCookbook/blob/master/chapter5
    /chapter5-recipe4/src/main/resources/control-node-topo.txt
    ```

27. This is what you should expect for the compute node:

    ```
    https://github.com/jgoodyear/OpenDaylightCookbook/blob/master/chapter5
    /chapter5-recipe4/src/main/resources/compute-node-topo.txt
    ```

How it works...

This deployment involves both OpenStack and OpenDaylight, and within those, respectively, networking-odl and neutron northbound are doing the wiring, so NetVirt is a consumer of the neutron events:

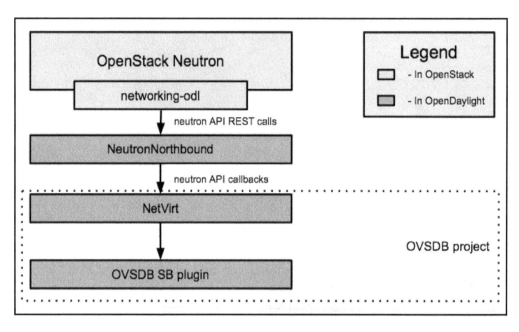

So the NetVirt project has listeners to get callbacks when events are happening, callbacks that will trigger and write into the OVSDB Southbound plugin, updating the OvS topology.

Service function chaining

End-to-end services usually require various service functions, network services such as load balancers or firewalls, as well as application-specific services. To provide the ability to spawn dynamic service function chains, less coupled to network topology and physical resources, the SFC project of OpenDaylight was created.

Leveraging VM and/or container networking, we can efficiently create network services as needed, having the service chain completely modular and dynamic.

In this recipe, we will perform a demonstration of the capability of the SFC project using the sfc103 demo provided within their repository:

`https://github.com/opendaylight/sfc/tree/release/beryllium-sr2/sfc-demo/sfc` `103`.

The global network topology for this recipe is as follows:

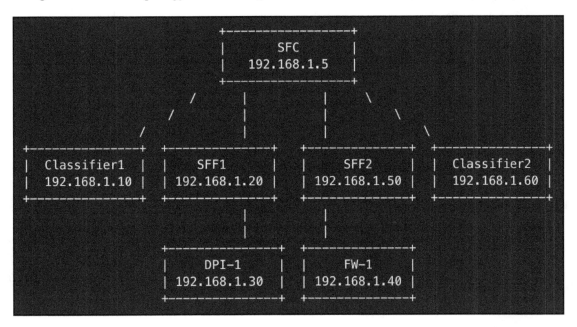

The following recipe has been tested with OpenDaylight Beryllium SR2 release. It is not guaranteed that the configuration will be the same in different releases.

Getting ready

This recipe requires VirtualBox and a machine with at least 8 GB of RAM. We will be using a trusty box, that can be found here:

`https://cloud-images.ubuntu.com/vagrant/trusty/current/trusty-server-cloudim` `g-amd64-vagrant-disk1.box`

How to do it...

Perform the following steps:

1. Now that you have downloaded all the required ingredients, and you have an environment to perform this recipe, let's build our VMs and create our service function chain.

2. Clone the SFC repository and checkout branch stable/beryllium, tag `release/beryllium-sr2`:

```
$ git clone https://git.opendaylight.org/gerrit/sfc
$ cd sfc
$ git checkout tabs/release/beryllium-sr2
```

3. Start the demonstration installation (it is automatic; skip this step to do it manually):

```
$ cd sfc-demo/sfc103/
$ ./demo.sh
```

4. From now until the setup is completely ready, it might take 5 to 10 minutes. In the meantime, the following step will explain what is automatically being done by the script we just started.

5. Everything starts with the environment setup; we have seven VMs to build and provide accordingly the functionality it performs.

6. Create the OpenDaylight VM:

   - Resources: 4 CPU and 4 GB of RAM
   - Private IP: `192.168.1.5`
   - Set up and run the SFC project:

```
$ wget
https://raw.githubusercontent.com/jgoodyear/OpenDaylightCookboo
k/master/chapter5/chapter5-
recipe5/src/main/resources/setup_odl.sh
$ ./setup_odl.sh
```

7. Create the classifier1 VM:

   - Resources: 1 CPU and 1 GB of RAM (default, no need to be specified)
   - Private IP: `192.168.1.10`

- Install the pre-requisites:

```
$ wget
https://raw.githubusercontent.com/jgoodyear/OpenDaylightCookboo
k/master/chapter5/chapter5-recipe5/src/main/resources/
setup_prerequisites.sh
$ ./setup_prerequisites.sh
```

- Install Open vSwitch patched to be `nsh-aware`:

```
$ rmmod openvswitch
$ find /lib/modules | grep openvswitch.ko | xargs rm -rf
$ curl
https://raw.githubusercontent.com/priteshk/ovs/nsh-v8/third-par
ty/start-ovs-deb.sh | bash
```

- Set OpenDaylight as OvS manager and create an initial bridge, `br-sfc`:

```
$ sudo ovs-vsctl set-manager tcp:192.168.1.5:6640
$ sudo ovs-vsctl add-br br-sfc
```

8. Create and configure an internal network namespace:

- Create a new network namespace named `app`:

```
$ ip netns add app
```

- Assign an interface to the network namespace by creating a virtual network interface pair, `veth-app`:

```
$ ip link add veth-app type veth peer name veth-br
```

Using the `ip link` command list you should see a pair of virtual ethernet namespaces. Right now they belong to either the default or global network namespace. In order to connect the global namespace to the `app` namespace created, do the following:

```
$ ip link set veth-app netns app
```

- Create ports named `veth-br` in `br-sfc`:

```
$ sudo ovs-vsctl add-port br-sfc veth-br
```

- Set port `veth-br` to up:

  ```
  $ ip link set dev veth-br up
  ```

- Configure our `app` namespace using the following commands by assigning an IP address and the `veth-app` interface and set it up:

  ```
  $ ip netns exec app ifconfig veth-app 192.168.2.1/24 up
  ```

- Assign a mac address to the link layer of the `veth-app` interface:

  ```
  $ ip netns exec app ip link set dev veth-app addr
  00:00:11:11:11:11
  ```

- Create an ARP address mapping entry for `veth-app`:

  ```
  $ ip netns exec app arp -s 192.168.2.2 00:00:22:22:22:22 -i
  veth-app
  ```

- Bring the `veth-app` and `lo` interfaces up:

  ```
  $ ip netns exec app ip link set dev veth-app up
  $ ip netns exec app ip link set dev lo up
  ```

- Set the **maximum transfer unit** (**MTU**) for the `veth-app` interface:

  ```
  $ ip netns exec app ifconfig veth-app mtu 1400
  ```

9. Create the classifier2 VM (the steps are similar to those done in step 4):

- Private IP: `192.168.1.10`
- Modify the values while going through the following steps:
    1. Use IP address `192.168.2.2/24`.
    2. Use mac address `00:00:22:22:22:22`.
    3. Use this command to create the ARP mapping:

       ```
       $ ip netns exec app arp -s 192.168.2.1 00:00:11:11:11:11-i
       veth-app
       ```

- Set up a simple HTTP server and bind it behind port `80`:

  ```
  $ ip netns exec app python -m SimpleHTTPServer 80
  ```

10. Once the preceding steps are done, we have the following architecture:

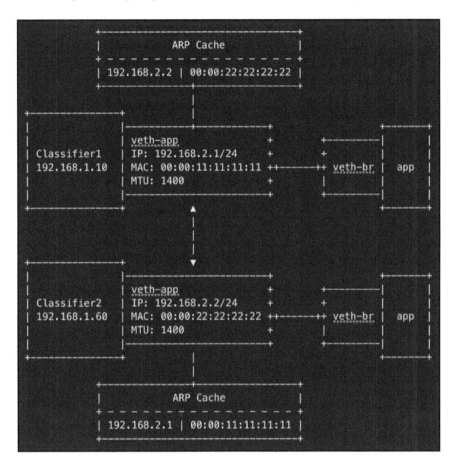

11. Create the service function forwarder VM1:

- Resources: 1 CPU and 1 GB of RAM (default, no need to be specified)
- Private IP: `192.168.1.20`
- Install pre-requisites:

```
$ wget
https://raw.githubusercontent.com/jgoodyear/OpenDaylightCookboo
k/master/chapter5/chapter5-recipe5/src/main/resources/
setup_prerequisites.sh
$ ./setup_prerequisites.sh
```

- Install OpenVSwitch patched to be `nsh-aware`:

```
$ rmmod openvswitch
$ find /lib/modules | grep openvswitch.ko | xargs rm -rf
$ curl
https://raw.githubusercontent.com/priteshk/ovs/nsh-v8/third-par
ty/start-ovs-deb.sh | bash
```

- Set OpenDaylight as OvS manager and create an initial bridge, `br-sfc`:

```
$ sudo ovs-vsctl set-manager tcp:192.168.1.5:6640
```

12. Create the service function forwarder VM2:

- Resources: 1CPU and 1 GB of RAM (default, no need to be specified)
- Private IP: `192.168.1.50`
- Install pre-requisites:

```
$ wget
https://raw.githubusercontent.com/jgoodyear/OpenDaylightCookboo
k/master/chapter5/chapter5-recipe5/src/main/resources/
setup_prerequisites.sh
$ ./setup_prerequisites.sh
```

- Install OpenVSwitch patched to be `nsh-aware`:

```
$ rmmod openvswitch
$ find /lib/modules | grep openvswitch.ko | xargs rm -rf
$ curl
https://raw.githubusercontent.com/priteshk/ovs/nsh-v8/third-par
ty/start-ovs-deb.sh | bash
```

- Set OpenDaylight as OvS manager and create an initial bridge, `br-sfc`:

```
$ sudo ovs-vsctl set-manager tcp:192.168.1.5:6640
```

13. Create the service functions VM1 and VM2. One will be a **Deep Inspection Package** (**DPI**) and the other will be a firewall.
14. Repeat the following operations for both VMs:

- Resources: 1 CPU and 1 GB of RAM (default, no need to be specified)
- VM1 Private IP: `192.168.1.30`
- VM2 Private IP: `192.168.1.40`

- Install pre-requisites:

  ```
  $ wget
  https://raw.githubusercontent.com/jgoodyear/OpenDaylightCookboo
  k/master/chapter5/chapter5-
  recipe5/src/main/resources/setup_sf.sh
  $ ./setup_sf.sh
  ```

15. At this point, a verification of all the VM configuration can be performed, ensuring we haven't missed something. To do so, open VirtualBox and make sure the VMs are running and configured as required.

16. Now that we have all the topology created and deployed, let's configure OpenDaylight, using the following nine requests.

17. For any of the following PUT requests, in order to verify the configuration was correctly processed by the OpenDaylight controller, you could send the request again, but using a GET operation without the payload. That request should return the configuration you pushed.

18. To verify that configuration was applied, you can send the GET request to the same URL but change the data store type from configuration to operational. Instead of having `http://${CONTROLLER_IP}:8181/restconf/config/...` you would have `http://${CONTROLLER_IP}:8181/restconf/operational/...`.

19. Create the service nodes for our six previously created nodes, the seventh being the OpenDaylight controller itself:

- Type: PUT
- Headers:

  Authorization: Basic YWRtaW46YWRtaW4=

- URL:
  `http://192.168.1.5:8181/restconf/config/service-node:service-nodes`
- Payload:

  ```
  {
    "service-nodes":{
      "service-node":[
        {
          "name":"node0",
          "service-function":[

          ],
  ```

```
            "ip-mgmt-address":"192.168.1.10"
        },
        {
          "name":"node1",
          "service-function":[

          ],
          "ip-mgmt-address":"192.168.1.20"
        },
        {
          "name":"node2",
          "service-function":[
            "dpi-1"
          ],
          "ip-mgmt-address":"192.168.1.30"
        },
        {
          "name":"node3",
          "service-function":[
            "firewall-1"
          ],
          "ip-mgmt-address":"192.168.1.40"
        },
        {
          "name":"node4",
          "service-function":[

          ],
          "ip-mgmt-address":"192.168.1.50"
        },
        {
          "name":"node5",
          "service-function":[

          ],
          "ip-mgmt-address":"192.168.1.60"
        }
      ]
    }
  }
```

20. Create the two service functions (DPI and firewall):

- Type: PUT
- Headers:

  Authorization: Basic YWRtaW46YWRtaW4=

- URL:
  `http://192.168.1.5:8181/restconf/config/service-function:service-functions`

- Payload:

```json
{
    "service-functions":{
        "service-function":[
            {
                "name":"dpi-1",
                "ip-mgmt-address":"192.168.1.30",
                "rest-uri":"http://192.168.1.30:5000",
                "type":"dpi",
                "nsh-aware":"true",
                "sf-data-plane-locator":[
                    {
                        "name":"sf1-dpl",
                        "port":6633,
                        "ip":"192.168.1.30",
                        "transport":"service-locator:vxlan-gpe",
                        "service-function-forwarder":"SFF1"
                    }
                ]
            },
            {
                "name":"firewall-1",
                "ip-mgmt-address":"192.168.1.40",
                "rest-uri":"http://192.168.1.40:5000",
                "type":"firewall",
                "nsh-aware":"true",
                "sf-data-plane-locator":[
                    {
                        "name":"sf2-dpl",
                        "port":6633,
                        "ip":"192.168.1.40",
                        "transport":"service-locator:vxlan-gpe",
                        "service-function-forwarder":"SFF2"
                    }
                ]
            }
        ]
    }
}
```

21. Create the service function forwarder:

- Type: PUT
- Headers:

    Authorization: Basic YWRtaW46YWRtaW4=

- URL:
  http://192.168.1.5:8181/restconf/config/service-function-forwar
  der:service-function-forwarders
- Payload:
  https://raw.githubusercontent.com/jgoodyear/OpenDaylightCookbook/maste
  r/chapter5/chapter5-recipe5/src/main/resources/sff.json

22. Create the service function chain:

- Type: PUT
- Headers:

    Authorization: Basic YWRtaW46YWRtaW4=

- URL:
  http://192.168.1.5:8181/restconf/config/service-function-chain:
  service-function-chains/
- Payload:

```
{
    "service-function-chains":{
      "service-function-chain":[
          {
            "name":"SFC1",
            "symmetric":"true",
            "sfc-service-function":[
                {
                  "name":"dpi-abstract1",
                  "type":"dpi"
                },
                {
                  "name":"firewall-abstract1",
                  "type":"firewall"
                }
            ]
          }
      ]
    }
}
```

}

23. Create the service function metadata:

- Type: PUT
- Headers:

  Authorization: Basic YWRtaW46YWRtaW4=

- URL:
  http://192.168.1.5:8181/restconf/config/service-function-path-m
  etadata:service-function-metadata/
- Payload:

```
{
    "service-function-metadata":{
      "context-metadata":[
          {
            "name":"NSH1",
            "context-header1":"1",
            "context-header2":"2",
            "context-header3":"3",
            "context-header4":"4"
          }
      ]
    }
}
```

24. Create the service function paths:

- Type: PUT
- Headers:

  Authorization: Basic YWRtaW46YWRtaW4=

- URL:
  http://192.168.1.5:8181/restconf/config/service-function-path:s
  ervice-function-paths/
- Payload:

```
{
    "service-function-paths":{
      "service-function-path":[
          {
            "name":"SFP1",
            "service-chain-name":"SFC1",
```

```
                    "classifier":"Classifier1",
                    "symmetric-classifier":"Classifier2",
                    "context-metadata":"NSH1",
                    "symmetric":"true"
                }
            ]
        }
    }
```

25. Create the service function **access control list** (**ACL**):

- Type: PUT
- Headers:

    Authorization: Basic YWRtaW46YWRtaW4=

- URL:
  `http://192.168.1.5:8181/restconf/config/ietf-access-control-list:access-lists/`
- Payload:
  `https://raw.githubusercontent.com/jgoodyear/OpenDaylightCookbook/master/chapter5/chapter5-recipe5/src/main/resources/acl.json`

26. Create the rendered service path:

- Type: POST
- Headers:

    Authorization: Basic YWRtaW46YWRtaW4=

- URL:
  `http://192.168.1.5:8181/restconf/operations/rendered-service-path:create-rendered-path/`
- Payload:

```
    {
        "input": {
            "name": "RSP1",
            "parent-service-function-path": "SFP1",
            "symmetric": "true"
        }
    }
```

27. Create the service function classifier:

- Type: PUT
- Headers:

  Authorization: Basic YWRtaW46YWRtaW4=

- URL:
  http://192.168.1.5:8181/restconf/config/service-function-classi
  fier:service-function-classifiers/
- Payload:

```
{
  "service-function-classifiers": {
    "service-function-classifier": [
      {
        "name": "Classifier1",
        "scl-service-function-forwarder": [
          {
            "name": "SFF0",
            "interface": "veth-br"
          }
        ],
        "access-list": "ACL1"
      },
      {
        "name": "Classifier2",
        "scl-service-function-forwarder": [
          {
            "name": "SFF3",
            "interface": "veth-br"
          }
        ],
        "access-list": "ACL2"
      }
    ]
  }
}
```

28. Using the DLUX SFC UI application, you can have an overview of the whole service function chain you have just created.

29. To view the service chain, navigate to the following URL:

    `http://192.168.1.5:8181/index.html#/sfc/servicechain`

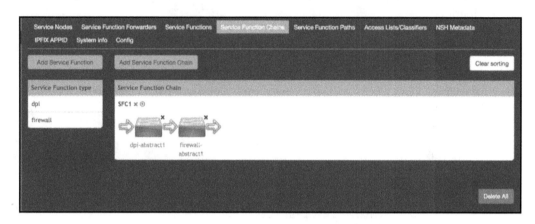

30. To view the service chain, navigate to the following URL:

    `http://192.168.1.5:8181/index.html#/sfc/servicenode`

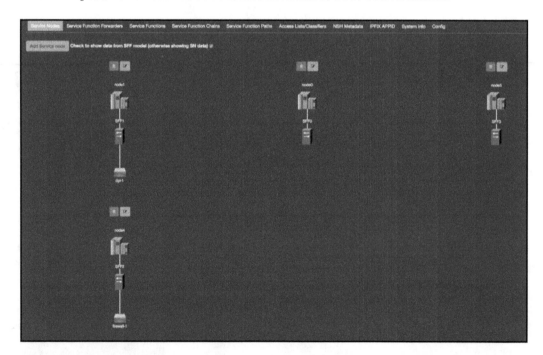

31. There are also other tabs that can be used to see other information, such as ACL and the NSH metadata.

32. Verify the deployment and environment:

- Within the classifiers and service function forwarder VM, look at the flows:

```
$ sudo ovs-ofctl dump-flows -Openflow13 br-sfc
```

- From classifier1, send a `wget` query to the classifier2, within the created `app` network namespace. As we've started a simple HTTP server within classifier2 while setting it up, it will respond, thus creating traffic that will flow within the created service function chain.

- Use Wireshark to observe packets.

33. Tear down the deployment:

```
$ vagrant destroy -f
```

How it works...

First, we had to create the environment using VirtualBox and some Linux networking commands in order to set up the classifiers. Once done, we configured the service node, functions, functions forwarders, chains, metadata, paths, ACL, classifiers, and renderer service path within the OpenDaylight data store. To do so we have used the REST APIs provided by OpenDaylight's SFC YANG models. They can be found here:

```
https://github.com/opendaylight/sfc/tree/release/beryllium-sr2/sfc-model/src/main/yang
```

Regarding the instance of OpenVSwitch used in our classifiers and service function forwarder, it has been modified to enable **Network Services Headers** (**NSH**) in order to be able to encapsulate and decapsulate a VXLAN tunnel from OpenFlow rules.

5

Virtual Core and Aggregation

This chapter will cover the following recipes:

- Configuring and retrieving BGP information
- Managing and visualizing topologies using BGP-LS
- Adding and removing BGP routes to/from the network
- Configuring and retrieving PCEP information
- Managing LSP tunnels with PCEP
- Network-wide programming with PCEP
- Getting BGP and PCEP statistics using the Java management extension
- Enabling TCP MD5 authentication for secure BGP and PCEP connectivity
- BGP component configuration using the OpenConfig implementation
- Implementing new extensions to the BGP and PCEP protocols

Introduction

The BGP-PCEP project in OpenDaylight implements two southbound plugins: **Border Gateway Protocol** (**BGP**) Linkstate Distribution to manage Layer 3 topology information, and **Path Computation Element Protocol** (**PCEP**) as a way to instantiate paths into the underlying network. Both protocols offer extensibility features to add new behaviors.

BGP is the routing protocol that makes the internet work. As per RFC, the primary function of BGP is to exchange network reachability information with other BGP systems.

PCEP is a TCP-based protocol defined by the IETF and it has the capability to remove the path computation function from network elements such as routers to an external entity known as the **Path Computation Engine** (**PCE**). A PCE is capable of computing network paths or routes for a given network. Using the PCEP protocol, a client known as **Path Computation Client** (**PCC**) can request path computation by a PCE. The PCEP protocol is designed for communication between PCC and PCE. Using PCEP, path computation can be centralized on the OpenDaylight controller, thereby offering the benefits of SDN.

The recipes in this chapter will primarily focus on fundamental use cases for BGP and PCEP using the OpenDaylight SDN controller.

Configuring and retrieving BGP information

This recipe will guide you through the manual configuration of the OpenDaylight controller XML files to connect with a router using PCEP. Both the router and OpenDaylight need to be configured. Once the connection is established, the controller can receive route information from the router, which can be retrieved using the RESTCONF.

Getting ready

The ingredients of this recipe require a router and the OpenDaylight controller with the BGP-PCEP implementation. You could also use the Quagga router. To use BGP-PCEP, the OpenDaylight controller can be configured manually or using RESTCONF.

How to do it...

Follow the given instructions to configure BGP using OpenDaylight's BGP XML configurations files:

1. Start the OpenDaylight distribution using the `karaf` script. Using this client will give you access to the Karaf CLI:

```
$ ./bin/karaf
```

```
\/|__|  \/  \/  \/  \/\/   /____/  \/
Hit '<tab>' for a list of available commands
and '[cmd] --help' for help on a specific command.
Hit '<ctrl-d>' or type 'system:shutdown' or 'logout' to   shut
down OpenDaylight.
opendaylight-user@root>
```

2. Install the user-facing features responsible for pulling in all dependencies needed to connect to a router using BGP-LS:

```
opendaylight-user@root>feature:install odl-bgpcep-bgp-all odl-
bgpcep-pcep-all odl-restconf-all odl-netconf-all
```

It might take a few minutes to complete the installation. To make sure the installation went well check the logs using the following command, which will list the BGP features that are installed:

```
opendaylight-user@root>feature:list -i | grep bgp
```

Karaf logs can be accessed to check for any errors using the following command:

```
opendaylight-user@root>log:tail
```

3. Configuration for a BGP connection initiated by OpenDaylight:

The OpenDaylight Karaf edition comes with preconfigured baseline BGP settings. The XML configuration files can be accessed from the karaf root folder at the path etc/opendaylight/karaf. For BGP configuration there are two files of interest to us: 31-bgp.xml and 41-bgp-example.xml.

Update the specified sections of the 41-bgp-example.xml to set up a BGP-LS connection with a peer IP address, that is, the router.

- **BGP Peer Configuration**: The XML file is configured with a default host IP of `192.0.2.1`. Update the following section with the IP address of your BGP speaker to which OpenDaylight should connect. In this example we use: `192.168.1.119` as the BGP peer or the router IP address:

```
<module>
<type
xmlns:prefix="urn:opendaylight:params:xml:ns:yang:controller:bg
p:rib:impl">prefix:bgp-peer</type>
<name>example-bgp-peer</name>
<host>192.168.1.119</host>
<holdtimer>180</holdtimer>
```

More BGP peers can be configured by adding a new module with different instance names and IP addresses:

```
<module>
<type
xmlns:prefix="urn:opendaylight:params:xml:ns:yang:controller:bg
p:rib:impl">prefix:bgp-peer</type>
<name>example-bgp-peer-2</name>
<host>(IP address of BGP speaker #2)</host>
<holdtimer>180</holdtimer>
```

The `<name>` tag refers to a unique BGP peer name.

- **RIB Configuration**: Update the XML file to set BGP open message fields in the following section:

```
<module>
<type
xmlns:prefix="urn:opendaylight:params:xml:ns:yang:controller:bg
p:rib:impl">prefix:rib-impl</type>
<name>example-bgp-rib</name>
<rib-id>example-bgp-rib</rib-id>
<local-as>65504</local-as>
<bgp-rib-id>192.168.1.102</bgp-rib-id>
```

The `local-as` field refers to the local autonomous-system number of where the OpenDaylight controller is deployed and its value should be the same as the BGP AS configuration of your router.

The `bgp-rib-id` is set to a default IP address of `192.0.2.2` and must be updated with the management IP address of the OpenDaylight controller instance; in our example this is set to `192.168.1.102`.

- Verify on your router, using appropriate commands, that its BGP peers are configured correctly to match the values in the aforementioned instructions.
- Note that the baseline BGP peer configuration is commented in the XML file to prevent the client from starting with the default configuration. Once the desired configuration settings are made, uncomment the module containing the BGP peer settings. In our example, this refers to the module named `example-bgp-peer`.

Additionally, the timers can be configured to the desired values. For example, to update the interval between BGP client and reconnection attempts (in seconds) set the retry timer field in the BGP peer module.

Enabling `TRACE` mode in Karaf logs can be useful for debugging. To do so edit the `etc/org.ops4j.pax.logging.cfg` file to add the following lines to the end of the file:

```
log4j.logger.org.opendaylight.bgpcep = TRACE
log4j.logger.org.opendaylight.protocol = TRACE
```

Once the changes are made to these files restart `karaf` for the new configurations to take effect and reinstall the features as mentioned previously. Type `log:tail` on the `karaf` console; you should be able to see the following `TRACE` log to confirm the setting were successful:

```
2016-06-12 13:25:09,503 | TRACE | oupCloseable-2-1 |
BGPSessionImpl    | 185 - org.opendaylight.bgpcep.bgp-rib-impl
- 0.5.2.Beryllium-SR2 | Message Keepalive [augmentation=[]]
sent to socket [id: 0x47daf78a, /192.168.1.102:51336 =>
/192.168.1.119:179]
```

Note in the preceding log that the default BGP binding port is `179` as per the BGP RFC specifications. `karaf` logs can also be accessed from the Karaf root folder at `/data/log/karaf.log`.

4. The data from BGP can be accessed through RESTCONF at the following URL. To retrieve Network Topology Information use the following `GET` request:

URL:
`http://<ODL_IP>:8181/restconf/operational/network-topology:network-topology/`

Method: GET

A sample JSON Response Body can be found at the GitHub link for the recipe:

```
https://github.com/jgoodyear/OpenDaylightCookbook/blob/master/chapter6
/chapter6-recipe1/samples/network_topology.txt
```

To retrieve BGP **Routing Information Base** (**RIB**) data use the following GET request:

URL:
```
http://<ODL_IP>:8181/restconf/operational/bgp-rib:bgp-rib/rib/e
xample-bgp-rib/
```

Method: GET

A sample JSON response for the GET operation can be found at the GitHub for the recipe at:

```
https://github.com/jgoodyear/OpenDaylightCookbook/blob/master/chapte
r6/chapter6-recipe1/samples/rib_data.txt
```

The BGP RIB data can be further accessed in a more granular way as described here for different types of route supported:

- For retrieving IPv4 route information use a GET request at URI:

```
http://<ODL_IP>:8181/restconf/operational/bgp-rib:bgp-rib/rib/e
xample-bgp-rib/loc-rib/tables/bgp-types:ipv4-address-
family/bgp-types:unicast-subsequent-address-family/ipv4-routes
```

For IPv6 route information: use a GET request at URI:

```
http://<ODL_IP>:8181/restconf/operational/bgp-rib:bgp-rib/rib/e
xample-bgp-rib/loc-rib/tables/bgp-types:ipv6-address-
family/bgp-types:unicast-subsequent-address-family/ipv6-routes
```

- For retrieving IPv4 flowspec information use a GET request at URI:

```
http://<ODL_IP>:8181/restconf/operational/bgp-rib:bgp-rib/rib/e
xample-bgp-rib/loc-rib/tables/bgp-types:ipv4-address-
family/bgp-flowspec:flowspec-subsequent-address-family/bgp-
flowspec:flowspec-routes
```

For IPv6 flowspec information: use a GET request at URI:

```
http://<ODL_IP>:8181/restconf/operational/bgp-rib:bgp-rib/rib/e
xample-bgp-rib/loc-rib/tables/bgp-types:ipv6-address-
family/bgp-flowspec:flowspec-subsequent-address-family/bgp-
flowspec:flowspec-ipv6-routes
```

- For retrieving IPv4 BGP Labeled unicast routes: use a GET request at URI:

```
http://localhost:8181/restconf/operational/bgp-rib:bgp-rib/rib/
example-bgp-rib/loc-rib/tables/bgp-types:ipv4-address-
family/bgp-labeled-unicast:labeled-unicast-subsequent-address-
family/bgp-labeled-unicast:labeled-unicast-routes
```

- For retrieving the BGP Linkstate: use a GET request at URI:

```
http://localhost:8181/restconf/operational/bgp-rib:bgp-rib/rib/
example-bgp-rib/loc-rib/tables/bgp-linkstate:linkstate-address-
family/bgp-linkstate:linkstate-subsequent-address-
family/linkstate-routes
```

How it works...

By installing `odl-bgpcep-bgp-all`, all the necessary dependencies to enable BGP implementation are pulled in. The following are the main dependencies:

- The BGP project defines YANG models for modeling BGP. It depends on OpenDaylight's "yangtools" project to generate Java APIs from the YANG models. The OpenDaylight "controller" **Model Driven Service Abstraction Layer (MD-SAL)** is used to store and manage BGP information.
- The `odl-restconf-all` feature needs to be installed to access the RESTful API exposed by the BGP project.
- The protocol-framework of the BGP project uses the `netty` library underneath.
- For the BGP-PCEP configuration there is a dependency on OpenDaylight's "config-subsystem."
- There is also a dependency on the `tcpmd5` project since BGP and PCEP support MD5 authentication.

Once the features are installed, the baseline XML configuration files are created. The BGP connection can be set up by configuring the BGP router and the OpenDaylight XML config files.

BGP implementation in OpenDaylight provides two main configuration files for BGP and RIB settings as follows:

- `31-bgp.xml`: This file defines the settings for the basic parser and RIB. Unless you need to change **Address Family Identifier** (**AFI**) and **Subsequent Address Family Identifier** (**SAFI**), this file will remain the same.
- `41-bgp-example.xml`: This file contains a sample configuration that must be edited to suit your deployment.

Once the configuration is made and the Karaf instance is rebooted, these parameters are picked by OpenDaylight. Using the RESTful API, the BGP routes and parameter can be managed as will be discussed in the recipes to follow.

See also

For this and the following recipes, the Quagga router has been used as a BGP peer. Any router of your choice could be used. Quagga is a handy and open source solution with which to try out the recipes. For instructions for configuring the Quagga router with BGP and for integrating it with OpenDaylight's BGP implementation, refer to:

`https://github.com/jgoodyear/OpenDaylightCookbook/tree/master/chapter6/chapter6-recipe1/quagga`

Managing and visualizing topologies using BGP-LS

In this recipe, we will review the topologies that were configured in the first recipe and provide details of the kind of information they store.

Getting ready

The first recipe is a prerequisite for this recipe. It is assumed that the BGP Peer and RIB are configured as described before.

Start the OpenDaylight distribution using the `karaf` script and install the features mentioned in the first recipe. We will be using the BGP RESTful API to view the different topologies managed by BGP-LS implementation.

How to do it...

The three main topologies that we configured earlier are as follows. It is imperative that these are well understood to be able to manage routes for each of the topologies:

- `example-linkstate-topology`: This topology is used to manage the nodes and links when the network-topology information is advertised through Linkstate messages.

  Note that the name of the topology matches the module that was defined for it in `41-bgp-example.xml`. OpenDaylight's implementation of the Linkstate `network-topology` can be accessed at the following URI:

  `http://<ODL_IP>:8181/restconf/operational/network-topology:network-topology/topology/example-linkstate-topology`

- `example-ipv4-topology`: This topology is used to manage the IPv4 addresses of the nodes in `network-topology`.

  Again, note that the name of the topology matches the module that was defined for it in `41-bgp-example.xml`. OpenDaylight's implementation of the IPv4 network-topology can be accessed at the following URI. Since we have configured the BGP peer routers and the local BGP (OpenDaylight instance attributes), the IPv4 `network-topology` will list their IP addresses as shown in the following sample response:

  URI:
  `http://<ODL_IP>:8181/restconf/operational/network-topology:network-topology/topology/example-ipv4-topology`

- `example-ipv6-topology`: As the name indicates, this topology is used to manage the IPv6 addresses of the nodes in the `network-topology`.

  Note that the name of the topology matches the module that was defined for it in `41-bgp-example.xml`. OpenDaylight's implementation of the Linkstate `network-topology` can be accessed at the following URI:

  `http://<ODL_IP>:8181/restconf/operational/network-topology:network-topology/topology/example-ipv6-topology`

A sample responses to the preceding GET REST operations can be accessed at the GitHub link for the recipe:

```
https://github.com/jgoodyear/OpenDaylightCookbook/tree/master/chapter6/chapt
er6-recipe2/samples
```

How it works...

Each BGP provider instance is configured in the OpenDaylight implementation with a unique RIB ID; for example, in our case rib-id is example-bgp-rib. For every BGP provider instance a unique topology is defined. In our case we define three topologies: example-ipv4-topology of type bgp-reachability-ipv4, example-linkstate-topology of type bgp-linkstate-topology, and example-ipv6-topology of type bgp-reachability-ipv6. Each of the topology types refers to the YANG models defined for these topologies in the BGP implementation in OpenDaylight. For every rib-id configured, an application BGP peer (of module type bgp-application-peer) is configured with a unique application rib-id. Each of these can then be accessed using the RESTful API generated by the OpenDaylight implementation of these topology providers.

Adding and removing BGP routes to/from the network

This recipe will address how to add IPv4 routes using the BGP RESTful API. As a prerequisite the recipe will guide you through the manual configuration to enable the OpenDaylight controller to accept incoming BGP connections, which essentially means allowing it to behave like a BGP Speaker.

Getting ready

As a prerequisite for this recipe, it is assumed that the RIB is configured and a regular BGP is also configured as described in the first recipe. In order to add IPv4 routes, that is, to populate the application RIB of a BGP peer, we need to configure the BGP speaker and set up an application peer.

BGP Speaker functionality configuration: This functionality can be enabled using the XML file `41-bgp-example.xml`. Update the default binding address from `0.0.0.0` to localhost, that is, `127.0.0.1` and change the default binding port from `179` to `1790`:

```
<module>
<type
xmlns:prefix="urn:opendaylight:params:xml:ns:yang:controller:bgp:rib:impl">
prefix:bgp-peer-acceptor</type>
<name>bgp-peer-server</name>
<binding-address>127.0.0.1</binding-address>
<binding-port>1790</binding-port>
...
</module>
```

From the first recipe where we configured a BGP peer into its own module, let's have a look at the tag for peer-registry. Each BGP peer module gets registered into the peer registry so that any incoming BGP connections that are handled by the BGP speaker are allowed. The following is a sample of what we configured in the first recipe:

```
<module>
<type
xmlns:prefix="urn:opendaylight:params:xml:ns:yang:controller:bgp:rib:impl">
prefix:bgp-peer</type>
<name>example-bgp-peer</name>
<host>192.168.1.119</host>
<holdtimer>180</holdtimer>
<peer-role>ibgp</peer-role>
<rib>
<type
xmlns:prefix="urn:opendaylight:params:xml:ns:yang:controller:bgp:rib:impl">
prefix:rib-instance</type>
<name>example-bgp-rib</name>
</rib>
<peer-registry>
<type
xmlns:prefix="urn:opendaylight:params:xml:ns:yang:controller:bgp:rib:impl">
prefix:bgp-peer-registry</type>
<name>global-bgp-peer-registry</name>
</peer-registry>
...
</module>
```

BGP application peer configuration: Since the BGP speaker needs to register all the peers that it needs to communicate with, we will be adding a BGP Application Peer in its own module.

In the following section replace the tags with appropriate information:

- `bgp-peer-id`: Refers to the IP address of the OpenDaylight instance, which is the local BGP identifier
- `target-rib`: Refers to the RIB identifier where the data will be stored
- `application-rib-id`: Refers to the RIB identifier of the local application peer RIB where the route information will be stored

More BGP peers can be configured to advertise the routes from the application peers:

```
<module>
<type
xmlns:x="urn:opendaylight:params:xml:ns:yang:controller:bgp:rib:impl">x:bgp
-application-peer</type>
<name>example-bgp-peer-app</name>
<bgp-peer-id>192.168.1.102</bgp-peer-id>
<target-rib>
<type
xmlns:x="urn:opendaylight:params:xml:ns:yang:controller:bgp:rib:impl">x:rib
-instance</type>
<name>example-bgp-rib</name>
</target-rib>
<application-rib-id>example-app-rib</application-rib-id>
<data-broker>
<type
xmlns:sal="urn:opendaylight:params:xml:ns:yang:controller:md:sal:dom">sal:d
om-async-data-broker</type>
<name>pingpong-broker</name>
</data-broker>
</module>
```

Restart the OpenDaylight distribution using the `karaf` script and install the necessary features, as described in the first recipe.

How to do it...

We will be using the BGP RESTful API to add and remove routes. The routes can be verified on the peer router:

1. To add IPv4 Unicast routes, use the following RESTful API:

   URI:
   ```
   http://<ODL_IP>:8181/restconf/config/bgp-rib:application-rib/ex
   ample-app-rib/tables/bgp-types:ipv4-address-family/bgp-
   types:unicast-subsequent-address-family
   ```

   Method: `PUT`

   A sample JSON body for the PUT operation can be accessed at the GitHub location for the recipe at:

   ```
   https://github.com/jgoodyear/OpenDaylightCookbook/blob/master/chapte
   r6/chapter6-recipe3/samples/add-ipv4-unicast-route.txt
   ```

   Deleting IPv4 routes:

   On the same URI for adding routes, issue a `DELETE` request to delete all the routes that were added. To delete a specific route, use the URI and append to it the network prefix-id. For example, if the prefix is `2.1.1.1/32` the prefix ID to append will be `2.1.1.1%2F32`.

2. To add IPv6 Unicast routes use the following RESTful API:

   URI:
   ```
   http://<ODL_IP>:8181/restconf/config/bgp-rib:application-rib/ex
   ample-app-rib/tables/bgp-types:ipv6-address-family/bgp-
   types:unicast-subsequent-address-family
   ```

   Method: `PUT`

   Access a sample JSON request body at GitHub:

   ```
   https://github.com/jgoodyear/OpenDaylightCookbook/blob/master/chapte
   r6/chapter6-recipe3/samples/add-ipv6-unicast-route.txt
   ```

Deleting IPv6 routes:

Performing a `DELETE` operation on the previously mentioned REST URI will remove all IPv6 routes. Prefixing the URI with the IPv6 prefix will remove only the route for the mentioned prefix. For example: to remove `2001:db8:60::5/128` the URI should be appended with `2001:db8:60::5%2F128`.

3. To add IPv4 Labeled Unicast routes use the following RESTful API:

URI:
```
http://<ODL_IP>:8181/restconf/config/bgp-rib:application-rib/ex
ample-app-rib/tables/bgp-types:ipv4-address-family/bgp-labeled-
unicast:labeled-unicast-subsequent-address-family
```

Method: `PUT`

A sample JSON request body can be accessed at the GitHub for the recipe at:

```
https://github.com/jgoodyear/OpenDaylightCookbook/blob/master/chapte
r6/chapter6-recipe3/samples/add-ipv4-labelled-unicast-route.txt
```

Deleting IPv4 Labeled Unicast routes:

Use the `DELETE` operation for the URI mentioned previously to delete all labeled routes. To delete a specific IPv4 labeled Unicast route append the URI with `bgp-labeled-unicast:labeled-unicast-route/<route-key_value>`.

4. Adding IPv4 flowspec (BGP-FS):

Change the attribute values for destination and source prefix, protocols, and port values as per your environment. The extended-communities attributes can be used to set traffic rates and marking and redirect attributes:

URI:
```
http://<ODL_IP>:8181/restconf/config/bgp-rib:application-rib/ex
ample-app-rib/tables/bgp-types:ipv4-address-family/bgp-
flowspec:flowspec-subsequent-address-family/bgp-
flowspec:flowspec-routes
```

Method: PUT

A sample JSON body for the PUT request is available at the GitHub link:

```
https://github.com/jgoodyear/OpenDaylightCookbook/blob/master/chapte
r6/chapter6-recipe3/samples/add-ipv4-flowspec.txt
```

Deleting IPv4 flowspec:

Use the same URI as for the DELETE operation to delete all the BGP-FS routes. In order to delete a specific route append the URI with `bgp-flowspec:flowspec-route/route-key_value`.

5. To add IPv6 flowspec (BGP-FS), use the given RESTful API:

URI:
```
http://<ODL_IP>:8181/restconf/config/bgp-rib:application-rib/ex
ample-app-rib/tables/bgp-types:ipv6-address-family/bgp-
flowspec:flowspec-subsequent-address-family/bgp-
flowspec:flowspec-ipv6-routes
```

Method: PUT

A sample JSON body for the previous PUT request can be accessed at the following GitHub link:

```
https://github.com/jgoodyear/OpenDaylightCookbook/blob/master/chapte
r6/chapter6-recipe3/samples/add-ipv6-unicast-route.txt
```
Deleting IPv6 flowspec:

Use the DELETE operation on the preceding link to delete all BGP-FS routes. To delete a specific route prefix the URI with `bgp-flowspec:flowspec-route/<route-key_value>`.

How it works...

In implementation the RIB the routes are stored in OpenDaylight's MD-SAL datastore. The implementation supports four types of route: IPv4Routes, IPv6Routes, LinkstateRoutes, and FlowspecRoutes. The routes can be managed by the RESTful API exposed by the implementation.

See also

A handy postman collection for managing routes using the RESTful API can be downloaded to your postman application from the GitHub link at `https://github.com/jg oodyear/OpenDaylightCookbook/tree/master/chapter6/chapter6-recipe3/postman`. Be sure to change the OpenDaylight IP address in the URLs and the parameter values in the content of the JSON request body to suit your setup. Additionally, the implementation also exposes a Java binding, which could be used to manage the routes programmatically.

Configuring and retrieving PCEP information

This recipe will guide you through the manual configuration of the OpenDaylight controller XML files to connect with a router using PCEP. Both the router and OpenDaylight need to be configured. Once the connection is established, the controller can be used to view Label Switched Paths and Path computation client information. The PCEP RESTful API can also be used to perform CRUD types of operation for tunnel management.

Getting ready

The ingredients in this recipe require a router and the OpenDaylight controller with the BGP-PCEP implementation. OpenDaylight comes preconfigured with the basic PCEP settings, and this recipe will review the attribute descriptions.

How to do it...

Follow these instructions to edit OpenDaylight XML files to configure PCEP:

1. Start the OpenDaylight distribution using the `karaf` script, which will give you access to the karaf CLI.
2. Install the user-facing features responsible for pulling in all dependencies needed to connect to a router using PCEP:

```
opendaylight-user@root>feature:install odl-bgpcep-bgp-all odl-
bgpcep-pcep-all odl-restconf-all odl-netconf-all
```

Allow a few minutes to complete the installation.

3. Configuring files for PCEP:

Once OpenDaylight `karaf` successfully installs the features, the XML configuration files are created in the `karaf` root directory at the path `etc/opendaylight/karaf`. The XML config files relevant to PCEP configuration are: `32-pcep.xml`, `39-pcep-provider.xml`, and `33-pcep-segment-routing.xml`.

Update to the specified sections of the `39-pcep-provider.xml` to set up the address on which the PCE will be initialized and the port on which it will listen. Add the tags for `listen-address` and `listen-port` as follows:

```
<module>
<type
xmlns:prefix="urn:opendaylight:params:xml:ns:yang:controller:pc
ep:topology:provider">prefix:pcep-topology-provider</type>
<name>pcep-topology</name>
<listen-address>172.17.13.25</listen-address>
<listen-port>2086</listen-port>
...
</module>
```

Restart OpenDaylight Karaf and reinstall the features for the configurations to take effect.

4. Retrieving PCEP topology data using OpenDaylight:

OpenDaylight defines a `pcep-topology` for storing the operational state of PCEP topology. Each node in the topology is a PCC and within each the PCC tunnels initiated by it are also displayed. If there is no PCC configured the PCEP topology will have no entries.

Use the following URI to access the PCEP topology:

```
http://<ODL_IP>:8181/restconf/operational/network-topology:netw
ork-topology/topology/pcep-topology
```

How it works...

By installing `odl-bgpcep-pcep-all`, all the necessary dependencies to enable PCEP implementation are pulled in. The `odl-restconf-all` feature needs to be installed to access the RESTful API exposed by the PCEP implementation. Once the features are installed, the baseline XML configuration files are created. PCEP implementation in OpenDaylight provides three main configuration files as follows:

- `32-pcep.xml`: This file defines the basic PCEP configurations such as the session parameters and they need not be modified.
- `39-pcep-provider.xml`: This file contains a sample configuration for a PCEP provider. The PCEP default settings are meant for a stateful (stateful07) PCEP extension. It needs to be updated with server binding settings to suit your deployment.
- `33-pcep-segment-routing.xml`: This file contains the PCEP provider configuration for segment routing and it need not be changed.

Once the configuration is made and the Karaf instance is rebooted, these parameters are picked by OpenDaylight. Each PCC client is added as a node to the PCEP topology provided by the implementation.

Managing LSP tunnels with PCEP

This recipe will guide you through the instructions to create, update, and delete label-switched paths for `draft-ietf-pce-stateful-pce-07` and `draft-ietf-pce-pce-initiated-lsp-00`. PCC needs to be configured and running. The PCE is the OpenDaylight PCEP implementation. Once the PCC to PCE connection is established, the PCEP remote procedure call implementation can be used to manage the LSPs.

Getting ready

The ingredients of this recipe require a PCC client to be set up and the OpenDaylight controller with the BGP-PCEP implementation. Here we are using the `pcc-mock` test tool bundled along with the PCEP implementation for creating, updating, and deleting tunnels. The See also section of this recipe provides a step-by-step guide to configuring the `pcc-mock` tool to run the recipe.

How to do it...

PCEP implementation provides the following remote procedure calls to be able to manage LSPs:

1. To create an LSP use the RPC by called: `add-lsp`, accessible at the following URI, and use the given JSON input:

   URI:
   `http://<ODL_IP>:8181/restconf/operations/network-topology-pcep:add-lsp`

   Method: `POST`

   Content Type: `application/xml`

   A sample input body:

```xml
<input
xmlns="urn:opendaylight:params:xml:ns:yang:topology:pcep">
<node>pcc://192.168.1.208</node>
<name>tunnel-1</name>
<arguments>
<lsp
xmlns="urn:opendaylight:params:xml:ns:yang:pcep:ietf:stateful">
<delegate>true</delegate>
<administrative>true</administrative>
</lsp>
<endpoints-obj>
<ipv4>
<source-ipv4-address>192.168.1.208</source-ipv4-address>
<destination-ipv4-address>39.39.39.39</destination-ipv4-
address>
</ipv4>
</endpoints-obj>
<ero>
<subobject>
<loose>false</loose>
  <ip-prefix><ip-prefix>201.24.160.40/32</ip-prefix></ip-
prefix>
</subobject>
<subobject>
<loose>false</loose>
  <ip-prefix><ip-prefix>195.20.160.33/32</ip-prefix></ip-
prefix>
</subobject>
<subobject>
```

```
<loose>false</loose>
  <ip-prefix><ip-prefix>39.39.39.39/32</ip-prefix></ip-prefix>
</subobject>
</ero>
</arguments>
<network-topology-ref
xmlns:topo="urn:TBD:params:xml:ns:yang:network-
topology">/topo:network-topology/topo:topology[topo:topology-
id="pcep-topology"]</network-topology-ref>
</input>
```

2. In order to update the LSP that was created in the previous step, use the RPC `update-lsp` and the JSON request given here:

URI:
`http://<ODL_IP>:8181/restconf/operations/network-topology-pcep:update-lsp`

Method: `POST`

Content Type: `application/xml`

A sample input body:

```
<input
xmlns="urn:opendaylight:params:xml:ns:yang:topology:pcep">
<node>pcc://192.168.1.208</node>
<name>tunnel-1</name>
<arguments>
<lsp
xmlns="urn:opendaylight:params:xml:ns:yang:pcep:ietf:stateful">
<delegate>true</delegate>
<administrative>true</administrative>
</lsp>
<ero>
<subobject>
<loose>false</loose>
  <ip-prefix><ip-prefix>200.20.160.41/32</ip-prefix></ip-
prefix>
</subobject>
<subobject>
<loose>false</loose>
  <ip-prefix><ip-prefix>196.20.160.39/32</ip-prefix></ip-
prefix>
</subobject>
<subobject>
<loose>false</loose>
```

```
        <ip-prefix><ip-prefix>39.39.39.39/32</ip-prefix></ip-prefix>
    </subobject>
    </ero>
    </arguments>
    <network-topology-ref
    xmlns:topo="urn:TBD:params:xml:ns:yang:network-
    topology">/topo:network-topology/topo:topology[topo:topology-
    id="pcep-topology"]</network-topology-ref>
    </input>
```

3. To delete this LSP use the RPC `remove-lsp` with the JSON request as follows:

URI:
`http://<ODL_IP>:8181/restconf/operations/network-topology-pcep:remove-lsp`

Method: `POST`

Content Type: `application/xml`

A sample input body:

```
    <input
    xmlns="urn:opendaylight:params:xml:ns:yang:topology:pcep">
    <node>pcc://192.168.1.208</node>
    <name>tunnel-1</name>
    <network-topology-ref
    xmlns:topo="urn:TBD:params:xml:ns:yang:network-
    topology">/topo:network-topology/topo:topology[topo:topology-
    id="pcep-topology"]</network-topology-ref>
    </input>
```

A handy PostMan collection with the preceding REST operations for managing LSPs is available at:

`https://github.com/jgoodyear/OpenDaylightCookbook/tree/master/chapter6/chapter6-recipe5/postman`

See also

The PCC client tool `pcep-mock` can be downloaded as an executable JAR from the following link:

`https://github.com/jgoodyear/OpenDaylightCookbook/tree/master`

Refer to the RFC drafts for PCEP, `draft-ietf-pce-stateful-pce-07` and `draft-ietf-pce-pce-initiated-lsp-00`, for details about the parameters and the README for `pcc-mock` for argument details. It is assumed that the OpenDaylight controller is running and the necessary features for BGP-PCEP are installed. For this recipe we run `pcc-mock`, as shown in the following a sample:

```
$ java -jar pcep-pcc-mock-0.5.3-executable.jar --local-address
192.168.1.208
  --remote-address 192.168.1.102 --state-sync-avoidance 2 2 2 --incremental-
sync-procedure 2 2 2 --triggered-initial-sync --triggered-re-sync
```

> The local address is the PCC IP address and the PCE address should be the OpenDaylight IP address.

You should now be able to see the following output on your console:

```
06:11:52.119 [main] INFO  o.o.t.jni.NativeKeyAccessFactory - Library /tmp/libt
cpmd5-jni.so2285157135999201656.tmp loaded
06:11:52.332 [nioEventLoopGroup-2-1] INFO  o.o.p.p.impl.PCEPSessionNegotiator
- Replacing bootstrap negotiator for channel [id: 0xba788ebc, L:/192.168.1.208
:54663 - R:/192.168.1.102:4189]
06:11:52.478 [nioEventLoopGroup-2-1] INFO  o.o.p.p.i.AbstractPCEPSessionNegoti
ator - PCEP session with [id: 0xba788ebc, L:/192.168.1.208:54663 - R:/192.168.
1.102:4189] started, sent proposal Open [_deadTimer=120, _keepalive=30, _sessi
onId=0, _tlvs=Tlvs [augmentation=[Tlvs1 [_stateful=Stateful [_lspUpdateCapabil
ity=true, augmentation=[Stateful1 [_deltaLspSyncCapability=true, _includeDbVer
sion=true, _triggeredInitialSync=true, _triggeredResync=true], Stateful1 [_ini
tiation=true]]]], Tlvs3 [_lspDbVersion=LspDbVersion [_lspDbVersionValue=1, aug
mentation=[]]]]], augmentation=[]]
06:11:52.756 [nioEventLoopGroup-2-1] INFO  o.o.p.p.i.AbstractPCEPSessionNegoti
ator - PCEP peer [id: 0xba788ebc, L:/192.168.1.208:54663 - R:/192.168.1.102:41
89] completed negotiation
06:11:52.761 [nioEventLoopGroup-2-1] INFO  o.o.p.pcep.impl.PCEPSessionImpl - S
ession /192.168.1.208:54663[0] <-> /192.168.1.102:4189[0] started
```

Network-wide programming with PCEP

This recipe will guide you through the instructions to create, update, and delete label switched paths for `draft-ietf-pce-segment-routing-01`. This draft refers to the PCEP extension for performing segment routing and extends the two drafts in the preceding recipe: `draft-ietf-pce-stateful-pce-07` and `draft-ietf-pce-pce-initiated-lsp-00`.

Getting ready

The ingredients of this recipe require a running instance of the `pcc-mock` test tool as described in the previous recipe.

How to do it...

PCEP implementation provides the following remote procedure calls to manage segment routing LSPs:

1. To create a segment routing LSP `add-lsp` RPC; the given sample JSON input can be used.

   URI:
   `http://<ODL_IP>:8181/restconf/operations/network-topology-pcep:add-lsp`

   Method: `POST`

   Content Type: `application/xml`

   A sample input body:

   ```xml
   <input
   xmlns="urn:opendaylight:params:xml:ns:yang:topology:pcep">
   <node>pcc://192.168.1.208</node>
   <name>tunnel-0</name>
     <arguments>
       <lsp
   xmlns="urn:opendaylight:params:xml:ns:yang:pcep:ietf:stateful">
       <delegate>true</delegate>
       <administrative>true</administrative>
       </lsp>
   <endpoints-obj>
   ```

```
    <ipv4>
      <source-ipv4-address>192.168.1.208</source-ipv4-address>
      <destination-ipv4-address>39.39.39.39</destination-ipv4-
address>
    </ipv4>
  </endpoints-obj>
    <path-setup-type
xmlns="urn:opendaylight:params:xml:ns:yang:pcep:ietf:stateful">
      <pst>1</pst>
    </path-setup-type>
  <ero>
    <subobject>
      <loose>false</loose>
      <sid-type
xmlns="urn:opendaylight:params:xml:ns:yang:pcep:segment:routing
">ipv4-node-id</sid-type>
      <m-flag
xmlns="urn:opendaylight:params:xml:ns:yang:pcep:segment:routing
">true</m-flag>
      <sid
xmlns="urn:opendaylight:params:xml:ns:yang:pcep:segment:routing
">12</sid>
      <ip-address
xmlns="urn:opendaylight:params:xml:ns:yang:pcep:segment:routing
">39.39.39.39</ip-address>
    </subobject>
  </ero>
    </arguments>
  <network-topology-ref
xmlns:topo="urn:TBD:params:xml:ns:yang:network-
topology">/topo:network-topology/topo:topology[topo:topology-
id="pcep-topology"]</network-topology-ref>
  </input>
```

2. To update the segment routing LSP created previously, use the RPC `update-lsp` with the given sample JSON input:

URI:
`http://<ODL_IP>:8181/restconf/operations/network-topology-pcep:update-lsp`

Method: POST

A sample input body:

```
<input
xmlns="urn:opendaylight:params:xml:ns:yang:topology:pcep">
<node>pcc://192.168.1.208</node>
<name>tunnel-0</name>
  <arguments>
    <lsp
xmlns="urn:opendaylight:params:xml:ns:yang:pcep:ietf:stateful">
    <delegate>true</delegate>
    <administrative>true</administrative>
    </lsp>
    <path-setup-type
xmlns="urn:opendaylight:params:xml:ns:yang:pcep:ietf:stateful">
      <pst>1</pst>
    </path-setup-type>
      <ero>
  <subobject>
    <loose>false</loose>
    <sid-type
xmlns="urn:opendaylight:params:xml:ns:yang:pcep:segment:routing
">ipv4-node-id</sid-type>
    <m-flag
xmlns="urn:opendaylight:params:xml:ns:yang:pcep:segment:routing
">true</m-flag>
    <sid
xmlns="urn:opendaylight:params:xml:ns:yang:pcep:segment:routing
">11</sid>
    <ip-address
xmlns="urn:opendaylight:params:xml:ns:yang:pcep:segment:routing
">200.20.160.41</ip-address>
  </subobject>
  <subobject>
    <loose>false</loose>
    <sid-type
xmlns="urn:opendaylight:params:xml:ns:yang:pcep:segment:routing
">ipv4-node-id</sid-type>
    <m-flag
xmlns="urn:opendaylight:params:xml:ns:yang:pcep:segment:routing
">true</m-flag>
    <sid
xmlns="urn:opendaylight:params:xml:ns:yang:pcep:segment:routing
">12</sid>
    <ip-address
xmlns="urn:opendaylight:params:xml:ns:yang:pcep:segment:routing
">39.39.39.39</ip-address>
```

```
      </subobject>
        </ero>
      </arguments>
    <network-topology-ref
    xmlns:topo="urn:TBD:params:xml:ns:yang:network-
    topology">/topo:network-topology/topo:topology[topo:topology-
    id="pcep-topology"]</network-topology-ref>
    </input>
```

3. To delete the segment routing LSP use the RPC `remove-lsp`. Use the same URI and inputs as mentioned in the previous recipe.

4. `trigger-sync` operation: This operation is used by the PCE to trigger LSP-DB initial synchronization:

URI:
```
http://<ODL_IP>:8181/restconf/operations/network-topology-pcep:
trigger-sync
```

Method: `POST`

A sample input body:

```
    <input
    xmlns="urn:opendaylight:params:xml:ns:yang:topology:pcep">
      <node>pcc://192.168.1.208</node>
      <network-topology-ref
    xmlns:topo="urn:TBD:params:xml:ns:yang:network
      -topology">/topo:network-topology/topo:topology[topo:topology
      -id="pcep-topology"]</network-topology-ref>
    </input>
```

To trigger a resync operation use the same RPC with the following sample inputs. The LSP database resynchronization triggered by the PCE works the same way as the initial synchronization:

A sample input Body:

```
    <input
    xmlns="urn:opendaylight:params:xml:ns:yang:topology:pcep">
      <node>pcc://192.168.1.208</node>
      <name>re-sync-lsp</name>
      <network-topology-ref
      xmlns:topo="urn:TBD:params:xml:ns:yang:network
      -topology">/topo:network-topology/topo:topology[topo:topology
      -id="pcep-topology"]</network-topology-ref>
    </input>
```

Getting BGP and PCEP statistics using the Java management extension

BGP statistics store the state of BGP Peers in the network topology and are exposed to Java management console as a runtime bean. For every BGP peer, a runtime MBean is registered when the BGP session is successfully established. These statistics can be accessed via the JMX using JConsole and Jolokia as runtime beans. They are also accessible through RESTCONF as operational data for the configured bgp-peer module. BGP Peer session state and BGP peer state list various statistics as modeled in `odl-bgp-rib-impl-cfg.yang` in the BGP-PCEP implementation in OpenDaylight.

BGP Statistics also provides two reset operations, `resetSession` and `resetStats`. These will be described in the following section along with sample screenshots.

PCEP statistics provides statistics for each PCC to PCE connection. For each such connection a runtime bean named in accordance with the IP address of the PCC is generated.

PCEP also provides two RPC operations, `resetStats` and `tearDownSession`, that will be described shortly.

Getting ready

To view BGP statistics it is assumed that OpenDaylight is configured with BGP peer and RIB settings. Optionally, routes are also added as explained in an earlier recipe.

How to do it...

Perform the following steps:

1. Start the OpenDaylight controller using the `karaf` script and by specifying the -jmx flag. Using the `-jmx` flag starts the JMX server in the controller.
2. Start the OpenDaylight distribution using the `karaf` script. Using this client will give you access to the karaf CLI:

    ```
    $ ./bin/karaf -jmx
    ```

    Reinstall the features to pull the dependencies for BGP-PCEP as mentioned in the first recipe.

JConsole can then be used to attach to the JMX server started by the preceding controller to access the runtime beans. The JConsole utility is shipped with JDK by default and can be launched from the Java home directory as follows:

```
$ $JAVA_HOME/bin/jconsole
```

Connect to the running Karaf process by selecting it. The following is a screenshot of the JConsole tool used to connect to the Karaf container:

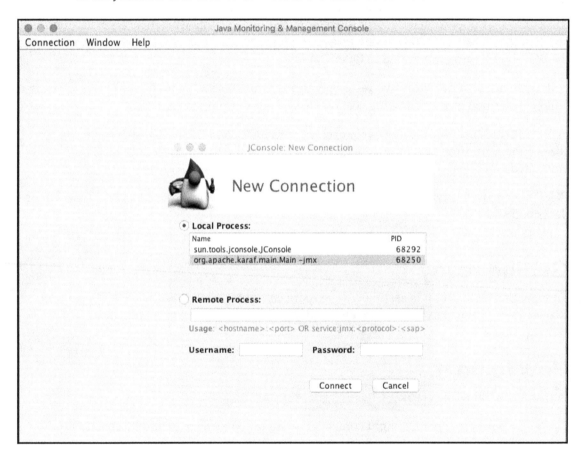

If prompted, choose to select the **Insecure connection** option. This will lead you to the JMX console:

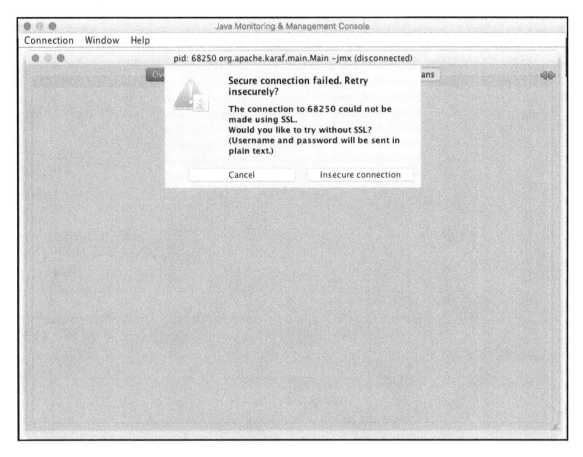

3. For each BGP peer a runtime bean is available named in line with the peer. As per our configuration described in the Configuring and retrieving BGP information recipe, we will be able to see an MBean called `example-bgp-peer`. The following screenshots show the available BGP statistics.

The attributes for **BgpPeerState** can be accessed from the **Attributes** options under the `example-bgp-peer` MBean:

Similarly, **BgpSessionState** also can be accessed under the **Attributes** option. Each statistic lists the attributes by key-value pairs, as can be seen in the following screenshot:

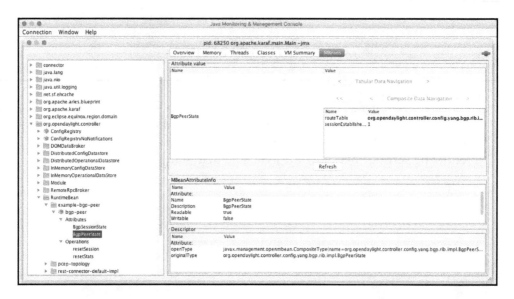

4. Reset RPC operations can be accessed from the same MBean, as shown in the following screenshot.

Use the `resetSession` RPC to restart the client session. After this operation is performed the client can reconnect as per its reconnection strategy:

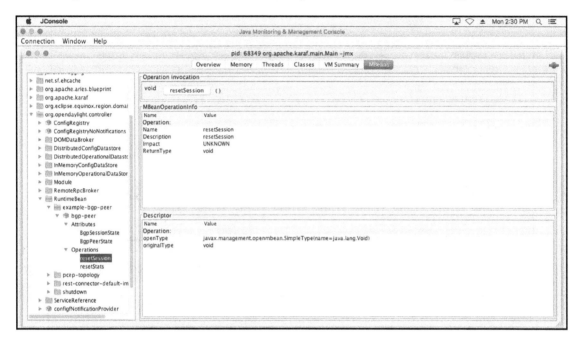

Use the **resetStats** RPC to reset the peer statistics by emptying message counters and timestamp values:

5. Access the attributes for the PCC node by the IP address added to pcep-topology:

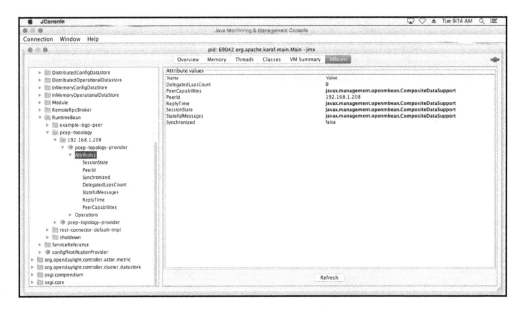

The `resetStats` remote procedure call implementation for PCEP can be accessed from the runtime bean from the PCC IP address under **Operations**, as shown in the following screenshot. This operation can be used to reset statistics such as message counters and timestamps to 0:

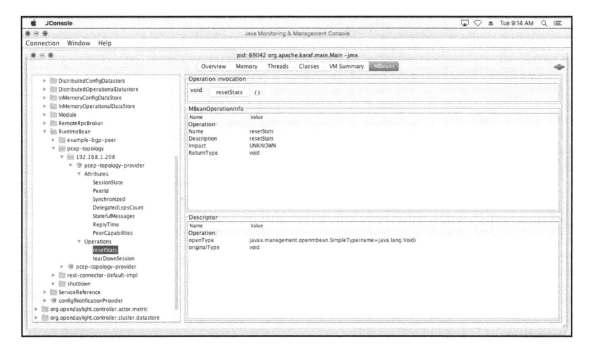

In a similar way, access the RPC implementation for the **tearDownSession** operation in order to close the connection between a PCC and PCE:

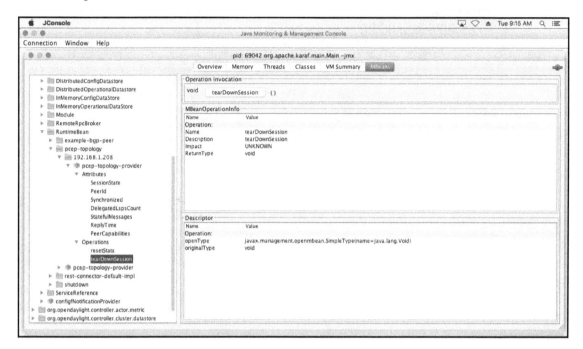

Enabling TCP MD5 authentication for secure BGP and PCEP connectivity

By default, TCP MD5 authentication is disabled for BGP and PCEP implementation in OpenDaylight. This configuration is very useful to secure a BGP connection. It can be enabled manually or by using RESTCONF. In the following recipe we will describe the manual way of configuring these attributes.

Getting ready

As a prerequisite, make sure that BGP and PCEP are configured as described in the first recipe. Additionally, to allow TCP MD5 authentication between BGP peers, the router also needs to be configured accordingly. This is however beyond the scope of this recipe.

How to do it...

In the following section, we will look at how to manually configure the BGP-PCEP to enable TCP MD5 authentication. Each section will describe the files of interest and will also address the details of the parameters that need to be updated.

OpenDaylight BGP configuration for TCP MD5 authentication:

1. Make sure you have started the OpenDaylight distribution using the karaf script and followed the instructions in earlier recipes to configure BGP.
2. In addition to the XML files, 31-bgp.xml and 41-bgp-example.xml, which were described in previous recipes, we will need another file called 20-tcpmd5.xml to enable TCP MD5. Be default the contents of 20-tcpmd5.xml are commented; they need to be uncommented.

   To reiterate, note that all of these XML files can be found under the etc/opendaylight/karaf folder from the Karaf root directory. The files will be only generated when Karaf is started and the features for BGP and PCEP are installed as mentioned in the first recipe.

3. Configuring the TCP MD5 section in the XML file 31-bgp.xml:
   Uncomment the TCP MD5 section as shown in the following snippet to set the md5-channel-factory service attributes:

   ```
   <!--
   ```

Uncomment this block to enable TCP MD5 signature support:

   ```
   -->
   ......
   <services
   xmlns="urn:opendaylight:params:xml:ns:yang:controller:config">
   <service>
   <type
   xmlns:prefix="urn:opendaylight:params:xml:ns:yang:controller:tc
   pmd5:cfg">prefix:key-access-factory</type>
   <instance>
   <name>global-key-access-factory</name>
     <provider> /modules/module[type='native-key-access-
   factory'] [name='global-key-access-factory']</provider>
   </instance>
   </service>
   <service>
   <type
   xmlns:prefix="urn:opendaylight:params:xml:ns:yang:controller:tc
   ```

```
pmd5:netty:cfg">prefix:md5-channel-factory</type>
<instance>
<name>md5-client-channel-factory</name>
  <provider>/modules/module[type='md5-client-channel-
factory'][name='md5-client-channel-factory']</provider>
</instance>
</service>
<service>
<type
xmlns:prefix="urn:opendaylight:params:xml:ns:yang:controller:tc
pmd5:netty:cfg">prefix:md5-server-channel-factory</type>
<instance>
<name>md5-server-channel-factory</name>
  <provider> /modules/module[type='md5-server-channel-factory-
impl'][name='md5-server-channel-factory']</provider>
</instance>
</service>
</services>
```

4. Configuring the TCP MD5 section in the XML file `41-bgp-example.xml`:

Create a password tag to the BGP peer configuration in the XML file and set the password attribute to the tag. The BGP peer that is the router also needs to be configured with the same password for the connection to be established. This needs to be done for every BGP peer configuration to enable TCP MD5 authentication. Finally, reboot the Karaf instance and reinstall BGP features for the new settings to be picked up:

```
<module>
  <type
xmlns:prefix="urn:opendaylight:params:xml:ns:yang:controller:bg
p:rib:impl">prefix:bgp-peer</type>
  <name>example-bgp-peer</name>
  <host>192.168.1.119</host>
  <holdtimer>180</holdtimer>
  <password>md5_auth_passwd</password>
```

OpenDaylight PCEP Configuration for TCP MD5 authentication:

1. Make sure you have started the OpenDaylight distribution using the `karaf` script and followed the instructions in earlier recipes to configure PCEP.
2. Ensure that the contents of `20-tcpmd5.xml` are uncommented.

3. Configure the TCP MD5 section in the XML file `32-pcep.xml`:

Just like in the BGP configuration, uncomment the TCP MD5 section to set `md5-channel-factory` service attributes:

```
<!--
```

Uncomment this block to enable TCP MD5 signature support:

```
-->
<md5-channel-factory>
  <type
xmlns:prefix="urn:opendaylight:params:xml:ns:yang:controller:tc
pmd5:netty:cfg">prefix:md5-channel-factory</type>
  <name>md5-client-channel-factory</name>
</md5-channel-factory>
<md5-server-channel-factory>
  <type
xmlns:prefix="urn:opendaylight:params:xml:ns:yang:controller:tc
pmd5:netty:cfg">prefix:md5-server-channel-factory</type>
  <name>md5-server-channel-factory</name>
</md5-server-channel-factory>
```

4. Configure the TCP MD5 section in the XML file `39-pcep-provider.xml`:
Add the PCC client entries to include their IP addresses along with their passwords. Note that the PCC clients also need to be set to reflect the same password for a successful TCP MD5 authentication to take place.

Restart Karaf and reinstall PCEP features for the configurations to take effect:

```
<!--
```

For TCP-MD5 support make sure the dispatcher has the `md5-server-channel-factory` attribute set and then set the appropriate client entries here. Note that, if this option is configured, the PCCs connecting here must have the same password configured; otherwise they will not be able to connect at all:

```
-->
<client>
  <address><PCC_IP_address></address>
  <password>pcc_client_passwd</password>
</client>
```

BGP component configuration using the OpenConfig implementation

In addition to manual configuration and configuration via RESTCONF, OpenDaylight provides an alternative way of BGP provisioning using OpenConfig.

OpenConfig is an initiative to define vendor-neutral data models to allow seamless network management and configuration. An RFC draft that defines a YANG data model for BGP is implemented by OpenDaylight's BGP project in order to support this (`https://tools.ietf .org/html/draft-ietf-idr-bgp-model-00`).

Getting ready

In order to make use of the OpenConfig implementation, two features need to be installed: `odl-restconf` and `odl-netconf-connector-ssh`. The RESTful API will be used to configure BGP component attributes to OpenDaylight, which in turn uses the NETCONF protocol to manage the network device configuration.

How to do it...

The following instructions will guide through the steps to configure BGP using OpenConfig:

1. Start the OpenDaylight distribution using the `karaf` script as described in the earlier recipes.
2. Install the user-facing features responsible for pulling in all dependencies needed to provide OpenConfig implementation:

   ```
   opendaylight-user@root>feature:install odl-restconf odl-
   netconf-connector-ssh
   ```

3. Configure one instance of BGP RIB. Use the following PUT request to set the RIB attributes. Set the `router-id` and as attributes to suit your environment. The router-id corresponds to the BGP identifier `bgp-rib-id` and as maps to autonomous system number `local-as` as described in the first recipe:

   URL:
   `http://<ODL_IP>:8181/restconf/config/openconfig-bgp:bgp/global/ config`

Method: PUT

Content-Type: application/xml

Body:

```
<config xmlns="http://openconfig.net/yang/bgp">
  <router-id>192.168.1.119</router-id>
  <as>65504</as>
</config>
```

4. BGP Peer attributes configuration: Use the following PUT request to add new BGP peer instance information:

 <ODL_IP> refers to the IP address at which the OpenDaylight Controller can be accessed.

URL:
http://<ODL_IP>:8181/restconf/config/openconfig-bgp:bgp/openconfig-bgp:neighbors

Method: POST

Content-Type: application/xml

Body:

```
<neighbor xmlns="http://openconfig.net/yang/bgp">
<neighbor-address>172.16.17.31</neighbor-address>
<afi-safis>
<afi-safi>
  <afi-safi-name
xmlns:x="http://openconfig.net/yang/bgp-types">x:IPV4
  -UNICAST</afi-safi-name>
</afi-safi>
<afi-safi>
  <afi-safi-name
xmlns:x="http://openconfig.net/yang/bgp-types">x:IPV6
  -UNICAST</afi-safi-name>
</afi-safi>
<afi-safi>
  <afi-safi-name
xmlns:x="http://openconfig.net/yang/bgp-types">x:IPV4
  -LABELLED-UNICAST</afi-safi-name>
</afi-safi>
```

```
<afi-safi>
  <afi-safi-name
xmlns:x="http://openconfig.net/yang/bgp-types">L2VPN
  -EVPN</afi-safi-name>
</afi-safi>
<afi-safi>
  <afi-safi-name
  xmlns:x="urn:opendaylight:params:xml:ns:yang:bgp:openconfig
  -extensions">x:linkstate</afi-safi-name>
</afi-safi>
<afi-safi>
  <afi-safi-name
  xmlns:x="urn:opendaylight:params:xml:ns:yang:bgp:openconfig
  -extensions">x:ipv4-flow</afi-safi-name>
</afi-safi>
<afi-safi>
  <afi-safi-name
  xmlns:x="urn:opendaylight:params:xml:ns:yang:bgp:openconfig
  -extensions">x:ipv6-flow</afi-safi-name>
</afi-safi>
</afi-safis>
<route-reflector>
  <config>
    <route-reflector-client>false</route-reflector-client>
  </config>
</route-reflector>
<timers>
  <config>
    <hold-time>180</hold-time>
  </config>
</timers>
<transport>
  <config>
    <passive-mode>false</passive-mode>
  </config>
</transport>
  <config>
    <peer-type>INTERNAL</peer-type>
    <peer-as>65504</peer-as>
  </config>
</neighbor>
```

5. BGP Application Peer configuration: If OpenDaylight is configured to behave as a BGP Speaker, that is, to allow any incoming BGP connections, then the application peer configuration also needs to be applied. The following `PUT` request can be used to configure application peers to OpenDaylight. Note that the OpenConfig API uses the application peer neighbor that belongs to a peer-group called `application-peers`:

URL:
`http://<ODL_IP>:8181/restconf/config/openconfig-bgp:bgp/openconfig-bgp:neighbors`

Method: `POST`

Content-Type: `application/xml`

Body:

```
<neighbor xmlns="http://openconfig.net/yang/bgp">
<neighbor-address>172.16.17.31</neighbor-address>
  <config>
    <peer-group>application-peers</peer-group>
  </config>
</neighbor>
```

Implementing new extensions to the BGP and PCEP protocols

The BGP and PCEP protocols offer extensibility features to add new behavior. There are many RFCs and drafts available for extensions to these two protocols. The OpenDaylight BGP-PCEP implementation offers a way to support these extensions. In this recipe, we will look at some implementation guidelines to add new extensions to BGP and PCEP protocols in OpenDaylight.

The BGP parser module implementation presently supports the following RFCs:

- RFC3107: Carrying Label Information in BGP-4
- RFC4271: A **Border Gateway Protocol 4 (BGP-4)**
- RFC4724: Graceful Restart Mechanism for BGP
- RFC4760: Multiprotocol Extensions for BGP-4
- RFC1997: BGP Communities Attribute
- RFC4360: BGP Extended Communities Attribute

- RFC6793: BGP Support for Four-Octet **Autonomous System** (**AS**) Number Space
- RFC4486: Subcodes for BGP Cease Notification Message
- RFC5492: Capabilities Advertisement with BGP-4
- RFC5668: 4-Octet AS Specific BGP Extended Community
- RFC6286: Autonomous-System-Wide Unique BGP Identifier for BGP-4
- RFC5575: Dissemination of Flow Specification Rules
- RFC7311: The Accumulated IGP Metric Attribute for BGP
- RFC7674: Clarification of the Flowspec Redirect Extended Community

And the PCEP base parser supports the following RFCs:

- RFC5440: PCE and PCEP
- RFC5541: Encoding of Objective Functions in the Path Computation Element Communication Protocol
- RFC5455: Diffserv-Aware Class-Type Object for the Path Computation Element Communication Protocol
- RFC5521: Extensions to the Path Computation Element Communication Protocol (PCEP) for Route Exclusions
- RFC5557: Path Computation Element Communication Protocol (PCEP) Requirements and Protocol Extensions in Support of Global Concurrent Optimization
- RFC5886: A Set of Monitoring Tools for Path Computation Element-Based Architecture

Getting ready

As a prerequisite, make sure that you have cloned the BGP-PCEP project from the OpenDaylight GitHub using the `git clone` command:

git clone `https://git.opendaylight.org/gerrit`

To implement extensions to BGP and PCEP you will need to set up your development environment for OpenDaylight development. The necessary tools and utilities include: Java JDK 8, Maven v3.3.1 or later, the Git client, and an IDE of your choice.

How to do it...

The following subsections highlight some implementation guidelines for extending BGP and PCEP protocols with an RFC or draft.

Guidelines to write a new BGP extension:

- Creating a separate Maven bundle for the extension you want to implement:

  Add the base-parser bundles as dependencies to the pom file of the new bundle created:

  ```
  <dependency>
    <groupId>${project.groupId}</groupId>
    <artifactId>bgp-parser-api</artifactId>
  </dependency>
  <dependency>
    <groupId>${project.groupId}</groupId>
    <artifactId>bgp-parser-spi</artifactId>
  </dependency>
  ```

- YANG modeling for the extension:

  You could write a new YANG model or new elements, or augment the existing ones based on your requirements. Once the YANG models are created, build the new bundle using the Maven command: `mvn clean install`. This will generate Java classes from the YANG models defined.

- Implementing parsers and serializers:

  The `bgp-parser-spi` bundle provides Java interfaces for parsing and serializing by names: `*Parser.java` and `*Serializer.java`. These interface names are prefixed with the names of the protocol elements, for example:
  `BGPKeepAliveMessageParser.java` implements `MessageParser.java` and `MessageSerializer.java`.
  Any new element of the extension that needs to be added should implement their `*Parser` and `*Serializer` interfaces.

- Registering parsers and serializers:

  Add a new Activator class that inherits from the `AbstractBGPExtensionProviderActivator` class. It is in this new activator class that the parsers and serializers will be registered.

  To register new address and subsequent address families, you will want to add **Address Family Identifiers/Subsequent Address Family Identifiers (AFI/SAFI)**. To do so create another Activator that inherits from the `AbstractRIBExtensionProviderActivator` class.

- Updating BGP XML configuration files:

  Register the new parser as a new module in the `31-bgp.xml` file as follows:

  ```
  <module>
  <type
  xmlns:prefix="urn:opendaylight:params:xml:ns:yang:controller:bg
  p:new-extension-parser">prefix:bgp-new-extension-
  parser</type><name>new-extension-parser</name>
  </module>
  ```

  Add the module as a new extension to the `bgp-parser-base` as follows:

  ```
  <extension>
  <type
  xmlns:bgpspi="urn:opendaylight:params:xml:ns:yang:controller:bg
  p:parser:spi">bgpspi:extension</type>
  <name>bgp-new-extension-parser</name>
  </extension>
  ```

  Add the instance of the new extension to the services section as follows:

  ```
  <instance>
  <name>bgp-new-extension-parser</name>
  <provider>/modules/module[type='bgp-new-extension-
  parser'][name='bgp-new-extension-parser']</provider>
  </instance>
  ```

If adding new AFI/SAFI be sure to register them to RIB, as shown in the following example:

```
<module>
<type
xmlns:prefix="urn:opendaylight:params:xml:ns:yang:controller:bg
p:rib:impl">prefix:bgp-table-type-impl</type>
<name>new-extension</name>
<afi xmlns:new-
extension="urn:opendaylight:params:xml:ns:yang:bgp-new-
extension">new-extension:new-extension-address-family</afi>
<safi xmlns:new-
extension="urn:opendaylight:params:xml:ns:yang:bgp-new-
extension">new-extension:new-extension-subsequent-address-
family</safi>
</module>
```

- For the new extension parser, augment the configuration datastore, as shown in the following snippet, and create a configuration file by adding the following parameters to the YANG model. This will generate *Module and *ModuleFactory classes:

```
identity bgp-new-extension-parser {
  base config:module-type;
  config:provided-service bgpspi:extension;
  config:provided-service ribspi:extension; // for new AFI/SAFI
  config:java-name-prefix NewExtensionParser;
}
  augment "/config:modules/config:module/config:configuration"
{
  case bgp-new-extension-parser {
  when "/config:modules/config:module/config:type = 'bgp-new-
extension
  -parser'";
  }
}
```

Build the new artifact using the Maven command: mvn clean install. This will generate the Module and ModuleFactory classes.

In the `createInstance` method of the `*Module` class create a new instance of the parser activator created earlier, as follows:

```
@Override
public java.lang.AutoCloseable createInstance() {
return new NewExtensionParserActivator();
}
```

Guidelines for writing a new PCEP extension:

- Creating a separate Maven bundle/artifact for the extension you want to implement:

  Add the base-parser bundles as dependencies to the new bundle:

  ```
  <dependency>
    <groupId>${project.groupId}</groupId>
    <artifactId>pcep-api</artifactId>
  </dependency>
  <dependency>
    <groupId>${project.groupId}</groupId>
    <artifactId>pcep-spi</artifactId>
  </dependency>
  ```

- Create a new YANG model for new elements or augment the existing ones based on your requirements. Build the new bundle using Maven command: `mvn clean install` to generate Java classes from the YANG models defined.

- Implementing parsers and serializers:

  The `pcep-spi` bundle provides Java interfaces for parsing and serializing by names `*Parser.java` and `*Serializer.java`. Any new element of the extension that needs to be added should implement their `*Parser` and `*Serializer` interfaces.

- Registering parsers and serializers:

  Add a new Activator class that inherits from the `AbstractPCEPExtensionProviderActivator` class where the parsers and serializers will be registered.

- Updating PCEP XML configuration files:

Register the new parser as a new module in the `32-pcep.xml` file as follows

```
<module>
<type
xmlns:prefix="urn:opendaylight:params:xml:ns:yang:controller:pc
ep:impl">prefix:pcep-new-extension-parser</type>
<name>pcep-new-extension-parser</name>
</module>
```

Add the module as a new extension to the `pcep-parser-base` as follows

```
<extension>
<type
xmlns:pcepspi="urn:opendaylight:params:xml:ns:yang:controller:p
cep:spi">pcepspi:extension</type>
<name>pcep-new-extension-parser</name>
</extension>
```

Add the instance of the new extension to services as follows:

```
<instance>
<name>pcep-new-extension-parser</name>
<provider>/modules/module[type='pcep-new-extension-
parser'][name='pcep-new-extension-parser']</provider>
</instance>
```

- For the new extension parser, augment the configuration datastore in `odl-pcep-impl-cfg.yang`, as shown in the following snippet. This will generate the `*Module` and `*ModuleFactory` classes:

```
identity pcep-new-extension-parser {
  base config:module-type;
  config:provided-service pcepspi:extension;
  config:java-name-prefix PcepNewExtensionParser;
}
  augment "/config:modules/config:module/config:configuration"
{
  case pcep-new-extension-parser {
  when "/config:modules/config:module/config:type = 'pcep-new
  -extension-parser'";
  }
}
```

Build the new artifact using the Maven command: `mvn clean install` to generate the `Module` and `ModuleFactory` classes.

In the `createInstance` method of the `*Module` class create a new instance of the parser activator created earlier, as shown in the following snippet:

```
@Override
  public java.lang.AutoCloseable createInstance() {
  return new NewPcepExtensionParserActivator();
}
```

See also

In its current implementation, the BGP project supports two extensions as follows. Listed alongside them is the OpenDaylight GitHub repository for their implementation:

- Linkstate OpenDaylight GitHub repository:

  `https://github.com/opendaylight/bgpcep/tree/stable/beryllium/bgp/linkstate`

- Flowspec OpenDaylight GitHub repository:

  `https://github.com/opendaylight/bgpcep/tree/stable/beryllium/bgp/flowspec`

The PCEP implementation supports two extensions:

- Stateful RFCs:

  `https://tools.ietf.org/html/draft-ietf-pce-stateful-pce-14` and `https://tools.ietf.org/html/draft-ietf-pce-pce-initiated-lsp-05`

  The OpenDaylight GitHub repository:

  `https://github.com/opendaylight/bgpcep/tree/stable/beryllium/pcep/ietf-stateful07`

- Segment routing RFCs:

  `https://tools.ietf.org/html/draft-ietf-pce-segment-routing-01`
  The OpenDaylight GitHub repository:

  `https://github.com/opendaylight/bgpcep/tree/stable/beryllium/pcep/se`
  `gment-routing`

These extensions, implementation can also be looked at for reference.

6
Intent and Policy Networking

In this chapter, we will cover the following recipes:

- Simple firewall with NIC
- MPLS intents and label management
- Traffic redirection with intents
- End-to-end intents
- NIC and OpenStack integration
- QoS operation with intents
- LOG action using NIC
- VTN renderer using NIC

Introduction

The NIC provides some features to enable the controller to manage and direct network services and resources based on intent. Intents can be defined as "what" to do, not "how" to do it, it's directly related to the user's desires. Intents are described to the controller through a new northbound interface, which provides generalized and abstracted policy semantics instead of OpenFlow-like rules. This project includes integration with OpenStack neutron, **Service Function Chaining** (**SFC**), and **Group Based Policy** (**GBP**). The NIC project uses the existing OpenDaylight network service functions and southbound plugins to control both virtual and physical network devices.

The NIC provides these features:

- `odl-nic-core-hazelcast`: Provides a distributed intent mapping service, implemented using hazelcast (used to share data in an in-memory data grid), which stores metadata needed by the `odl-nic-core` feature

- `odl-nic-core-mdsal`: Provides an intent REST backend

- `odl-nic-console`: Provides a Karaf CLI extension for intent CRUD operations and mapping service operations

- `odl-nic-renderer-of - Generic OpenFlow Renderer`: This renderer is responsible for communicating with the OpenDaylight OpenFlow plugin and pushing rules to switches

- `odl-nic-renderer-vtn`: A feature that transforms an intent to a network modification using the VTN project

- `odl-nic-renderer-gbp`: A feature that transforms an intent to a network modification using the group policy project

- `odl-nic-renderer-nemo`: A feature that transforms an intent to a network modification using the NEMO project.

- `odl-nic-listeners`: This adds support for event listening, (depends on: `odl-nic-renderer-of`).

- `odl-nic-neutron-integration`: Allow integration with OpenStack neutron to allow coexistence between existing neutron security rules and intents pushed by OpenDaylight applications.

Some useful commands used on NIC:

- `intent:add`:

```
--[cut]--
DESCRIPTION
  intent:add
Adds an intent to the controller.
Examples: --actions [ALLOW] --from <subject> --to <subject>
  --actions [BLOCK] --from <subject>
SYNTAX
  intent:add [options]
```

```
OPTIONS
  -a, --actions
    Action to be performed.
    -a / --actions BLOCK/ALLOW
    (defaults to [BLOCK])
--help
    Display this help message
-t, --to
    Second Subject.
    -t / --to <subject>
    (defaults to any)
-f, --from
    First subject.
    -f / --from <subject>
    (defaults to any)
--[cut]--
```

- intent:remove:

```
--[cut]--
DESCRIPTION
  intent:remove
Removes an intent from the controller.
SYNTAX
  intent:remove id
ARGUMENTS
  Id: Intent Id
--[cut]---
```

- intent:show:

```
--[cut]--
DESCRIPTION
  intent:show
Shows detailed information about an intent.
SYNTAX
  intent:show id
ARGUMENTS
  id :Intent Id
--[cut]--
```

- intent:list:

```
--[cut]--
DESCRIPTION
  intent:list
Lists all intents in the controller.
SYNTAX
```

```
        intent:list [options]
OPTIONS
   -c, --config
     List Configuration Data (optional).
     -c / --config <ENTER>
   --help
     Display this help message
--[cut]--
```

For the Boron release, just a single renderer feature should be installed at a time.

Simple firewall with NIC

In order to have a simple firewall feature using intents, we will create a simple topology that consists of two hosts and one OpenFlow switch. You can create commands using MAC addresses or endpoint groups.

Getting ready

The ingredients of this recipe require an OpenFlow switch. If you don't have any, you can use a Mininet-VM with OvS installed. You can download Mininet-VM from the website `htt ps://github.com/mininet/mininet/wiki/Mininet-VM-Images`. Any version should work.

The following recipe will be presented using a Mininet-VM with OvS 2.3.2.

The sample code for this recipe is available at:

`https://github.com/jgoodyear/OpenDaylightCookbook/tree/master/chapter1`

How to do it...

Perform the following steps:

1. Start the OpenDaylight distribution using the `karaf` script. Using this client will give you access to the Karaf CLI:

   ```
   $ ./bin/karaf
   ```

2. Install the user-facing feature responsible for pulling in all dependencies needed to connect an OpenFlow switch:

   ```
   opendaylight-user@root>feature:install odl-nic-core-mdsal odl-
   nic-console odl-nic-renderer-of
   ```

It might take a few minutes to complete the installation.

To make sure the installation went well, check the logs using the following command:

```
opendaylight-user@root>log:tail
--[cut]--
of-renderer - 1.1.3.SNAPSHOT | Creating Open flow renderer
2016-05-23 12:46:32,725 | INFO | config-pusher |
OFRendererFlowManagerProvider | 284 - org.opendaylight.nic.of-
renderer - 1.1.3.SNAPSHOT | OF Renderer Provider Session
Initiated
2016-05-23 12:46:32,794 | INFO | config-pusher |
ConfigPusherImpl     | 122 -
org.opendaylight.controller.config-persister-impl -
0.4.3.SNAPSHOT | Successfully pushed configuration snapshot 91-
of-renderer.xml(odl-nic-renderer-of,odl-nic-renderer-of)
--[cut]--
```

3. Have your topology up and running. To make sure your Mininet topology use the following command:

```
sudo mn --controller=remote,ip=<CONTROLLER_IP> --topo linear,2
--switch ovsk,protocols=OpenFlow13
--[cut]--
2016-05-23 13:10:47,002 | INFO | ofEntity-0  | OfEntityManager
| 261 - org.opendaylight.openflowplugin - 0.2.3.SNAPSHOT |
sendNodeAddedNotification: Node Added notification is sent for
ModelDrivenSwitch openflow:1
2016-05-23 13:10:47,006 | INFO | ofEntity-1  | OfEntityManager
| 261 - org.opendaylight.openflowplugin - 0.2.3.SNAPSHOT |
sendNodeAddedNotification: Node Added notification is sent for
ModelDrivenSwitch openflow:2
--[cut]--
```

4. Install intents to allow unidirectional flows from h1 to h2 and block flows from h2 to h1 using their respective MAC addresses:

```
intent:add -f ce:25:6a:e8:17:a9 -t 02:4d:f8:00:81:8e -a ALLOW
intent:add -f 02:4d:f8:00:81:8e -t ce:25:6a:e8:17:a9 -a BLOCK
```

5. Verify connectivity between hosts:

```
--[cut]--
mininet> pingall
*** Ping: testing ping reachability
h1 -> h2
h2 -> X
*** Results: 50% dropped (1/2 received)
--[cut]--
```

This result means that all the pings between h2 and h1 have dropped.

How it works...

The `odl-nic-console` enables the NIC command-line feature. It provides several commands to interact with intents, such as `add`, `list`, `show`, `remove intents`, and many more.

Using the `odl-nic-core-mdsal` feature, we have pulled in all the necessary dependencies to enable NIC to communicate with the MD-SAL.

Using the `odl-nic-of-listeners` feature, we have pulled in all the necessary dependencies to enable NIC to listen to network events.

Using the `odl-nic-of-renderer` feature, we have pulled in all the necessary dependencies to enable NIC to render intents in OpenFlow switches. Once a new intent is installed, this module creates OpenFlow messages and pushes them into OpenFlow switches.

MPLS intents and label management

NIC's mapping service should make the creation of intents between two endpoints to be handled by the OpenFlow renderer possible. Thus, this renderer can generate OpenFlow rules for push or pop labels to the MPLS endpoint nodes. After an IPv4 Prefix match and forward to port rule once MPLS label match, all the switches that form the shortest path between the endpoints using the Dijkstra algorithm.

Getting ready

Some constraints were added to the intent model for protection and failover mechanism to ensure end-to-end connectivity between endpoints. These constraints aim to reduce the risk of connectivity failure due to a single link or port-down event on a forwarding device. The constraints implemented are:

- **Protection constraint**: Requires an end-to-end connectivity to be protected by providing redundant paths

- **Failover**: Uses disjoint path calculation algorithms such as Suurballe to provide alternate end-to-end routes

- **Fast-reroute**: Uses failure detection features in hardware forwarding devices through OF group table features

How to do it...

Perform the following steps:

1. Start `karaf` and install related features:

   ```
   karaf> feature:install odl-nic-core-mdsal odl-nic-listerners
   odl-nic-console
   karaf> feature:install odl-dlux-all old-dlux-core odl-dlux-
   yangui odl-dlux-yangvisualizer
   ```

2. Start the Mininet topology and verify in the DLUX topology page for the nodes and link.

   The sample code for this recipe is available at:

   https://github.com/jgoodyear/OpenDaylightCookbook/tree/master/chapte r9/chapter9-recipe2

   Use the file `shortest_path.py` to create your topology:

   ```
   mn -controller=remote,ip=<controller_ip> --custom
   shortest_path.py --topo shortest_path.py --switch
   ovsk,protocols=OpenFlow13
   ```

3. Update the mapping service with required information using the file, `mapping_service_config.json`.

4. Create bidirectional intents using the `karaf` command line or RestCONF:

   ```
   karaf> intent:add -f uva -t eur -a ALLOW
   karaf>intent:add -f eur -t uva -a ALLOW
   ```

5. Verify the flows by running the `ovs` command on `mininet` if the flows were pushed correctly to the nodes that form the shortest path:

   ```
   mininet> dpctl dump-flows
   ```

How it works...

The file `mapping_service_config.json` contains code in JSON format to create groups for endpoints. Once those endpoints are mapped on NIC, you are able to create intents using these groups. The bundle `intent-listerners` will notify the `of-renderer` about this intent creation, and then, the `of-renderer` will extract all information for this endpoint to create the OpenFlow rules. Those steps are similar to the recipe, *MPLS intents and label management*.

Traffic redirection with intents

In order to have a simple traffic redirection using intents, we will create a simple topology that consists of three hosts and one OpenFlow switch. We will use commands using the MAC address.

Getting ready

The sample code for this recipe is available at:

`https://github.com/jgoodyear/OpenDaylightCookbook/tree/master/chapter9/chapter9-recipe3`

This demo requires an OpenFlow switch. If you don't have any, you can use a Mininet-VM with OvS installed.

How to do it...

Perform the following steps:

1. Start the OpenDaylight distribution using the `karaf` script. Using this client will give you access to the Karaf CLI.
2. Install the features responsible for intent creation on the command line in order to generate the OpenFlow rule.

3. Have your topology running using Mininet and check the connectivity with the OpenDaylight controller.

4. Start your Mininet topology using the file `redirect_test.py`:

```
sudo mn --controller=remote,ip=<controller-ip> --custom
redirect_test.py --topo mytopo
```

5. Check if all nodes are `mininet` console using the following command:

```
--[cut]--
mininet> net
h1 h1-eth0:s1-eth1
h2 h2-eth0:s1-eth2
h3 h3-eth0:s2-eth1
h4 h4-eth0:s2-eth2
h5 h5-eth0:s2-eth3
srvc1 srvc1-eth0:s3-eth3 srvc1-eth1:s4-eth3
s1 lo: s1-eth1:h1-eth0 s1-eth2:h2-eth0 s1-eth3:s2-eth4 s1-
eth4:s3-eth2
s2 lo: s2-eth1:h3-eth0 s2-eth2:h4-eth0 s2-eth3:h5-eth0 s2-
eth4:s1-eth3 s2-eth5:s4-eth1
s3 lo: s3-eth1:s4-eth2 s3-eth2:s1-eth4 s3-eth3:srvc1-eth0
s4 lo: s4-eth1:s2-eth5 s4-eth2:s3-eth1 s4-eth3:srvc1-eth1
c0
--[cut]--
```

6. Start the OpenDaylight distribution using the `karaf` script. Using this client will give you access to the Karaf CLI and then install all needed features:

```
--[cut]--
/bin karaf
feature:install odl-nic-core-mdsal odl-nic-console odl-nic-
listeners
--[cut]--
```

7. Configure the service node. All the traffic will be redirected to this node:

```
--[cut]--
mininet> srvc1 ip addr del 10.0.0.6/8 dev srvc1-eth0
mininet> srvc1 brctl addbr br0
mininet> srvc1 brctl addif br0 srvc1-eth0
mininet> srvc1 brctl addif br0 srvc1-eth1
mininet> srvc1 ifconfig br0 up
mininet> srvc1 tc qdisc add dev srvc1-eth1 root netem delay
200ms
--[cut]--
```

8. Now configure the service using the SFC API, using the file,
   `service_config.json`:

   ```
   --[cut]--
   curl -i -H "Content-Type: application/json" -H "Cache-Control:
   no-cache" --data @service_config.json -X PUT --user admin:admin
   http://localhost:8181/restconf/config/service-function:service-
   functions/
   --[cut]--
   ```

9. Now configure all switches and port information for the service functions using
   the file, `service_functions_config.json`:

   ```
   --[cut]--
   curl -i -H "Content-Type: application/json" -H "Cache-Control:
   no-cache" --data @service_functions_config.json -X PUT --user
   admin:admin
   http://localhost:8181/restconf/config/service-function-forwarde
   r:service-function-forwarders/
   --[cut]--
   ```

10. Use the Karaf CLI:

    ```
    --[cut]--
    intent:add -f 00:00:00:00:00:01 -t 00:00:00:00:00:05 -a
    REDIRECT -s srvc1
    --[cut]--
    ```

11. Now, `h1` should ping to `h5`, if it works properly after intent creation, it means
    that all traffic between `h1` and `h5` is redirected to `srvc1`:

    ```
    --[cut]--
    mininet> h1 ping h5
    PING 10.0.0.5 (10.0.0.5) 56(84) bytes of data.
    64 bytes from 10.0.0.5: icmp_seq=2 ttl=64 time=201 ms
    64 bytes from 10.0.0.5: icmp_seq=3 ttl=64 time=200 ms
    64 bytes from 10.0.0.5: icmp_seq=4 ttl=64 time=200 ms
    --[cut]--
    ```

How it works...

The host `srvc1` was created to emulate similar behavior to a service. It will be used to receive all redirected packets. Before intent creation, you have to use the REST API to describe the current topology. For this example, we have two different VLANs (`100` and `200`). At step 9, you are defining the `egress` and `ingress` service function data-planes for the service `srvc1`. At NIC to create an intent to use the service `srvc1`. At step 11, your `h1` and `h5` using the parameter `-s` followed by the service (`srvc1` in this case). Once the intent has been created, all traffic between `h1` and `h5` will be redirected to `srvc1` with a `200 ms`.

End-to-end intents

In order to ensure the connectivity between two nodes using intents, we will create a simple topology that consists of two hosts and one OpenFlow switch. You can create commands using endpoint groups.

Getting ready

The ingredients of this recipe require an OpenFlow switch. If you don't have any, you can use a Mininet-VM with OvS installed. You can download Mininet-VM from the website `https://github.com/mininet/mininet/wiki/Mininet-VM-Images`. Any version should work.

The following recipe will be presented using a Mininet-VM with OvS 2.3.2.

The sample code for this recipe is available at:

`https://github.com/jgoodyear/OpenDaylightCookbook/tree/master/chapter1`

How to do it...

Perform the following steps:

1. Start the OpenDaylight distribution using the `karaf` script. Using this client will give you access to the Karaf CLI:

   ```
   $ ./bin/karaf
   ```

2. Install the user-facing feature responsible for pulling in all dependencies needed to connect an OpenFlow switch:

    ```
    opendaylight-user@root>feature:install odl-nic-core-mdsal odl-
    nic-console odl-nic-renderer-of
    ```

It might take a few minutes to complete the installation.

To make sure the installation was finished with success, check the logs using the following command:

```
opendaylight-user@root>log:tail
--[cut]--
of-renderer - 1.1.3.SNAPSHOT | Creating Open flow renderer
2016-05-23 12:46:32,725 | INFO | config-pusher |
OFRendererFlowManagerProvider | 284 - org.opendaylight.nic.of-
renderer - 1.1.3.SNAPSHOT | OF Renderer Provider Session
Initiated
2016-05-23 12:46:32,794 | INFO | config-pusher |
ConfigPusherImpl  | 122 - org.opendaylight.controller.config-
persister-impl - 0.4.3.SNAPSHOT | Successfully pushed
configuration snapshot 91-of-renderer.xml(odl-nic-renderer-
of,odl-nic-renderer-of)
--[cut]--
mininet> pingall
*** Ping: testing ping reachability
h1 -> h2
h2 -> h1
*** Results: 0% dropped (2/2 received)
--[cut]--
```

3. Have your topology up and running. To make sure your Mininet topology was created with success, use the following command:

```
sudo mn --controller=remote,ip=<CONTROLLER_IP> --topo linear,2
--switch ovsk,protocols=OpenFlow13
--[cut]--
2016-05-23 13:10:47,002 | INFO | ofEntity-0 | OfEntityManager
| 261 - org.opendaylight.openflowplugin - 0.2.3.SNAPSHOT |
sendNodeAddedNotification: Node Added notification is sent for
ModelDrivenSwitch openflow:1
2016-05-23 13:10:47,006 | INFO | ofEntity-1 | OfEntityManager
| 261 - org.opendaylight.openflowplugin - 0.2.3.SNAPSHOT |
sendNodeAddedNotification: Node Added notification is sent for
ModelDrivenSwitch openflow:2
--[cut]--
```

4. Map endpoint groups:

```
opendaylight-user@root>intent:map --add-key developers --value
"MAC => 00:00:00:00:00:01"
developers = [[ {MAC=00:00:00:00:00:01} ]]
opendaylight-user@root>intent:map --add-key hr --value "MAC =>
00:00:00:00:00:02"
developers = [[ {MAC=00:00:00:00:00:01} ]]
hr = [[ {MAC=00:00:00:00:00:02} ]]
```

5. Install intents to allow unidirectional flows from h1 to h2 and block flows from h2 to h1, using their respective MAC addresses:

```
opendaylight-user@root>intent:add -f developers -t hr -a ALLOW
Intent created (id: 2df29b4f-217a-4633-9461-3230c35647be)
opendaylight-user@root>intent:add -f hr -t developers -a ALLOW
Intent created (id: 1dc6e387-d7e9-40c0-ae31-637cc5b1f2e5)
```

6. Verify connectivity between hosts:

```
--[cut]--
mininet> pingall
*** Ping: testing ping reachability
h1 -> h2
h2 -> h1
*** Results: 0% dropped (2/2 received)
--[cut]--
```

How it works...

The `odl-nic-console` feature enables the NIC command-line feature. It provides several commands to interact with intents, such as add, list, show, remove intents, and many more.

The `odl-nic-core-mdsal` feature enables NIC to communicate with OpenDaylight's MD-SAL.

The `odl-nic-of-listeners` feature enables NIC to listen to network events.

The `odl-nic-of-renderer` feature enables NIC to render intents in OpenFlow switches. Once a new intent is installed, this module creates OpenFlow messages and pushes them into OpenFlow switches.

Using the `intent:add -f 02:4d:f8:00:81:8e -t 02:4d:f8:00:81:8e -a ALLOW` we are creating an intent where the parameter `-f` defines the source device (`from`), `-t` defines the target device (`to`), and `-a` defines the action of this intent. In other words: Add a new intent to `ALLOW` all traffic where the source MAC address is `02:4d:f8:00:81:8e` and destination MAC address is `02:4d:f8:00:81:8e`.

After intent creation, the `odl-nic-of-listeners` feature will send this intent to the `odl-nic-of-renderer` feature to extract all needed information to compose an OpenFlow rule and send it to the switches.

NIC and OpenStack integration

In order to demonstrate the integration of the NIC project with OpenStack, you have to set up the OpenStack environment installing an Ubuntu server 14.04+ on a VM using VirtualBox 4.3+ (preferably 4 core, 32 GB NIC interfaces).

Getting ready

Once you have OpenStack set up on your machine and VirtualBox installed, you are ready to start the configuration.

How to do it...

Perform the following steps:

1. Install Ubuntu 14.04+ server.
2. Configure the IP address and the gateway for your two NIC interfaces. One interface should be an NAT address while the other one should be attached on the host-only adapter and be on the same network as your host.
3. Configure the required environment variables and proxies:

```
--[cut]--
export http_proxy= {YOUR_HTTP_PROXY}
export https_proxy= {YOUR_HTTP_PROXY}
export ftp_proxy= {YOUR_FTP_PROXY}
export no_proxy=localhost,127.0.0.1,{IP of host}
--[cut]--
```

4. Update /etc/apt/apt.conf with the proxy detail:

```
--[cut]--
Acquire::http::proxy "YOUR_PROXY";
--[cut]--
```

5. Update the apt repository:

```
--[cut]--
# apt-get update
--[cut]--
```

6. Install git:

```
--[cut]--
# apt-get install git
--[cut]--
```

7. Clone into the openstack repository:

```
--[cut]--
git clone https://git.openstack.org/openstack-dev/devstack -b
stable/liberty
--[cut]--
```

8. Change the GIT_BASE variable to https in the file stackrc:

```
--[cut]--
GIT_BASE=${GIT_BASE:-https://git.openstack.org}
--[cut]--
```

9. Create a local.conf file in the ~/devsctack directory with the following contents.

10. Use the following local.conf example on this link:

   https://github.com/jgoodyear/OpenDaylightCookbook/tree/master/chapter9/chapter9-recipe6

11. Modify the fields of local.conf as per your setup:

```
--[cut]--
HOST_IP= {YOUR_NAT_IP}
HOST_NAME= {YOUR_HOST_NAME}
ODL_MGR_IP= {HOST_ONLY_IP}
--[cut]--
```

12. Run the `stack.sh` script. Once that is done, you can `lock down` the stack repository used by changing the following values in `local.conf`:

```
--[cut]--
OFFLINE=True
RECLONE=no
--[cut]--
```

13. In case the `br-int` interface does not come up or takes a long time, manually add the bridge and set its controller:

```
--[cut]--
sudo ovs-vsctl add-br br-int
sudo ovs-vsctl set-controller br-int tcp:192.168.56.1:6653
--[cut]--
```

You can verify that the manager is set and check the flows using the following:

```
--[cut]--
sudo ovs-vsctl show
sudo ovs-ofctl dump-flows br-int -O Openflow13
--[cut]--
```

14. Once stacking runs correctly, you will be able to log into the OpenStack dashboard.

15. Run the Karaf container for NIC (`./karaf clean`) inside the host machine and install the following features in the corresponding order:

```
--[cut]--
feature:install odl-neutron-serviceodl-nic-core-service-mdsal
odl-nic-console odl-nic-neutron-integration
--[cut]--
```

16. Create the security rules using the OpenStack instance dashboard navigating into the default group:

```
--[cut]--
http://{YOUR_VM_NAT}:80/dashboard/project/access_and_security/
--[cut]--
```

17. Verify the created OpenFlow rules using the following command:

```
--[cut]--
#ovs-ofctl dump-flows br-int
--[cut]--
```

How it works...

Once you have the OpenStack environment configured as well, you are able to create the policies using the OpenStack dashboard. Following all the described steps, you will have the OpenDaylight controller integrated with OpenStack over the OpenVSwitch port `br-int`. After creating the security rule using the OpenStack dashboard, the module `intent-listeners` will handle an intent creation and send this intent to `of-renderer`. Once the module `of-renderer` receives this intent originated from the OpenStack dashboard, some new OpenFlow rules will be created on OpenVSwitch.

QoS operation with intents

The QoS attribute mapping currently supports DiffServ. It uses a 6-bit **differentiated services code point** (**DSCP**) in the 8-bit **differentiated services field** (**DS field**) in the IP header.

Getting ready

The following steps explain the QoS attribute mapping function:

- Initially configure the QoS profile, which contains the profile name and DSCP value
- When a packet is transferred from a source to destination, the flow builder evaluates whether the transferred packet matches the condition such as actions and endpoints in the flow
- If the packet matches the endpoints, the flow builder applies the flow matching action and DSCP value

Start Mininet, and create three switches (s1, s2, and s3) and four hosts (h1, h2, h3, and h4) in it:

```
sudo mn --mac --topo tree,2 --
controller=remote,ip=192.168.0.100,port=6633
```

 Replace `192.168.0.100` with the IP address of the OpenDaylight controller based on your environment.

You can check the topology you created by executing the `net` command in the `mininet` console:

```
mininet> net
h1 h1-eth0:s2-eth1
h2 h2-eth0:s2-eth2
h3 h3-eth0:s3-eth1
h4 h4-eth0:s3-eth2
s1 lo:  s1-eth1:s2-eth3  s1-eth2:s3-eth3
s2 lo:  s2-eth1:h1-eth0  s2-eth2:h2-eth0  s2-eth3:s1-eth1
s3 lo:  s3-eth1:h3-eth0  s3-eth2:h4-eth0  s3-eth3:s1-eth2
```

- Run `karaf`:

```
--[cut]--
./bin/karaf
--[cut]--
```

- Once the console is up, type the following to install features:

```
--[cut]--
feature:install odl-nic-core-mdsal odl-nic-console odl-nic-
listeners
--[cut]--
```

How to do it...

Perform the following steps:

- To apply the QoS constraint, configure the QoS profile:

```
--[cut]--
Intent:qosConfig -p <qos_profile_name> -d <valid_dscp_valud>
--[cut]--
```

Example:

```
--[cut]--
Intent:qosConfig -p High_Quality -d 46
--[cut]--
```

The valid DSCP values range from 0-63.

- To provision the network for the two hosts (h1 and h3), add intents that allow traffic in both directions by executing the following CLI command.

  Demonstrate the ALLOW action with constraint QOS and QoS profile name:

  ```
  --[cut]--
  Intent:add -f <SOURCE_MAC> -t <DESTINATION_MAC> -a ALLOW -q QOS
  -p <qos_profile_name>
  --[cut]--
  ```

Example:

```
--[cut]--
Intent:add -f 00:00:00:00:00:01 -t 00:00:00:00:00:02 -a ALLOW -
q QOS -p High_Quality
--[cut]--
```

Verification

- As we have applied the action type ALLOW, now you can ping between hosts h1 and h3:

  ```
  --[cut]--
  mininet> h1 ping h3
  PING 10.0.0.3 (10.0.0.3) 56(84) bytes of data.
  64 bytes from 10.0.0.3: icmp_req=1 ttl=64 time=0.984 ms
  64 bytes from 10.0.0.3: icmp_req=2 ttl=64 time=0.110 ms
  64 bytes from 10.0.0.3: icmp_req=3 ttl=64 time=0.098 ms
  --[cut]--
  ```

- Verify the flow entry and ensure that mod_nw_tos is part of the actions:

  ```
  --[cut]--
  mininet> dpctl dump-flows
  *** s1 -----------------------------------------------------------
  ------------------
  NXST_FLOW reply (xid=0x4):
  cookie=0x0, duration=21.873s, table=0, n_packets=3,
  n_bytes=294, idle_age=21,
  priority=9000,dl_src=00:00:00:00:00:03,dl_dst=00:00:00:00:00:01
  ```

```
actions=NORMAL,mod_nw_tos:184
cookie=0x0, duration=41.252s, table=0, n_packets=3,
n_bytes=294, idle_age=41,
priority=9000,dl_src=00:00:00:00:00:01,dl_dst=00:00:00:00:00:03
actions=NORMAL,mod_nw_tos:184
--[cut]--
```

How it works...

When you define QoS constraints using the parameter -d 46, it means that all rules that compose that intent will contain a filed mod_nw_tos:184. The value 46 defines that you are creating rules to perform QoS for a broadcast video, this value could vary according to the desired service (between 0-63). To use the defined QoS constraint, you have to create a new intent to allow all traffic between the devices that need QoS constraints, thus, once you make use of the parameter -q to create a new intent with the constraint, it means that packets that will be sent to those devices will be tagged with a DSCP value.

LOG action using NIC

This topic will demonstrate how to use the LOG action in OF Renderer. It enables the communication between two hosts and logging the flow statistics of the particular traffic.

Getting ready

Have your Mininet topology configured and the last NIC version compiled on your machine.

How to do it...

Start your Mininet network with three hosts, and then, create an intent to allow all traffic between two nodes setting LOG as the action. Create two intents to allow traffic in both directions:

1. Start karaf:

   ```
   --[cut]--
   ./karaf clean
   --[cut]--
   ```

2. Create a new intent to allow bidirectional traffic between two endpoints:

```
--[cut]--
karaf> intent:add -f 00:00:00:00:00:01 -t 00:00:00:00:00:03 -a
ALLOW
karaf> intent:add -f 00:00:00:00:00:03 -t 00:00:00:00:00:01 -a
ALLOW
--[cut]--
```

3. Create a new intent to LOG all activities between those two endpoints:

```
--[cut]--
karaf> intent:add -f 00:00:00:00:00:01 -t 00:00:00:00:00:03 -a
LOG
--[cut]--
```

4. Verify the communication between both:

```
--[cut]--
mininet> h1 ping h3 PING 10.0.0.3 (10.0.0.3) 56(84) bytes of
data.
64 bytes from 10.0.0.3: icmp_req=1 ttl=64 time=0.104 ms
64 bytes from 10.0.0.3: icmp_req=2 ttl=64 time=0.110 ms
64 bytes from 10.0.0.3: icmp_req=3 ttl=64 time=0.104 ms
--[cut]--
```

5. View the flow statistics log details in Karaf's log:

```
--[cut]--
2016-08-29 23:12:40,256 | INFO | lt-dispatcher-22 |
IntentFlowManager | 264 - org.opendaylight.nic.of-renderer -
1.1.0.SNAPSHOT | Creating block intent for endpoints:
source00:00:00:00:00:01 destination 00:00:00:00:00:03
2016-08-29 23:12:40,252 | INFO | lt-dispatcher-25 |
FlowStatisticsListener | 264 - org.opendaylight.nic.of-renderer
- 1.1.0.SNAPSHOT | Flow Statistics gathering for Byte
Count:Counter64 [_value=238]
2016-08-29 23:12:40,252 | INFO | lt-dispatcher-26 |
FlowStatisticsListener | 264 - org.opendaylight.nic.of-renderer
- 1.1.0.SNAPSHOT | Flow Statistics gathering for Packet
Count:Counter64 [_value=3]
--[cut]--
```

How it works...

Some initial rules are needed to ensure that the connectivity between all nodes connect to the topology, those rules will enable bidirectional traffic between all hosts. Thus, you have to create two intents to allow bidirectional traffic for some endpoints. In this case, we are using the h1 and h3, and after the intent creation, you are able to establish a connection between both. In this case, some events could be displayed in Karaf's log, just creating a new intent with LOG as the action. The of-renderer module will receive this intent and extract all needed information to create some flow statistics to monitor all traffic between both.

VTN renderer using NIC

This section will demonstrate how VTN works using intents on an NIC project to ALLOW or BLOCK packets of the traffic according to the specified flow conditions.

Getting ready

Have your Mininet topology configured and the last NIC version compiled on your machine.

How to do it...

Perform the following steps:

1. Start your Mininet topology with a minimum of three hosts. For this example, we will create a topology with three switches and three hosts and create an ALLOW rule using the VTN renderer and then, update these intents to BLOCK all traffic between both.

2. Execute the Mininet topology:

   ```
   --[cut]--
   $ mininet@admin:~$ sudo mn -controller=remote
   ,ip=<controller_ip> --topo tree,2
   --[cut]--
   ```

3. Start `karaf`:

```
--[cut]--
./karaf clean
--[cut]--
```

4. Install the NIC features:

```
--[cut]--
karaf> feature: install odl-nic-core-mdsal odl-nic-renderer-vtn
--[cut]--
```

5. Create the intents using the REST API:

```
--[cut]--
./provision_h1_and_h2.sh <your_controller_ip>
./provision_h2_and_h3.sh <your_controller_Ip>
--[cut]--
```

6. Verify the connectivity between all hosts:

```
--[cut]--
mininet> pingall
Ping: testing ping reachability
h1 -> h2 X X
h2 -> h1 h3 X
h3 -> X h2 X
h4 -> X X X
--[cut]--
```

7. Update the intent to `BLOCK` all traffic between `h1` and `h2`:

```
--[cut]--
./update_h1_and_h2.sh <your_controller_ip>
--[cut]--
```

8. Verify the connectivity between all hosts:

```
--[cut]--
mininet> pingall
Ping: testing ping reachability
h1 -> X X X
h2 -> X h3 X
h3 -> X h2 X
h4 -> X X X
--[cut]--
```

How it works...

The current NIC version supports just one renderer by instance. Once you define that the VTN renderer will be used to render all intents, you must use the REST API to provide the desired network state. In step 4, you are creating a new intent using the REST API. In this case, the module `intent-impl` will translate all parameters in a given intent. This intent will be sent the `vtn-renderer` module, this module will extract all needed information to create the OpenFlow rule according to the endpoint name and intent action. Each `subject` represents the endpoint, where the order will define the source and destination for each intent.

7

OpenDaylight Container Customizations

In this chapter, we will cover:

- Reconfiguring SSH access to OpenDaylight
- Creating your own branded OpenDaylight
- Customizing your OpenDaylight repositories
- Customizing your start up applications
- Installing OpenDaylight as a service
- Creating your own custom OpenDaylight command using the Maven archetype
- Deploying applications using features
- Using JMX to monitor and administer OpenDaylight
- Setting up Apache Karaf Decanter to monitor OpenDaylight

Introduction

Network engineers will tell you that, out of the box, OpenDaylight provides you with the features and tools you'll need to deploy your application; however, many will want to tweak their deployment.

The recipes in this chapter are devoted to network engineers, system builders, and integrators; the people who need to make their OpenDaylight deployment integrate even closer with their organization.

New to OpenDaylight and its Apache Karaf-based container?
Readers interested in obtaining a deeper understanding of OpenDaylight's
OSGi-based modular architecture and underlying technologies should
consult Packt Publishing's *Instant OSGi Starter, Learning Apache Karaf, and
Apache Karaf Cookbook* by *Jamie Goodyear, Johan Edstrom, Heath Kesler*, and
Achim Nierbeck.

Reconfiguring SSH access to OpenDaylight

Using OpenDaylight via its local console provides its user with superb commands and
control capabilities over their OSGi container. OpenDaylight's remote SSH-based console
extends this experience to remote terminals, and as such presents system builders with an
opportunity to further harden their systems. In this recipe, we'll change OpenDaylight's
default remote connection parameters.

Getting ready

The ingredients of this recipe include an OpenDaylight distribution kit, access to a JDK, and
a source code editor. Sample configuration for this recipe is available at:

```
https://github.com/jgoodyear/OpenDaylightCookbook/tree/master/chapter10/chapter
10-recipe1
```

How to do it...

The process for reconfiguring OpenDaylight's SSH access is a very quick two-step process;
edit the shell configuration and restart OpenDaylight. The steps are as follows:

1. Editing shell configuration.

    OpenDaylight ships with a default shell configuration file; it's a good practice to
    edit entries in `etc/org.apache.karaf.shell.cfg` to point to non-default ports
    as a security precaution:

    ```
    #
    # Via sshPort and sshHost you define the address you can login
    into Karaf.
    #
    sshPort = 8102
    sshHost = 192.168.1.110
    ```

In the preceding sample configuration, we define the port we'll open for SSH access to `8102` and set the `sshHost` to an IP address of the host machine (the default value `0.0.0.0` means the SSHD service is bound to all network interfaces). Restricting access to particular network interfaces can help reduce unwanted access.

2. Restart OpenDaylight.

   After editing the configuration, we must restart OpenDaylight.

   Once restarted, you'll be able to connect to OpenDaylight using an SSH client:

   ```
   ssh -p 8102 karaf@192.168.1.110
   ```

   Upon connection, you'll be prompted for your password.

How it works...

At boot time, Apache Karaf will read the SSH configuration, setting its runtime bindings according to the property values. As the properties file is in the `etc` folder, the Configuration Admin service inside of Apache Karaf will monitor for any runtime changes to its values - a change in this file will be propagated to the runtime service.

There's more...

Changing the default remote access configuration is a good start. However, system builders should also consider changing the default OpenDaylight user/password combination found in `users.properties`.

You may also decide to generate a server SSH key file to simplify remote access. Information regarding this configuration can be found here:

```
http://karaf.apache.org/manual/latest
```

Creating your own branded OpenDaylight

OpenDaylight at its core is a rebranded Apache Karaf 3.0 server. The Karaf community has made rebranding runtime a simple task; let's make our own for the OpenDaylight Cookbook.

Getting ready

The ingredients of this recipe include an OpenDaylight distribution kit, access to a JDK, Maven, and a source code editor. Sample code for this recipe is available at:

```
https://github.com/jgoodyear/OpenDaylightCookbook/tree/master/chapter10/chapter
10-recipe2
```

How to do it...

Branding Apache Karaf is a five-step process; generating a Maven-based project structure, adding a resource directive to our pom, configuring our bundle build parameters, creating a resource file containing our branding, then building and deploying our brand into Karaf. For this, the given steps must be followed:

1. Generate a Maven-based project structure.

    For this recipe, we need to only create the bare minimum of Maven pom files, setting its packaging to `bundle` and including a `build` section.

2. Add a resource directive to the pom `build` section.

    In our pom file, we add a `resource` directive to our `build` section:

    ```
    <resource>
      <directory>
        ${project.basedir}/src/main/resources
      </directory>
      <filtering>true</filtering>
      <includes>
        <include>**/*</include>
      </includes>
    </resource>
    ```

    We add a resource directive to our build to instruct Maven to process the contents of our resources folder, filter any wildcards, and include the result in a generated bundle.

3. Configure the maven bundle plugin.

    Next, we configure the maven bundle plugin to:

    ```
    <configuration>
      <instructions>
    ```

```
    <Bundle-SymbolicName>
      ${project.artifactId}
    </Bundle-SymbolicName>
  <Import-Package>*</Import-Package>
  <Private-Package>!*</Private-Package>
    <Export-Package>
      org.apache.karaf.branding
    </Export-Package>
    <Spring-Context>
      *;publish-context:=false
    </Spring-Context>
  </instructions>
</configuration>
```

We configure the maven bundle plugin to export `Bundle-SymbolicName` as the `artifactId` and set `Export-Package` to `org.apache.karaf.branding`. The symbolic name as the project's `artifactId` is a common convention among Karaf bundle developers. We export the Karaf branding package so that the Karaf runtime will identify the bundle, as containing custom branding.

4. Create our custom branding resource file.

Returning to our project, we'll create a `branding.properties` file in `src/main/resource/org/apache/karaf/branding`. This properties file will contain ASCII and Jansi (Jansi is a small library for using ANSI escape sequences) text characters, organized to produce your custom look. By using maven resource filtering, you can use variable substitutions in the format `${variable}`:

```
##
welcome = \
\u001B[33m\u001B[0m\n\
\u001B[33m          ___    ____   _          \u001B[0m\n\
\u001B[33m         / _ \\|  _ \\| |        \u001B[0m\n\
\u001B[33m        | | | | | | | |         \u001B[0m\n\
\u001B[33m        | |_| | |_| | |___      \u001B[0m\n\
\u001B[33m         \\___/|____/|_____|     \u001B[0m\n\
\u001B[33m                                       \u001B[0m\n\
\u001B[33m       OpenDaylight Cookbook          \u001B[0m\n\
\u001B[33m Packt Publishing -
http://www.packtpub.com\u001B[0m\n\
\u001B[33m       (version ${project.version})\u001B[0m\n\
\u001B[33m\u001B[0m\n\
\u001B[33mHit '\u001B[1m<tab>\u001B[0m' for a list of available
commands\u001B[0m\n\
\u001B[33mand '\u001B[1m[cmd] --help\u001B[0m' for help on a
specific command.\u001B[0m\n\
```

```
\u001B[33mHit '\u001B[1m<ctrl-d>\u001B[0m' or
'\u001B[1mosgi:shutdown\u001B[0m' to shutdown\u001B[0m\n\
\u001B[33m\u001B[0m\n\
```

In the preceding sample, branding properties file we use a combination of ASCII characters and Jansi text mark up to produce simple text effects:

When displayed in Karaf, the text will be rendered as shown in the preceding screenshot.

5. Build and deploy our custom branding.

We build our branding via the Maven invocation `mvn install`. After we build our branding bundle, we place a copy inside of OpenDaylight's `KARAF_HOME/lib` folder, move aside the existing `karaf.branding-1.2.0-Beryllium.jar`, and then start the container. Upon first boot, you will see our custom branding displayed.

How it works...

At the first boot, Apache Karaf will check for any bundle in its `lib` folder to export the `org.apache.karaf.branding` package. Upon detection of this resource, it will access the `branding.properties` content and display it as part of the runtime start up routine.

Customizing your OpenDaylight repositories

OpenDaylight uses a collection of Maven repositories to provision required libraries, frameworks, and other artifacts. To ease accessing your own organization's resources, you can configure your OpenDaylight installation to access the repositories your installation requires.

Getting ready

The ingredients of this recipe include an OpenDaylight distribution kit, access to a JDK, Maven, and a source code editor. Sample configuration for this recipe is available at:

`https://github.com/jgoodyear/OpenDaylightCookbook/tree/master/chapter10/chapter10-recipe3`

How to do it...

OpenDaylight defines its repositories in `$ODL_HOME/etc/org.ops4j.pax.url.mvn.cfg`. We can customize the repositories by editing the entries under the property `org.ops4j.pax.url.mvn.repositories`, adding, or removing entries as required.

For example, to add a new repository containing your SDN artifacts we'd edit `$ODL_HOME/etc/org.ops4j.pax.url.mvn.cfg` as follows:

```
org.ops4j.pax.url.mvn.repositories= \
file:${karaf.home}/${karaf.default.repository}@id=system.repository, \
file:${karaf.data}/kar@id=kar.repository@multi, \
http://repo1.maven.org/maven2@id=central, \
http://repository.springsource.com/maven/bundles/release@id=spring.ebr.rele
ase, \
http://repository.springsource.com/maven/bundles/external@id=spring.ebr.ext
ernal, \
http://zodiac.springsource.com/maven/bundles/release@id=Gemini, \
http://www.sdnrepo.org/repo
```

Once the file is written out, OpenDaylight will update its list of available repositories.

What about snapshot repositories?

By default, snapshot repositories are disabled. Enabling their use requires appending `@snapshots` to a repository entry. For example: `http://www.sdnrepo.org/repo@snapshots`.

How it works...

OpenDaylight utilizes a Maven URL Handler, which is used to resolve remote Maven repositories. This handler is configured via the properties contained in `$ODL_HOME/etc/org.ops4j.pax.url.mvn.cfg`. The key property for our recipe is `org.ops4j.pax.url.mvn.repositories`, which sets a comma separated list of remote repository URLs that the container will check in order of occurrence when resolving Maven artifacts. For example, when looking for a bundle `org.foo.bar`, it will check each configured repository as ordered in the list for the bundle. Upon finding the bundle (within a specified version range), it will download the resource.

Need to load resources from your local m2 repository?
In `$ODL_HOME/etc/org.ops4j.pax.url.mvn.cfg` comment out the line:
`org.ops4j.pax.url.mvn.localRepository=${karaf.home}/${karaf.default.repository}`.
This will allow OpenDaylight Beryllium or Boron to read from your local m2 repository.

There's more...

Once you have customized the available repositories to OpenDaylight, you may want to update the initial startup application that your container will boot at start. For more information on this, read the recipe *Customizing your start up applications*.

Customizing your start up applications

Out of the box, OpenDaylight deploys a minimal runtime environment. We can alter this base runtime to include applications that your environment requires to be present. For the purposes of this recipe, applications are considered as the set of feature targets that implement an application. See the recipe, *Deploying applications using features* for more information on the Apache Karaf feature mechanism.

Getting ready

The ingredients of this recipe include an OpenDaylight distribution kit, access to a JDK, Maven, and a source code editor. Sample configuration for this recipe is available at:

https://github.com/jgoodyear/OpenDaylightCookbook/tree/master/chapter10/chapter 10-recipe4

How to do it...

Startup applications are maintained as a comma separated list of feature targets in the `featuresBoot` property found in `$ODL_HOME/etc/org.apache.karaf.features.cfg`.

The list of available features in your OpenDaylight container can be found by executing the command `features:list` from the console. Each entry is a valid target for inclusion in your custom applications startup list.

For example, to add applications `foo` and `bar` to your OpenDaylight container's startup, we'd edit `$ODL_HOME/etc/org.apache.karaf.features.cfg` as follows:

```
#
# Comma separated list of features to install at startup
#
featuresBoot=config,standard,region,package,kar,ssh,management,foo,bar
```

Upon restarting OpenDaylight with the preceding changes, the feature targets `foo` and `bar` will be loaded during initial boot.

Feature targets `foo` and `bar` must be available to your container; otherwise OpenDaylight will fail to load the application. Configure your feature repositories! When customizing your boot features, you'll have to ensure that the feature targets are available within the feature repository locations listed in the `featuresRepositories` property.

How it works...

OpenDaylight defines its startup applications as a comma-separated list property found in `$ODL_HOME/etc/org.apache.karaf.features.cfg`. This list is processed late into the startup process; configuration properties, and core container bundles are initialized and started ahead of applications.

There's more...

Changing your startup applications may require updating your container's knowledge of available Maven repositories. See *Customizing your OpenDaylight repositories* for more information.

Installing OpenDaylight as a service

When we install OpenDaylight, we'll want it to operate as a system service on our host platform (Windows, Linux, and so on). In this recipe, we'll set up OpenDaylight to start when your system boots up.

Getting ready

The ingredients of this recipe include an OpenDaylight distribution kit and a source code editor. Sample wrapper configuration for this recipe is available at:

```
https://github.com/jgoodyear/OpenDaylightCookbook/tree/master/chapter10/chapter
10-recipe5
```

How to do it...

Installing OpenDaylight as a service is a three-step process; installing the service wrapper feature, installing the wrapper service, and then performing a set of system dependent operations to integrate OpenDaylight as a service into your host operating system. The steps are given as following:

1. Installing the `service-wrapper` feature.

   OpenDaylight utilizes a `service-wrapper` feature to handle gathering and deploying the required resources for your host-operating environment. We begin its installation by invoking the following command:

   ```
   opendaylight-user@root()> feature:install service-wrapper
   ```

   The `service-wrapper` feature URL is included in Karaf by default, so no additional steps are required to make it available to OpenDaylight.

2. Installing the wrapper service.

   Now, we must instruct the wrapper to configure and install the appropriate service scripts and resources for us:

   ```
   opendaylight-user@root()> wrapper:install -s AUTO_START -n ODL-
   BE -D "OpenDaylight Cookbook"
   ```

   The preceding `wrapper:install` invocation includes three flags; `-s` for start type, `-n` for service name, and `-D` for service description. The start type can be one of the two options; `AUTO_START` for automatically starting the service on boot and `DEMAND_START` for starting only when manually invoked. The service name is used as an identifier in the host's service registry. The description provides system administrators with a brief description of your OpenDaylight installation. After executing the `install` command, the OpenDaylight console will display the libraries, scripts, and configuration files that the wrapper generates. You'll now need to exit OpenDaylight to continue the service installation.

3. Integration with a host operating system.

   This step will require administrator level permissions to execute the generated OpenDaylight service wrapper installation scripts.

On Windows:

```
C:> C:\Path\To\distribution-karaf-0.4.0-Beryllium\bin\ODL-BE-
service.bat install
```

Installs the service natively into Windows:

```
C:> net start "ODL-BE"
C:> net stop "ODL-BE"
```

The net commands allow an administrator to start or stop the OpenDaylight service.

Linux integration will vary based on distribution, the following commands will work on Debian/Ubuntu-based systems:

```
jgoodyear@ubuntu1404:~$ ln -s /Path/To/distribution-
karaf-0.4.0-Beryllium /bin/ODL-BE-service /etc/init.d
jgoodyear@ubuntu1404:~$ update-rc.d ODL-BE-service defaults
jgoodyear@ubuntu1404:~$ /etc/init.d/ODL-BE-service start
jgoodyear@ubuntu1404:~$ /etc/init.d/ODL-BE-service stop
```

The first command creates a symbolic link from the service script in OpenDaylight's bin folder to the init.d directory, and then updates the startup scripts to include the OpenDaylight service for automatic starting during boot. The remaining two commands can be used to manually start or stop the OpenDaylight service.

How it works...

The wrapper service feature integrates OpenDaylight into the host operating systems service mechanism. This means that whether on a Windows or Linux-based system, OpenDaylight will avail of available fault detection, crashes, freezes, out of memory, or similar events, and automatically attempt to restart OpenDaylight.

The service-wrapper feature when installed to the container will actually install the installer to the service-wrapper. The wrapper:install console command performs the actual registering of OpenDaylight (Apache Karaf) as a system service/daemon.

There's more...

After installing OpenDaylight to your system, a wrapper configuration file will be created in `$ODL_HOME/etc` called `ODL-BE-wrapper.conf` (assuming service name `ODL-BE`). Editing this file, you can alter system variables and tune OpenDaylight's JVM.

> For more information on installing and tweaking Apache Karaf as a system service, please see:
> `http://karaf.apache.org/manual/latest-3.0.x/#_integration_in_the _operating_system_the_service_wrapper`

Creating your own custom OpenDaylight command using the Maven archetype

OpenDaylight's Karaf console provides a multitude of useful commands for interacting with the OSGi runtime, and managing deployed applications. You may want to develop custom commands that integrate directly with Karaf so that you may automate tasks, or interact directly with your applications.

Custom Karaf commands will appear in your container as a fully integrated component of the console:

```
●○○        bin — java -Djava.security.properties=/Users/jgoodyear/Documents/Packt/OpenDaylight-Cookbook/ODL-BE/distribution-karaf-0.4.0-B...
    java -Djava.security.properties=/Use...karaf.jar org.apache.karaf.main.Main      ...OpenDaylightCookbook/chapter10/chapter10-recipe6/command — -bash
[Cyberman:bin jgoodyear$ ./karaf
Java HotSpot(TM) 64-Bit Server VM warning: ignoring option MaxPermSize=512m; support was removed in
 8.0


    _____                    _____              .__  .__       .__     __
    \_____  \ _____   ____ ____ _____ \ _____  ___.__.| |__ |__| ____ | |___/  |_
     /   |   \\____ \_/ __ \/    \ |    |  \\__  \<   |  || |  \|  |/ ___\| |  \   __\
    /    |    \  |_> >  ___/|   |  \|    `   \/ __ \\___  ||   Y  \  / /_/  >   Y  \  |
    _____  /   __/ \___  >___|  /_____  (____  / ____||___|  /__\___  /|___|  /__|
            \/|__|        \/     \/        \/     \/\/           \/  /_____/      \/

Hit '<tab>' for a list of available commands
and '[cmd] --help' for help on a specific command.
Hit '<ctrl-d>' or type 'system:shutdown' or 'logout' to shutdown OpenDaylight.

[opendaylight-user@root>install -s mvn:com.packt/odl-be-command/1.0.0-SNAPSHOT
Bundle ID: 64
[opendaylight-user@root>cookbook:sample -o 4 test
Executing command sample
Option: 4
Argument: test
opendaylight-user@root>█
```

The preceding screenshot illustrates our sample cookbook command accepting an option flag and an argument; let's dive into building your own command.

Getting ready

The ingredients of this recipe include an OpenDaylight distribution kit, access to a JDK, Maven, and a source code editor. Sample code for this recipe is available at:

```
https://github.com/jgoodyear/OpenDaylightCookbook/tree/master/chapter10/chapter
10-recipe6
```

How to do it...

Building custom commands is a three-step process; generating a template command project, implementing your custom code, and then building and deploying it in Karaf:

1. Template command project.

   To encourage building custom commands, the community has provided a Maven archetype for generating `karaf` command projects:

   ```
   mvn archetype:generate \
       -DarchetypeGroupId=org.apache.karaf.archetypes \
       -DarchetypeArtifactId=karaf-command-archetype \
       -DarchetypeVersion=3.0.4 \
       -DgroupId=com.packt.chapter1 \
       -DartifactId=command \
       -Dversion=1.0.0-SNAPSHOT \
       -Dpackage=com.packt
   ```

   In the preceding archetype invocation, we supply the Maven project group and artifact names. The process will request you to supply a command name. Maven then generates a project template for your command.

2. Implement custom code.

   The custom command template project will supply you with a Maven pom file, blueprint wiring (in `src/main/resources/OSGI-INF/blueprint`), and custom command stub implementation (in `src/main/java/`). Edit these files as required to add your custom actions.

3. Build and deploy custom commands into Karaf.

We build our command via Maven invocation `mvn install`. Deploying into Karaf only requires issuing a well-formed install command; to do this invoke `install -s mvn:groupId/artifactId` on the Karaf console:

```
opendaylight-user@root()> install -s mvn:com.packt/odl-be-
command
   Bundle ID: 68
opendaylight-user@root()>
```

The preceding invocation has `groupId = com.packt, artifactId = odl-be-command`.

 You will need to edit `$ODL_HOME/etc/org.ops4j.pax.url.mvn.cfg` and comment out the line:
`org.ops4j.pax.url.mvn.localRepository=${karaf.home}/${kar af.default.repository}`
This will allow OpenDaylight Beryllium or Boron to read from your local m2 repository.

How it works...

The Maven archetype will have generated the pom build file, Java code, and blueprint file for your custom command. Let's take a look at these key components:

The generated pom file contains all of the essential dependencies that a `karaf` command requires, and sets up a basic maven-bundle-plugin configuration. Edit this file to bring in additional libraries that your command requires, and be sure to update your bundle's build parameters accordingly. When this project is built, a bundle will be produced that can be installed directly into Karaf.

Our custom command logic resides in a generated Java source file, which will be named after the command name you supplied. The generated command extends Karaf's `OSGICommandSupport` class, which provides us with access to the underlying command session, and OSGi environment. A command annotation adorns our code; this provides the runtime with scope, name, and description. Karaf provides `Argument` and `Option` annotations to simplify adding command-line arguments and option processing.

The blueprint container wires together our command implementation to the commands available in Karaf's console.

 For more information on extending Karaf's console, see
`http://karaf.apache.org/manual/latest-3.0.x/#_extending`.

There's more...

Thanks to Apache Karaf's SSHD service and remote client, your custom commands could be leveraged to provide external command and control of your applications. Just pass your command and parameters into the remote client and monitor the returned results.

See also

Custom commands are a perfect ingredient when customizing Karaf to your needs, so why not go further and make Karaf your own? For more information refer to the recipe, *Creating your own branded OpenDaylight*.

Deploying applications using features

Managing the assembly and deployment of repository locations, bundles, configuration, and other artifacts quickly becomes a major headache for system builders. To remedy this, the Karaf community has developed the concept of features:

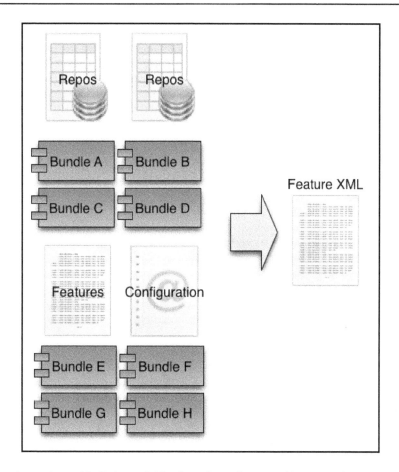

A feature descriptor is an XML-based file that describes a collection of artifacts to be installed together into the Karaf container. In this recipe, we'll learn how to make a feature, add it to Karaf, and then use it to install bundles.

Getting ready

The ingredients of this recipe include an OpenDaylight distribution kit, access to a JDK, Maven, and a source code editor. Sample code for this recipe is available at:

```
https://github.com/jgoodyear/OpenDaylightCookbook/tree/master/chapter10/chapter
10-recipe7
```

How to do it...

Making your application deployable as an Apache Karaf feature is a four-step process; generating a Maven-based project, editing pom build directives, creating a `features.xml` resource, and then building and deploying into Karaf:

1. Generating a Maven-based project.

    For this recipe, we need to only create a bare minimum of Maven pom files, setting its packaging to `bundle`, and including a `build` section.

2. Edit pom `build` directives.

    We add a resources directive to our pom `build` section, and the `maven-resources-plugin` and `build-helper-maven-plugin` to its plugin list:

    ```
    <resources>
        <resource>
            <directory>src/main/resources</directory>
            <filtering>true</filtering>
        </resource>
    </resources>
    ```

    The resources directive indicates the location of the features file that we'll create for processing:

    ```
    <plugin>
        <groupId>org.apache.maven.plugins</groupId>
        <artifactId>maven-resources-plugin</artifactId>
            <executions>
                <execution>
                    <id>filter</id>
                    <phase>generate-resources</phase>
                    <goals>
                        <goal>resources</goal>
                    </goals>
                </execution>
            </executions>
    </plugin>
    ```

    The `maven-resource-plugin` is configured to process our resources:

    ```
    <plugin>
        <groupId>org.codehaus.mojo</groupId>
        <artifactId>build-helper-maven-plugin</artifactId>
        <executions>
    ```

```
        <execution>
            <id>attach-artifacts</id>
            <phase>package</phase>
            <goals>
                <goal>attach-artifact</goal>
            </goals>
            <configuration>
                <artifacts>
                    <artifact>
                        <file>
${project.build.directory}/classes/${features.file}
                        </file>
                        <type>xml</type>
                        <classifier>features</classifier>
                    </artifact>
                </artifacts>
            </configuration>
        </execution>
    </executions>
</plugin>
```

Finally, the `build-helper-maven-plugin` completes the build of our
`features.xml` file.

3. Creating a `features.xml` resource.

Add to the `src/main/resources` folder a file named `features.xml` with the
details of your bundles:

```
<?xml version="1.0" encoding="UTF-8"?>
<features>
  <feature name='moduleA' version='${project.version}'>
<bundle>
  mvn:com.packt/opendaylight-moduleA/${project.version}
</bundle> </feature>
  <feature name='moduleB' version='${project.version}'>
    <bundle>
    mvn:com.packt/opendaylight-moduleB/${project.version}
    </bundle>
  </feature>
  <feature name='recipe4-all-modules'
  version='${project.version}'>
  <feature version='${project.version}'>moduleA</feature>
  <feature version='${project.version}'>moduleB</feature>
  </feature>
</features>
```

We provide each feature with a name that Karaf will use as a reference to install each element specified in the named feature's configuration. Features may reference other features, thus providing fine-grained control over installation. In the preceding features file, we can see three named features; one for `moduleA`, one for `moduleB`, and finally one that includes the content of both features under `recipe4-all-modules`.

 If you need to include a JAR that is not offered as a bundle, try using the wrap protocol to automatically provide them with OSGi manifest headers. For more information, see:
`https://ops4j1.jira.com/wiki/display/paxurl/Wrap+Protocol`

4. Build and deploy our feature.

Using our sample recipe project, we build our feature by executing `mvn install`. This performs all of the feature file variable substitutions, and installs a processed copy in your local m2 repository.

To make our feature available to Karaf, we'll add the feature file's Maven coordinates as follows:

```
opendaylight-user@root()> feature:repo-add
mvn:com.packt/opendaylight-features-file/1.0.0-
SNAPSHOT/xml/features
```

Now we can use Karaf's feature commands to install `moduleA` and `moduleB`:

```
opendaylight-user@root()> feature:install recipe4-all-modules
   Apache Karaf starting moduleA bundle
   Apache Karaf starting moduleB bundle
opendaylight-user@root()>
```

Using `feature:install` in this fashion helps to promote repeatable deployments, and avoid missing component installations that are not caught by the OSGi environment (if no bundle dependencies are missing, then as far as the container is concerned, all is well). We can verify our feature installed by invoking the command:

```
opendaylight-user@root()> feature:list | grep -i "recipe"
```

Then observing if our feature is listed.

How it works...

When Karaf processes a feature descriptor either as a bundle, hot deployment, or via system start-up property, the same processing and assembly functions occur:

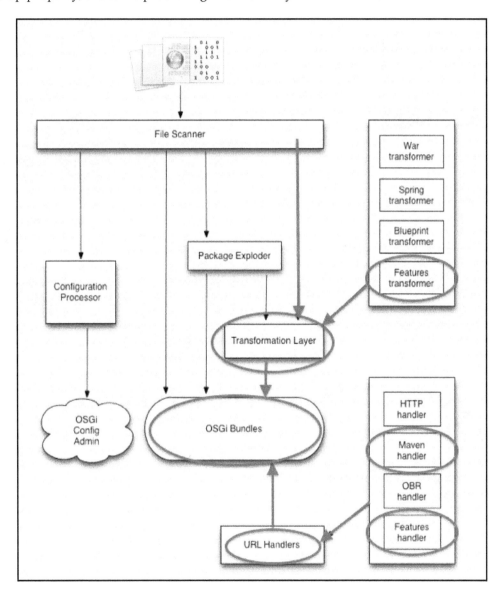

The feature descriptor invocation is transformed into a list of artifacts to be installed in the OSGi container (see the **Transformation Layer** in the preceding figure). At the lowest level, individual elements in a feature have a handler for obtaining the described artifact (bundle, JAR, configuration file, and so on). Our sample feature uses Maven coordinates for obtaining bundles; the Maven handler will be called to process these resources. If a HTTP URL was specified, then the HTTP handler would be called (see **URL Handlers** in the preceding figure). Each artifact in the specified feature will be installed until the entire list is processed.

There's more...

Our *How to do it...* steps outline a general methodology for producing a feature file for your projects and automating the filtering of resource versions. From Apache Karaf's point of view, it just processes a well-formatted features file - as such one could hand write the file and deploy it directly into Karaf.

Feature files have additional attributes that can be used to set bundle start levels, flagging as being a dependency, and setting configuration properties. For more information please visit `http://karaf.apache.org/manual/latest-3.0.x/#_provisioning`.

An advanced use case of Karaf feature files is to build a Karaf archive or KAR. A KAR file is the processed form of a feature file, collecting all required artifacts into a single deployable form. This archive is ideal for deployment when your Karaf instance will not have access to remote repositories, as all required resources are packaged in the KAR.

Using JMX to monitor and administer OpenDaylight

By default, OpenDaylight can be administered via JMX. Network engineers, however, often need to tweak the default configurations to get their deployment integrated into their network. In this recipe, we'll show you how to make these changes.

Getting ready

The ingredients of this recipe include an OpenDaylight distribution kit, access to a JDK, and a source code editor. Sample configuration for this recipe is available at:

`https://github.com/jgoodyear/OpenDaylightCookbook/tree/master/chapter10/chapter10-recipe8`

 Administrators should take care when exposing JMX access; SSL should be enabled, and strong passwords enforced.

How to do it...

Setting up OpenDaylight to use JMX for remote monitoring takes three steps; editing the management configuration, updating the users file, and then testing the configuration with your JMX management tool of choice:

1. Editing management configuration.

   Apache Karaf ships with a default management configuration; to make our modifications, we update `etc/org.apache.karaf.management.cfg`:

   ```
   #
   # Port number for RMI registry connection
   #
   rmiRegistryPort = 11099
   #
   # Port number for RMI server connection
   #
   rmiServerPort = 44445
   ```

   The default ports (`1099` and `44444`) are usually fine for general deployment; change these ports only if you are experiencing port conflicts on your deployment:

   ```
   #
   # Role name used for JMX access authorization
   # If not set, this defaults to the ${karaf.admin.role}
   configured in etc/system.properties
   #
   jmxRole=admin
   ```

Towards the bottom of the configuration file there will be a commented-out entry for `jmxRole`; enable this by removing the hash character.

2. Updating the users file.

   We must now update the `etc/users.properties` file:

   ```
   karaf = karaf,_g_:admingroup
   _g_\:admingroup = group,admin,manager,viewer,webconsole,jmxRole
   ```

   The `users.properties` file is used to configure users, groups, and roles in Karaf. We append `jmxRole` to the admin group.

   The syntax for this file is as follows:

   ```
   Username = password, groups
   ```

3. Testing our configuration.

   After making the previous configuration changes, we'll need to restart our Karaf instance. Now we can test our JMX setup:

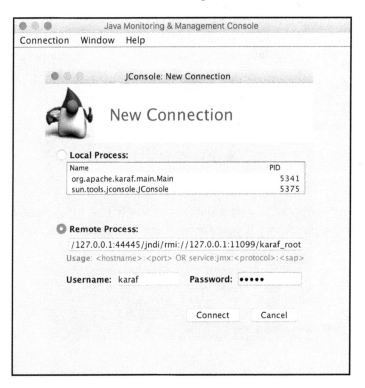

After restarting Karaf, use a JMX-based admin tool of your choice (the preceding figure is JConsole) to connect to the container. Due to image size restrictions, the full URL couldn't be displayed; as such we reproduce it here `service:jmx:rmi://127.0.0.1:44445/jndi/rmi://127.0.0.1:11099/ka raf-root`. The syntax of the URL is `service:jmx:rmi://host:${rmiServerPort}/jndi/rmi://host:${rmiRe gistryPort}/${karaf-instance-name}`.

How it works...

The Apache Karaf container provides a collection of **Managed Beans** (**MBeans**), which allow users to connect to the running JVM, accessing live metrics or executing operations from the MBeans.

 For more information on Java MBeans, please review the following Java tutorial:
`https://docs.oracle.com/javase/tutorial/jmx/mbeans/`

The configuration of `etc/org.apache.karaf.management.cfg` allows Apache Karaf to control how to access the Java runtime's JMX management facility.

There's more...

You can check your OpenDaylight installation's RMI ports at any time by executing the `instance:list` command:

```
opendaylight-user@root>instance:list
SSH Port | RMI Registry | RMI Server | State    | PID  | Name
-------------------------------------------------------------------
8101 |         11099 |      44445 | Started | 6079 | root
```

In the preceding invocation, we can see that the `RMI Registry` is set to port `11099` and `RMI Server` to port `44445`.

Setting up Apache Karaf Decanter to monitor OpenDaylight

Apache Karaf provides a monitoring and alerting solution called **Apache Karaf Decanter**. OpenDaylight users can configure this system to provide their deployments with an easy-to-read status dashboard and take advantage of advanced capabilities such as **Service Level Agreement (SLA)** alerting.

 As of OpenDaylight Beryllium, Decanter support is experimental. Platform level monitoring is possible; application specific monitoring requires custom Collectors (and/or configurations) and Kibana dashboard updates (Kibana is a browser-based analytics and search dashboard for Elasticsearch).

Getting ready

The ingredients of this recipe include an OpenDaylight distribution kit, web browser, access to a JDK, and a source code editor. Sample configuration(s) for this recipe is available at:

```
https://github.com/jgoodyear/OpenDaylightCookbook/tree/master/chapter10/chapter
10-recipe9
```

How to do it...

As OpenDaylight is effectively a custom Apache Karaf distribution, it can make use of Apache Karaf Decanter by following these essential installation and configuration steps:

1. Start OpenDaylight Container.

   The Decanter 1.x requires a running instance of OpenDaylight for installation.

2. Add Apache Karaf Decanter feature repository.

Decanter is distributed as an Apache Karaf feature repository, as such we need to make this feature available to our OpenDaylight container via the `repo-add` command:

```
opendaylight-user@root>feature:repo-add
mvn:org.apache.karaf.decanter/apache-karaf-
decanter/1.0.0/xml/features
```

Upon executing this command, the Decanter feature targets will become available to your OpenDaylight container.

Decanter 1.1.x and above use Kibana 4.x, which requires Apache Karaf 4.x or higher. OpenDaylight Beryllium can use Decanter 1.0.0.

3. Install the following Decanter feature targets:

After adding the feature repository, we may now install the following feature targets:

```
opendaylight-user@root>feature:install elasticsearch
opendaylight-user@root>feature:install kibana
opendaylight-user@root>feature:install decanter-appender-
elasticsearch
opendaylight-user@root>feature:install decanter-collector-log
opendaylight-user@root>feature:install decanter-collector-
system
opendaylight-user@root>feature:install decanter-collector-jmx
opendaylight-user@root>feature:install decanter-appender-log
opendaylight-user@root>feature:install decanter-appender-
elasticsearch
```

It is common to observe exceptions after installing the `decanter-collector-jmx` target. If you're using the Karaf client to connect to an OpenDaylight container then you can log in again to have those console messages disappear. More recent editions of Decanter have resolved these issues, which future OpenDaylight editions will be able to take advantage of.

4. Access Decanter via web browser:

Having installed Decanter's core dependencies, and a set of Collectors and Appenders, the Decanter service will now be available to view via web browser.

Using your choice of web browser, open `http://localhost:8181/kibana`.

Two of the default dashboards will be relevant to OpenDaylight; Karaf, and the operating system. The Karaf dashboard provides JVM metrics, while the operating system dashboard provides metrics for configured OS tests (disk free and temperature tests will only work on select host environments that support reporting these values):

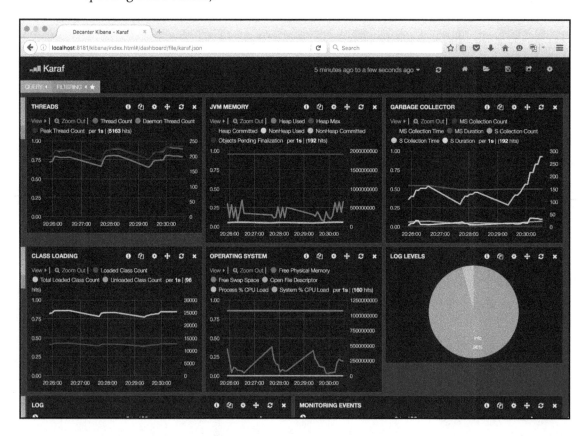

As shown in the preceding screenshot, Decanter displays all of the metrics it can gather for Karaf's JVM. This is a mix of data collected from the log and JMX Collectors, displayed using Kibana's built-in utilities.

An in-depth review of Kibana and Elasticsearch are beyond the scope of this cookbook. In brief, Kibana is a browser-based analytics and search dashboard for Elasticsearch. Elasticsearch is a search engine based upon Lucene; it provides a distributed, multi-tenant capable full-text search engine with an HTTP web interface and schema free JSON documents.

The Collectors and Appenders included earlier will be sufficient to provide Decanter with basic container metrics for JVM health and Karaf-based logging. OpenDaylight-specific application data collection will require custom Collectors to be developed and deployed into Decanter.

5. Adding an Alerter:

Having installed the core Decanter features, you now have the option of configuring a service level agreement checker via a Decanter Alerter.

We'll first install the Decanter SLA and SLA log feature targets:

```
opendaylight-user@root>feature:install decanter-sla
opendaylight-user@root>feature:install decanter-sla-log
```

Upon installation, a configuration file will be created in the `etc` folder called `org.apache.karaf.decanter.sla.checker.cfg`. You will have to edit this file to tell the Alerter what to monitor, and under which circumstance to fire an alert.

The syntax Decanter checker configurations use is:

`attribute.level=check`

Where `attribute` is the name of the attribute from the harvested data (this comes from Collectors into Decanter), `level` is the alert level (warn or error), and check is an expression of the form `checkType:value` (`checkType` may be one of `range`, `equal`, `notequal`, `match`, or `notmatch`. Value is the data property value of the attribute).

Let's configure our Alerter to monitor JVM threads. We'll set the SLA to alert if more than 60 threads are active. To do this, we'll add the following to `org.apache.karaf.decanter.sla.checker.cfg`:

```
ThreadCount.error=range:[0, 60]
```

This configuration entry tells the Alerter to check `ThreadCount`, and throw an error when the `ThreadCount` is outside of the range 0 to 60 threads.

Once configured, you should see log entries similar to the following:

```
2016-06-05 10:34:17,427 | ERROR | Thread-48          | Logger
| 110 - org.apache.karaf.decanter.sla.log - 1.0.0 | DECANTER
SLA ALERT: ThreadCount out of pattern range:[0,60]
2016-06-05 10:34:17,427 | ERROR | Thread-48          | Logger
| 110 - org.apache.karaf.decanter.sla.log - 1.0.0 | DECANTER
SLA ALERT: Details: hostName:Cyberman.local |
alertPattern:range:[0,60] | ThreadAllocatedMemorySupported:true
| ThreadContentionMonitoringEnabled:false |
TotalStartedThreadCount:560 | alertLevel:error |
CurrentThreadCpuTimeSupported:true |
CurrentThreadUserTime:46389834000 | PeakThreadCount:226 |
AllThreadIds:[J@24b50dea | type:jmx-local |
ThreadAllocatedMemoryEnabled:true |
CurrentThreadCpuTime:47637221000 |
ObjectName:java.lang:type=Threading |
ThreadCpuTimeSupported:true |
ThreadContentionMonitoringSupported:true | ThreadCount:220 |
ThreadCpuTimeEnabled:true | karafName:root |
ObjectMonitorUsageSupported:true | hostAddress:10.0.1.6 |
SynchronizerUsageSupported:true | alertAttribute:ThreadCount |
DaemonThreadCount:193 | event.topics:decanter/alert/error |
```

In the preceding log snippet, we observe that the `ThreadCount` being 560 threads - well outside of the range of 0 to 60, has triggered the Alerter.

If you'd like to generate an e-mail upon an alert condition, install `decanter-sla-email` and configure the `org.apache.karaf.decanter.sla.email.cfg` generated by the feature with e-mail addresses and SMTP information.

How it works...

Apache Karaf Decanter is a monitoring solution built for the deployment inside of Apache Karaf. OpenDaylight, as a custom Apache Karaf distribution can easily make use of Decanter.

Bringing together three parts builds the Decanter monitoring system: **Collectors**, **Appenders**, and **Alerters**:

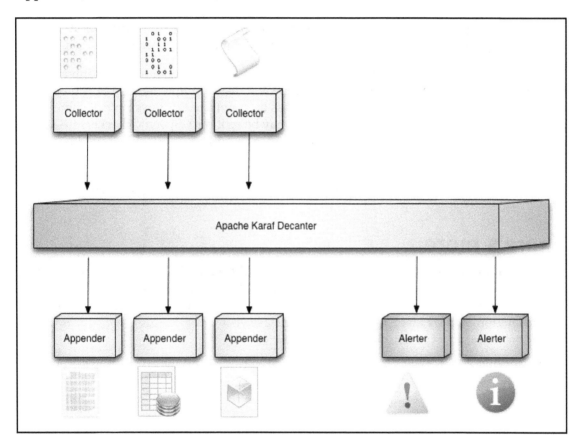

In the preceding architecture figure, we can see how these parts are arranged to perform system monitoring. Data enters via Collectors, and Decanter then sends it to Appenders for storage and/or Alerters for checking and possible alerting. Let's review these components in closer detail.

The Collectors, as their name suggests, harvest data and send it into Decanter. Decanter will take this data and send it to Appenders. Upon installing Collectors, there will be configuration files created in the OpenDaylight `etc` folder. Adjust these configurations as required to tune Collectors to gather the information you need. Please refer to Apache Karaf Decanter Collectors documentation to explore the configuration of each Collector.

The Appenders receive data from Decanter and are responsible for pushing/storing data to a backend. Upon installing Appenders, there will be configuration files created in the OpenDaylight `etc` folder. These will require configuration to connect them to their respective storage (for example, database credentials). Please refer to Apache Karaf Decanter Appenders documentation to explore the configuration of each Appender.

Finally, the Alerters are a special type of Appender; they receive data from Decanter. However, instead of trying to store the data, they will instead implement an SLA type analysis, sending alerts if a violation of policy has been detected (for example, if some metric is outside of some range then an e-mail may be sent out). Specific checkers (tests) are configured in the `org.apache.karaf.decanter.sla.checker.cfg` file (found in the OpenDaylight `etc` folder).

When fully assembled, Decanter provides a highly capable monitoring solution.

There's more...

Apache Karaf Decanter is an active subproject of Apache Karaf. Improvements made to the project will become accessible to OpenDaylight users. For more information on Apache Karaf Decanter, please visit `http://karaf.apache.org/projects.html#decanter`. For documentation on the 1.x version of Decanter, please visit `http://karaf.apache.org/manual/decanter/latest-1/`.

8
Authentication and Authorization

In this chapter, we will cover the following recipes:

- OpenDaylight identity manager
- Basic filtering for RBAC in OpenDaylight
- Token-based authentication in OpenDaylight
- OpenDaylight source IP authorization
- OpenDaylight with OpenLDAP environment federation
- OpenDaylight with FreeIPA environment federation

Introduction

Security of the software-defined network controller is at the heart of network security. However, the security architectures that can be used within the SDN are variants based on the business case. OpenDaylight comes with authentication and authorization mechanisms out of the box, which secure OpenDaylight and it also has federation with different authentication systems such as LDAP IPs and FreeIPA. In this chapter, you will learn how to use OpenDaylight built-in authentication and authorization functionality and how to integrate OpenDaylight with existing federation systems such as FreeIPA.

OpenDaylight identity manager

OpenDaylight has its own built-in identity manager that manages OpenDaylight users. OpenDaylight authenticates users based on a typical username and password architecture and authorizes the user based on its roles and domain. In this recipe, you will learn how to add a new user, update user information, add a new role, and add a new user domain.

Getting ready

To step through this recipe, you will need a new OpenDaylight Beryllium distribution and you will need to download the recipe folder from the book GitHub repository.

How to do it...

1. Start the OpenDaylight distribution using the `karaf` script. Using the following commands will give you access to the Karaf CLI:

```
$ cd distribution-karaf-0.4.1-Beryllium-SR1/
$ ./bin/karaf


 _____ _____  .__  .__  .__ __
 _____ \_____   ___ _____   _____ \ _____ __.__.|  |  |_|  |___
  |    |  _/  |_
 /    |  \\___  \_/ _ \ / \ |  |  \\_  \< |  | |  | |/ ___\|  |  \ _\
 /    |  \ |_> >  __/|  |  \|  `  \/ _ \\___  ||  |_| / /_/  >  Y  \ |
 _____  / __/  \___ >__| /_____  (____  / ___||___/__\_\__
 /|___| /__|
 \/|__| \/ \/ \/ \/\/ /_____/ \/
Hit '<tab>' for a list of available commands
and '[cmd] --help' for help on a specific command.
Hit '<ctrl-d>' or type 'system:shutdown' or 'logout' to
shutdown OpenDaylight.
opendaylight-user@root>
```

2. In order to easily test the OpenDaylight identity manager, we will install the OpenDaylight `dlux` feature using the following command:

```
opendaylight-user@root> feature:install odl-dlux-all
```

You can check `aaa` installed features in Karaf CLI using the following command:

opendaylight-user@root> feature:list -i | grep aaa

You should see something like this in your Karaf CLI:

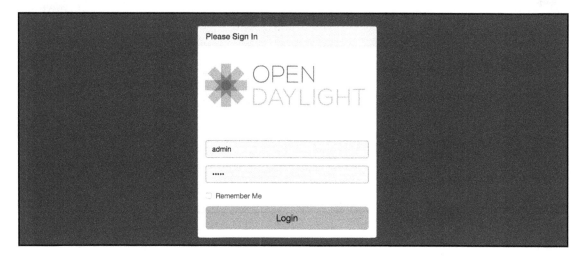

3. Now, in order to log in to the OpenDaylight `dlux`, open your browser and go to `http://localhost:8181/index.html#/login`. I'm sure as you've been through previous chapters, you already know that the default username is `admin` and password is `admin`:

4. You will need the PostMan or any REST API client to use the recipe PostMan collection that exists in the recipe directory `chapter11/chapter11-recipe1/aaa-idm.postman_collection.json`. After you import the JSON file you should be able to see the identity manager REST APIs `get`, `add`, and `delete` for users, domains, and roles:

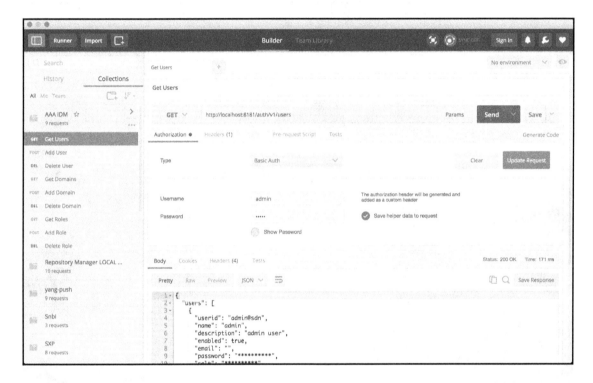

5. Now we will create a new user using the **Add User** Rest API. Click on **Add User** in the left tab on the PostMan, then click on the body's right tab and select raw. You can see the new user data, username, and password, and you can change it as you prefer:

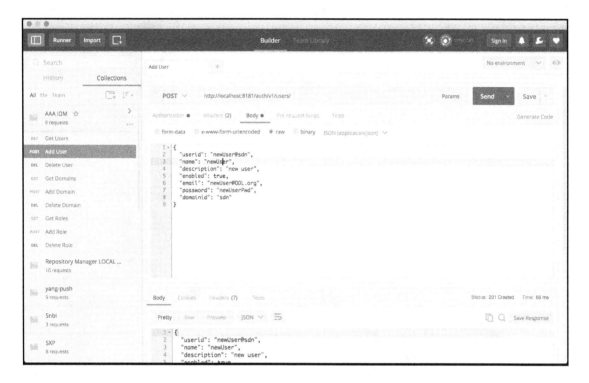

6. Now in order to test the new user authentication, open your browser and go to `http://localhost:8181/index.html#/login`. Use the new user identity to log in. You should be able to successfully log in:

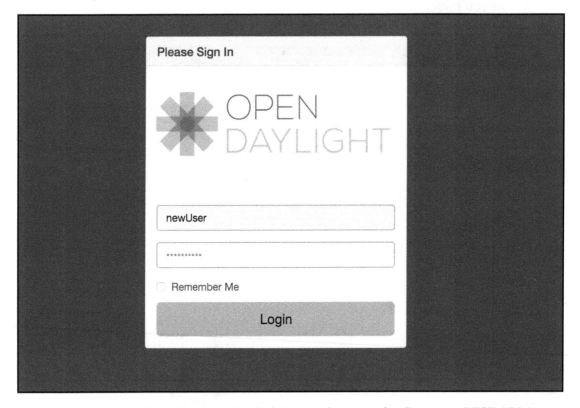

7. Now to retrieve the OpenDaylight's user data, use the **Get users** REST API. You should be able to see the default users information (`sdn`, `user`) and the new user information.

See also

As we create a new user, you can also create new domains and roles using **Add Domain** and **Add Role** REST APIs. The OpenDaylight default domain is `sdn` and default roles are `admin` and `user`. Creating different domains and roles will be helpful to distinguish between different user's roles.

Basic filtering for RBAC in OpenDaylight

RBAC in OpenDaylight is useful to authorize the user access to OpenDaylight resources. OpenDaylight relies on the Shiro framework to apply the RBAC based on the predefined URLs in Shiro configurations. In this recipe, you will learn how to restrict the user role from accessing specific OpenDaylight REST APIs.

Getting ready

This recipe required a new refresh OpenDaylight Beryllium distribution.

How to do it...

1. Start the OpenDaylight distribution using the `karaf` script. Using this client will give you access to the Karaf CLI:

   ```
   $ cd distribution-karaf-0.4.1-Beryllium-SR1/
   $ ./bin/karaf

   _____ _____ .__ .__ .__ __ __
   \_____  \ _____ \ ____ ___ _____ \ \ _____ __.__.| | |_|__| ____
   |   |  |_/  |_
   /   | \\___  \/  _ \ / \ |   | \\_  \< | || | | | |/ __\| | \  \_\
   /    | \ |_> > __/| | \|  `\/ _ \\__  || |_| / /_/ > Y \ |
   _____  / __/ \__ >__| /_____  (____ / ___||____/__\___
   /|___| /_|
   \/|__| \/ \/ \/ \/\/ /_____/ \/
   Hit '<tab>' for a list of available commands
   and '[cmd] --help' for help on a specific command.
   Hit '<ctrl-d>' or type 'system:shutdown' or 'logout' to
   shutdown OpenDaylight.
   opendaylight-user@root>
   ```

2. We will install the `restconf` and neutron features in order to show how we can restrict access to those features to the admin role only.

   Install the `odl-restconf` and `odl-neutron-service` features using the following command:

   ```
   opendaylight-user@root> feature:install odl-restconf odl-
   neutron-service
   ```

You can check for `aaa` installed features in Karaf CLI using the following command:

```
opendaylight-user@root> feature:list -i | grep aaa
```

You should see something like this in your Karaf CLI:

```
opendaylight-user@root>feature:list -i | grep aaa
odl-aaa-api              | 0.3.2-Beryllium-SR2 | x    | odl-aaa-0.3.2-Beryllium-SR2    | OpenDaylight :: AAA :: APIs
odl-aaa-shiro            | 0.3.2-Beryllium-SR2 | x    | odl-aaa-0.3.2-Beryllium-SR2    | OpenDaylight :: AAA :: Shiro
odl-aaa-authn            | 0.3.2-Beryllium-SR2 | x    | odl-aaa-0.3.2-Beryllium-SR2    | OpenDaylight :: AAA :: Authentication - NO
CLUSTER
```

3. We will test the admin and user roles authorization to the `restconf` and neutron REST APIs. For the admin user who has the admin role privilege and restconf streams APIs, run the following command:

```
$ curl -u admin:admin http://localhost:8181/restconf/streams
```

The response should be:

```
{
    "Streams": { }
}
```

For the user who has the user role privilege and `restconf` streams APIs, run the following command:

```
$ curl -u user:user http://localhost:8181/restconf/streams
```

The response should be the same as the admin user. In order to test the neutron REST APIs, we will create a dummy network then will retrieve its data.

Use the following command to create the dummy network:

```
$ curl -u admin:admin -X PUT -H "Content-Type:
application/json" -d '{
"networks": {
"network": [
{
"shared": "false",
"admin-state-up": "true",
"status": "UP",
"uuid": "e20ccd4b-c316-4df9-8e4c-f003b942a90d",
"name": "net1",
"tenant-id": "e20ccd4b-c316-4df9-8e4c-f003b942a90c",
"neutron-provider-ext:network-type": "vlan",
"neutron-provider-ext:segmentation-id": "100",
```

```
"neutron-L3-ext:external": "false"
}
]
}
}'
http://localhost:8181/restconf/config/neutron:neutron/networks
```

Then test the authorization of the neutron REST APIs for admin and user roles by using the following commands:

```
$ curl -u admin:admin -X GET
http://localhost:8181/restconf/config/neutron:neutron/networks
```

The response should be:

```
{
"networks": {
"network": [
{
"uuid": "e20ccd4b-c316-4df9-8e4c-f003b942a90d",
"tenant-id": "e20ccd4b-c316-4df9-8e4c-f003b942a90c",
"neutron-provider-ext:segmentation-id": "100",
"neutron-provider-ext:network-type": "neutron-provider-
ext:vlan",
"neutron-L3-ext:external": false,
"name": "net1",
"shared": false,
"admin-state-up": true,
"status": "UP"
}
]
}
}
$ curl -u user:user -X GET
http://localhost:8181/restconf/config/neutron:neutron/networks
```

The response should be the same as the admin role.

4. Now you will restrict the authorization for the streams and neutron REST APIs for the admin role only. Under the OpenDaylight distribution directory, we will modify the shiro.ini file to add the streams and neutron REST APIs URLs:

```
$ cd distribution-karaf-0.4.2-Beryllium-SR2/etc
$ vi shiro.ini
```

Under the URL authorization section, add the following lines:

```
/streams/ = authcBasic, roles[admin]
/config/neutron**/** = authcBasic, roles[admin]
```

Now save the `shiro.ini` file and exit. The Shiro framework configuration takes effect at startup time only, so we will need to restart the OpenDaylight distribution. Run the following command in the OpenDaylight console to restart OpenDaylight:

```
$ opendaylight-user@root> system:shutdown -r
```

5. We will re-test the user and admin roles authorization to the `restconf` and neutron REST APIs. For the admin role and restconf streams APIs, run the following command:

```
$ curl -u admin:admin http://localhost:8181/restconf/streams
```

The response should be:

```
{
  "Streams": { }
}
```

For the user who has the user role privilege and `restconf streams` APIs, run the following command:

```
$ curl -u user:user http://localhost:8181/restconf/streams
```

The response should be an unauthorized message like the following:

```
<html>
  <head>
    <meta http-equiv="Content-Type" content="text/html;
    charset=ISO-8859-1"/>
    <title>Error 401 Unauthorized</title>
  </head>
  <body><h2>HTTP ERROR 401</h2>
    <p>Problem accessing
    /restconf/config/neutron:neutron/networks/. Reason:
    <pre> Unauthorized</pre></p><hr /><i><small>Powered by
    Jetty://</small></i><br/>
  </body>
</html>
```

Then test the authorization of the neutron REST APIs for admin roles by using the following command:

```
$ curl -u admin:admin -X GET
http://localhost:8181/restconf/config/neutron:neutron/networks
```

The response should be as follows:

```
{
"networks": {
"network": [
{
"uuid": "e20ccd4b-c316-4df9-8e4c-f003b942a90d",
"tenant-id": "e20ccd4b-c316-4df9-8e4c-f003b942a90c",
"neutron-provider-ext:segmentation-id": "100",
"neutron-provider-ext:network-type": "neutron-provider-
ext:vlan",
"neutron-L3-ext:external": false,
"name": "net1",
"shared": false,
"admin-state-up": true,
"status": "UP"
}
]
}
}
For the user role:
$ curl -u user:user -X GET
http://localhost:8181/restconf/config/neutron:neutron/networks
```

The response should be an unauthorized message similar to the following:

```
<html>
  <head>
    <meta http-equiv="Content-Type" content="text/html;
    charset=ISO-8859-1"/>
    <title>Error 401 Unauthorized</title>
  </head>
    <body><h2>HTTP ERROR 401</h2>
    <p>Problem accessing
    /restconf/config/neutron:neutron/networks/. Reason:
    <pre> Unauthorized</pre></p><hr /><i><small>Powered by
    Jetty://</small></i><br/>
    </body>
</html>
```

How it works...

As OpenDaylight relies on the Shiro framework to authorize the users for the REST APIs, the `shiro.ini` file has the basic HTTP authentication filter configuration. The basic authentication for OpenDaylight exists in the main section of the `shiro.ini` file `authcBasic = org.opendaylight.aaa.shiro.filters.ODLHttpAuthenticationFilter`. In our recipe, we authorize the stream's REST APIs for the admin role by setting the streams URL to be authorized based on the basic authentication and the admin `role /streams/ = authcBasic, roles[admin]`. OpenDaylight, at startup, will authorize the user who has the admin role to access the stream's REST API URL. A reference for the `ODLHttpAuthenticationFilter` file exists under the `aaa` project in the OpenDaylight GitHub repository source code.

Token-based authentication in OpenDaylight

OpenDaylight has different techniques to authenticate different operations. Token-based authentication is used in the SDN production environment to control the lifetime of the authenticated operations in OpenDaylight. In this recipe, you will learn how to generate a token that can be used to authenticate OpenDaylight's HTTP requests.

Getting ready

This recipe requires a new OpenDaylight Beryllium distribution.

How to do it...

1. Start the OpenDaylight distribution using the `karaf` script. Using this client will give you access to the Karaf CLI:

```
$ cd distribution-karaf-0.4.1-Beryllium-SR1/
$ ./bin/karaf
```

```
        _____                       .__   .__   .__        __
_____ _____   ____    ____   _____ \ _____    ___.__.| | |__| ____ |___|____
 |   |__/  |_                 |   |__/  |_                      |__|
 / |  \\___  \/ / _ \ / \ |  | \\_ \< |  | |   |  |/  __\|  |  \  _\
 / |  \ |_> >  __/| | |\| ` \/  _  \\__  ||  |_| / /_/ >  Y  \ |
 _____ / _/ \___  >__| /_____  (___ / ____||___/__\___
 /|___| /__|
```

```
\/|__| \/ \/ \/ \/\/ /_____/ \/
Hit '<tab>' for a list of available commands
and '[cmd] --help' for help on a specific command.
Hit '<ctrl-d>' or type 'system:shutdown' or 'logout' to
shutdown OpenDaylight.
opendaylight-user@root>
```

2. We will install the `restconf` feature to show how we can use the token-based authentication to authenticate the stream REST API. Install the `odl-restconf` feature using the following command:

```
opendaylight-user@root> feature:install odl-restconf
```

You can check for `aaa` installed features in Karaf CLI using the following command:

```
opendaylight-user@root> feature:list -i | grep aaa
```

You should see something like this in your Karaf CLI:

```
opendaylight-user@root>feature:list -i | grep aaa
odl-aaa-api       | 0.3.2-Beryllium-SR2 | x    | odl-aaa-0.3.2-Beryllium-SR2    | OpenDaylight :: AAA :: APIs
odl-aaa-shiro     | 0.3.2-Beryllium-SR2 | x    | odl-aaa-0.3.2-Beryllium-SR2    | OpenDaylight :: AAA :: Shiro
odl-aaa-authn     | 0.3.2-Beryllium-SR2 | x    | odl-aaa-0.3.2-Beryllium-SR2    | OpenDaylight :: AAA :: Authentication - NO
CLUSTER
```

3. We will generate a granted token based on the admin user. We should specify the username, password, and the domain to generate the token:

```
$ curl -ik -d 'grant_type=password&username=admin&password=
admin&scope=sdn' http://localhost:8181/oauth2/token
```

The response contains the access token, token type, and expiry time in seconds. You should have something like the following:

```
HTTP/1.1 201 Created
Transfer-Encoding: chunked
Server: Jetty(8.1.15.v20140411)
{
  "access_token":"1d995bbe-e948-3ad0-a38e-0573932cb839",
  "token_type":"Bearer",
  "expires_in":3600
}
```

4. We will user the generated token to access the streams REST APIs:

```
$ curl -H 'Authorization:Bearer 1d995bbe-e948-3ad0-
a38e-0573932cb839' http://localhost:8181/restconf/streams/
```

The response should be as follows:

```
{
  "Streams": { }
}
```

How it works...

OpenDaylight's user presents credentials in a token request to the controller token service within a domain. The token request will be passed to the controller token endpoint that will validate the user credential and generate a claim. The controller token entity transforms the claim (user, domain, and roles) into a token that will be provided to the user. The token service configuration exists in the `org.opendaylight.aaa.tokens.cfg` file under the OpenDaylight distribution `directory /distribution-karaf-0.4.2-Beryllium-SR2/etc/ org.opendaylight.aaa.tokens.cfg`. The default configuration for the token expiry time is 3,600 seconds.

OpenDaylight source IP authorization

For many use cases, source IP based authorization is widely used to authorize the network elements access to OpenDaylight. For example, in some IoT cases you need to distinguish between different IoT devices based on their IPs to restrict access to OpenDaylight functionalities. In this recipe, you will learn how to set up OpenDaylight source IP authorization using Apache server.

Getting ready

For this recipe, you need a new refresh OpenDaylight distribution, Postman as REST API client, VirtualBox to set up a Ubuntu 14.04 VM, and vagrant if you use the predefined vagrant file from the recipe folder.

How to do it...

1. If you already have the pre-request installed, you can skip this step and start directly from step 4. If you use the predefined vagrant file to establish the environment, first, you need to install vagrant if it is not already installed. Then you need to go to the IPBased-VM directory under the recipe folder:

   ```
   $ cd chapter11-recipe4/IPBased-VM/
   ```

   You will need to change the network interface name in the Vagrant file to match your machine network interface:

   ```
   $ vi Vagrantfile
   ```

   Change the en0 to match your machine network interface and save the file. Then you need to start the VMs installation:

   ```
   $ vagrant up
   ```

   The installation time should take between 15-20 min so it is a good time to get a coffee.

2. Now use he vagrant ssh command to get access to the IPBased-VM:

   ```
   $ vagrant ssh
   ```

3. Inside the IPBased-VM the OpenDaylight distribution is ready to run. Start the OpenDaylight distribution using the karaf script. Using this script will give you access to the Karaf CLI:

   ```
   $ cd distribution-karaf-0.4.1-Beryllium-SR1/
   $ ./bin/karaf

   _____       ._-    ._-  ._-  _-
   _____ _____ ____ ___  _____ \ _____ ___.__.| |  |_|_|  ___
   |  |__/  |_
   /  |  \\___  \_/  _ \ /  \ |  |  \\__  \< |  ||  |  |  |/ __\| | \ _\
   /  |  \  |_> > ___/|  |  \| `  \/ _ \\__  || |_| /  /_/ > Y  \ |
   _____ /  __/ \__  >__| /_____  (____  /  ___||___/__\___
   /|___| /_|
   \/|__| \/ \/ \/ \/\/ /____/ \/
   Hit '<tab>' for a list of available commands
   and '[cmd] --help' for help on a specific command.
   Hit '<ctrl-d>' or type 'system:shutdown' or 'logout' to
   shutdown OpenDaylight.
   opendaylight-user@root>
   ```

4. Install the `odl-restconf` features using the following command:

   opendaylight-user@root> feature:install odl-restconf

   You can check for `aaa` installed features in Karaf CLI using the following command:

   opendaylight-user@root> feature:list -i | grep aaa

   You should see something like this in your Karaf CLI:

```
opendaylight-user@root>feature:list -i | grep aaa
odl-aaa-api              | 0.3.2-Beryllium-SR2 | x    | odl-aaa-0.3.2-Beryllium-SR2    | OpenDaylight :: AAA :: APIs
odl-aaa-shiro            | 0.3.2-Beryllium-SR2 | x    | odl-aaa-0.3.2-Beryllium-SR2    | OpenDaylight :: AAA :: Shiro
odl-aaa-authn            | 0.3.2-Beryllium-SR2 | x    | odl-aaa-0.3.2-Beryllium-SR2    | OpenDaylight :: AAA :: Authentication - NO
CLUSTER
```

5. Now open another console and use the `vagrant ssh` command to get access to the `IPBased-VM` as we will need to keep the other one for OpenDaylight Karaf.

6. Use the following command to check that `odl-restconf` REST API can be accessed with the default OpenDaylight authentication username and password:

   $ curl -u admin:admin https://localhost:8181/restconf/streams/

   The response should be as follows:

```
{
   "Streams": { }
}
```

7. Now we will enable the firewall by using the following command:

   $ sudo ufw enable

   The default password for sudo is `vagrant`.

8. We will install the firewall rules to only allow access to localhost through the `8181` port and `HTTP/SSH` access from anywhere:

```
$ sudo iptables -A INPUT -p tcp -s localhost --dport 8181 -j
ACCEPT
$ sudo iptables -A INPUT -p tcp --dport 8181 -j DROP
$ sudo iptables -A INPUT -p tcp --dport 80 -j ACCEPT
$ sudo iptables -A INPUT -p tcp --dport 22 -j ACCEPT
$ sudo iptables -A OUTPUT -p tcp --sport 22 -j ACCEPT
```

9. Now check if you still have access to the streams API:

```
$ curl -u admin:admin https://localhost/restconf/streams/
```

As you can see, there is no `8181` port in the URL as we forward the REST API request through the `80` port. Now check that you are unable to access the streams REST API from outside the `IPBased-VM` by executing the same command from your host machine. Open a new console and run this:

```
$ curl -u admin:admin https://< IPBased-VM IP
address>/restconf/streams/
```

This should not give you a **not found** message or may just hang:

```
<!DOCTYPE HTML PUBLIC "-//IETF//DTD HTML 2.0//EN">
<html>
  <head>
    <title>404 Not Found</title>
  </head>
    <body>
      <h1>Not Found</h1>
      <p>The requested URL /restconf/streams/ was not found on
      this server.</p>
      <hr>
      <address>Apache/2.4.7 (Ubuntu) Server at 192.168.1.6
      Port80
      </address>
    </body>
</html>
```

10. We will enable the Apache `proxy_http` module:

```
$ sudo a2enmod proxy_http
```

11. Now we will configure the Apache server to restrict access only to the localhost:

```
$ cd /etc/apache2/conf-available
$ sudo touch my_app.conf
$ sudo chown vagrant my_app.conf
$ vi my_app.conf
```

Add the following configuration to the `my_app.conf` file:

```
LoadModule proxy_http_module modules/mod_proxy_http.so
<LocationMatch "/*">
  Order allow,deny
  Allow from 127.0.0.1
```

```
</LocationMatch>
ProxyPass / http://localhost:8181/
ProxyPassReverse / http://localhost:8181/
```

Now save the `my_app.cong` file and exit. Then go to directory `conf-enable` and create a link to the `my_app.conf` file:

```
$ cd /etc/apache2/conf-enabled
$ sudo ln -s /etc/apache2/conf-available/my_app.conf
./my_app.conf
```

We will need to restart the Apache server to apply the new configuration:

```
$ sudo /etc/init.d/apache2 restart
```

12. Verify that the streams REST APIs can be accessed based on the new configuration we installed on the Apache server. At the `IPBased-VM`, run the following command:

```
$ curl -u admin:admin http://localhost/restconf/streams/
```

You should get the same stream response:

```
{
  "Streams": { }
}
```

Now run the same command in your host machine:

```
$ curl -u admin:admin https://< IPBased-VM IP
address>/restconf/streams/
```

You should get the forbidden access message:

```
<!DOCTYPE HTML PUBLIC "-//IETF//DTD HTML 2.0//EN">
<html>
  <head>
    <title>403 Forbidden</title>
  </head>
    <body>
      <h1>Forbidden</h1>
      <p>You don't have permission to access /restconf/streams/
      on this server.</p>
      <hr>
      <address>Apache/2.4.7 (Ubuntu) Server at 192.168.1.6 Port
      80</address>
    </body>
</html>
```

13. Now, you will let the host machine access OpenDaylight by adding its IP address subnet mask to the `my_app.conf` file:

```
$ cd /etc/apache2/conf-available/
$ vi my_app.conf
```

Update the `my_app.conf` file configuration as the following:

"The subnet mask based on the host machine subnet":

```
LoadModule proxy_http_module modules/mod_proxy_http.so
<LocationMatch "/*">
  Order allow,deny
  Allow from 127.0.0.1
  Allow from 192.168.1.0/16
</LocationMatch>
ProxyPass / http://localhost:8181/
ProxyPassReverse / http://localhost:8181/
```

We need to restart the Apache server to apply the new configuration:

```
$ sudo /etc/init.d/apache2 restart
```

14. Now re-check the access to OpenDaylight from the host machine:

```
$ curl -u admin:admin https://< IPBased-VM IP
address>/restconf/streams/
```

You should be able to access the streams REST APIs. If you tried to access OpenDaylight from any other host in your network with a different subnet, you should get the forbidden access message.

How it works...

The firewall rules we installed on the `IPBased-VM`, restrict the access from outside to port `80` for HTTP access and port `22` for `ssh` access. The Apache server has the proxy component that will be configured to allow access from an outside `IPBased-VM` based on IP address or subnet mask. OpenDaylight as an application server running in the same host with the firewall and the Apache server will be under the firewall rules and Apache server configurations umbrella.

OpenDaylight with OpenLDAP environment federation

Due to different authentication mechanisms and deployment environments, OpenDaylight can integrate with different identity providers to authenticate OpenDaylight's users. OpenLDAP is an application protocol that can be used as identity provider to authenticate and authorize OpenDaylight's users. In this recipe, we will learn how to set up the OpenLDAP server, define the SDN users, group, and configure OpenDaylight to authenticate the users by the OpenLDAP server.

Getting ready

For this recipe, you need a new OpenDaylight distribution, PostMan as REST API client, VirtualBox to set up a Ubuntu 14.04 VM, and vagrant if you use the predefined vagrant file from the recipe folder.

How to do it...

1. If you already have the pre-request installed, you can skip this step and start directly from step 4. If you use the predefined vagrant file to establish the environment, you need to install Vagrant if it is not already installed. Then you need to go to the `LDAP-VM` directory under the recipe folder:

   ```
   $ cd chapter11-recipe5/LDAP-VM/
   ```

   You will need to change the network interface name in the Vagrant file to match your machine network interface:

   ```
   $ vi Vagrantfile
   ```

   Change the `en0` to match your machine network interface and save the file. Then you need to start the VMs installation:

   ```
   $ vagrant up
   ```

   The installation time should take between 5-10 min so it is a good time to get a coffee.

2. Now use the `vagrant ssh` command to get access to the `LDAP-VM`:

```
$ vagrant ssh
```

3. Now we will set up and prepare the LDAP server to authorize the OpenDaylight users. In the `LDAB-VM` CLI, run the following commands:

```
$ sudo apt-get update
$ sudo apt-get install slapd ldap-utils
```

After the installation is done, we will configure the LDAP server. Run the following command:

```
$ sudo dpkg-reconfigure slapd
```

You will be asked the following questions through the configuration process:

- Omit `OpenLDAP` server configuration? No.
- DNS domain name? You can enter your preferable domain name. However, for this recipe we will enter `odl.ldap.org`.
- Organization name? Your own choice, we will use OpenDaylight.
- Administrator password? Enter `opendaylight` word as a password.
- Database backend to use? HDB.
- Remove the database when slapd is purged? No.
- Move old database? Yes.
- Allow LDAPv2 protocol? No.

4. To be able to create and manage the OpenDaylight users using a PHP user interface web page, we will install `PHPldapAdmin` package. Run the following command in the `LDAP-VM` CLI:

```
$ sudo apt-get install phpldapadmin
```

After the installation is done, we will need to configure the web interface configuration. Open the `config.php` file using the following command:

```
$ sudo vi /etc/phpldapadmin/config.php
```

Search for the following sections and modify them accordingly:

```
$servers->setValue('server','host','LDAP_VM_IP_Address');
$servers->setValue('server','base',array('dc=odl,dc=ldap,dc=org
'));
$servers->setValue('login','bind_id','cn=admin,dc=odl,dc=ldap,d
```

```
c=org');
$config->custom->appearance['hide_template_warning'] = true;
```

Also, you will need to modify the template render file. Open the
`TemplateRender.php` using the following command:

```
$ sudo vi /usr/share/phpldapadmin/lib/TemplateRender.php
```

Search for the following section and modify it as follows:

```
$default =
$this->getServer()->getValue('appearance','password_hash');
```

Change it to:

```
$default =
$this->getServer()->getValue('appearance','password_hash_custom
');
```

5. Now we will create the OpenDaylight users and groups in the LDAP server. In
   the host machine, open a browser and enter the following URL:

   ```
   http://<LDAP_VM_IP_Address>/phpldapadmin
   ```

   You should see the following web page:

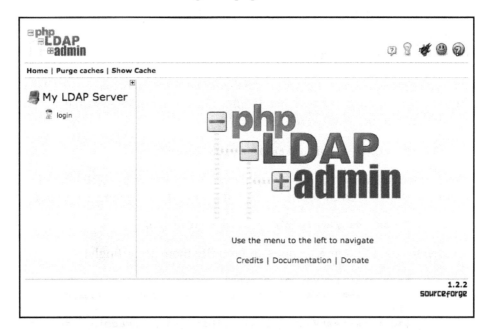

Click on the login link on the left panel, you will see the login **distinguished name** (**DN**) information. Enter OpenDaylight in the password field (if you didn't use OpenDaylight as password in the configurations step, enter the password you chose), then click authenticate:

Now we will create the groups and users organization units. Under the admin domain tree view, click on **Create new entry here**:

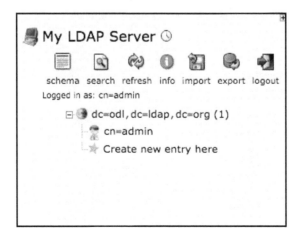

In the right template panel choose **Generic: Organisational Unit** and enter groups in the organization unit file, then press **create object**. Repeat the same step and enter users instead of groups. You should see the groups and users organization unit has been created in the left tree view panel:

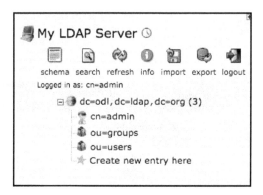

Click on the groups organization unit (ou=groups) and in the right panel, click on **Create a child entry**:

Choose the **Generic: Posix Group** template then enter `odlUsers` in the group field then press **Create Object**. You should see the `odlUsers` group created in the left tree view panel under the groups organization unit.

Now click on the users organization unit (`ou=users`) in the left panel tree view then click on **Create new child entry** and choose **Generic: User Account**. Fill in the user information as follows and for the password field, enter `opendaylight`:

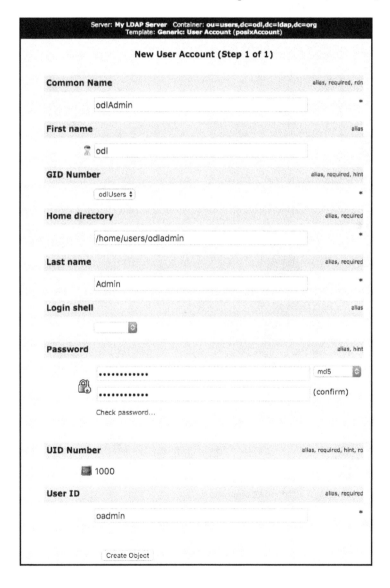

You should be able to see the `odlAdmin` user created under the users organization unit:

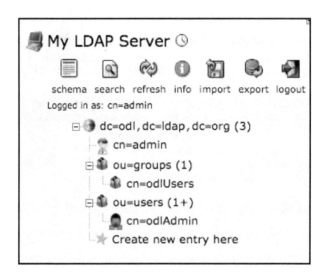

6. Now it's time for OpenDaylight to run and authenticate the `odlAdmin` user we created in the LDAP server. In the host machine, start the OpenDaylight distribution using the `karaf` script. Using this script will give you access to the Karaf CLI:

```
$ cd distribution-karaf-0.4.1-Beryllium-SR2/
$ ./bin/karaf
```

```
_____ _____    .__  .__   .__ __
\_____  \\_____  \ _____ ____ ____   _____  \ _____  ___.__. .__  .__ .__ ___
 | |___/ |_
/ | \\___  \/ _ \ /\ \ | | \\_  \<  | || | | | 1/ __\| | \ _\
/ | \ |_> >  __/| | \|` \/ __ \\__  || |_| / /_/ > Y \ |
_____/ _/\__  >__| /_____  (____ / ___||___/__\___
/|___| /__|
\/|__| \/ \/ \/ \/\/ /_____/ \/
Hit '<tab>' for a list of available commands
and '[cmd] --help' for help on a specific command.
Hit '<ctrl-d>' or type 'system:shutdown' or 'logout' to
shutdown OpenDaylight.
opendaylight-user@root>
```

7. For testing the LDAP Server authentication, we will install the `odl-dlux-all` feature in OpenDaylight. Install the `odl-dlux-all` feature using the following command:

```
opendaylight-user@root> feature:install odl-dlux-all
```

You can check for `aaa` installed features in Karaf CLI using the following command:

```
opendaylight-user@root> feature:list -i | grep aaa
```

You should see something like this in your Karaf CLI:

```
opendaylight-user@root>feature:list -i | grep aaa
odl-aaa-api           | 0.3.2-Beryllium-SR2 | x  | odl-aaa-0.3.2-Beryllium-SR2 | OpenDaylight :: AAA :: APIs
odl-aaa-shiro         | 0.3.2-Beryllium-SR2 | x  | odl-aaa-0.3.2-Beryllium-SR2 | OpenDaylight :: AAA :: Shiro
odl-aaa-authn         | 0.3.2-Beryllium-SR2 | x  | odl-aaa-0.3.2-Beryllium-SR2 | OpenDaylight :: AAA :: Authentication - NO
CLUSTER
```

8. Now we will update the OpenDaylight `shiro.ini` configuration file to connect to our LDAP server and ask for the user's authentication. Under the `distribution` directory, run the following command:

```
$ vi etc/shiro.ini
```

Update the `ldapRealm` and `securityManager` sections as follows then save the file:

```
ldapRealm = org.opendaylight.aaa.shiro.realm.ODLJndiLdapRealm
ldapRealm.userDnTemplate =
cn={0},ou=users,dc=odl,dc=ldap,dc=org
ldapRealm.contextFactory.url = ldap://<LDAP_VM_IP_Address>:389
ldapRealm.searchBase = dc=odl,dc=ldap,dc=org
ldapRealm.ldapAttributeForComparison = objectClass
securityManager.realms = $ldapRealm, $tokenAuthRealm
```

Now we will need to restart the OpenDaylight distribution to update its configuration. In the `karaf` console, run the following command:

```
opendaylight-user@root > shutdown -r
```

9. After the OpenDaylight distribution has been restarted, we will test the LDAP server authentication. In the host machine, open a browser and go to the following URL:

```
http://localhost:8181/index.html#/login
```

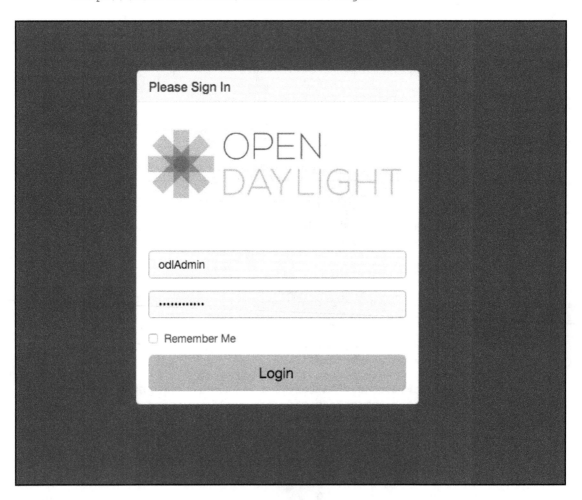

Now enter the `odlAdmin` user credentials as we created in the LDAP server and you should be able to log in.

How it works...

OpenDaylight relies on the Shiro framework to communicate with the LDAP server and authenticate the `odlAdmin` user. The LdapRealm section in the `shiro.ini` file has the basic configurations that OpenDaylight needs to connect to the LDAP server and validating the given user credentials. The implementation of the LdapRealm exists under the `aaa` project source code repository in GitHub:

```
https://github.com/opendaylight/aaa
```

Based on the `shiro.ini` configuration we provide in this recipe under the `securityManager.realms` section, OpenDaylight uses the default authentication realm that uses the local datastore and also uses the LdapRealm. To use the LdapRealm only, you will need to update the `securityManager.realms` to use only the LdapRealm:

```
securityManager.realms = $ldapRealm
```

OpenDaylight with FreeIPA environment federation

FreeIPA is another identity provider using the LDAP application protocol to manage the SDN environment authentication and authorization operations. In this recipe, we will learn how to set up a FreeIPA server, define the SDN users, groups, and configure OpenDaylight to authenticate the users by the FreeIPA server.

Getting ready

For this recipe, you need a new OpenDaylight distribution, PostMan as REST API client, VirtualBox to set up a Ubuntu 14.04 VM, and vagrant if you use the predefined Vagrant file from the recipe folder.

How to do it...

1. If you already have the pre-request installed, you can skip this step and start directly from step 4. If you use the predefined Vagrant file to establish the environment, you need to install Vagrant if it is not already installed. Then you need to go to the `FreeIPA-VM` directory under the recipe folder:

   ```
   $ cd chapter11-recipe6/FreeIPA-VM/
   ```

   You will need to change the network interface name in the Vagrant file to match your machine network interface:

   ```
   $ vi Vagrantfile
   ```

   Change the `en0` to match your machine network interface and save the file. Then you need to start the VMs installation:

   ```
   $ vagrant up
   ```

   The installation time should take between 5-10 min so it is a good time to get a coffee.

2. Now use the `vagrant ssh` command to get access to the `FreeIPA-VM`:

   ```
   $ vagrant ssh
   ```

3. The FreeIPA server requires that the host name should be set correctly. In the `FeeIPA-VM` console, run the following command:

   ```
   $ sudo vi /etc/hosts
   ```

   Make sure that the hosts file has the following configurations:

   ```
   127.0.0.1 localhost.localdomain localhost
   <FreeIPA_VM_IP_Address> ipa.example.com ipa
   ```

   Then set the network configuration using the following command:

   ```
   $ sudo vi /etc/sysconfig/network
   ```

   Make sure it has the following configurations:

   ```
   NETWORKING=yes
   HOSTNAME=ipa.example.com
   ```

4. Now we will configure the FreeIPA server to authorize the OpenDaylight users. In the `FreeIPA-VM` console, run the following command:

```
$ sudo ipa-server-install --setup-dns
```

You will be asked the following questions through the configuration process:

- Existing BIND configuration detected, overwrite? [no]: yes
- Server host name [`ipa.example.com`]: `ipa.example.com`
- Please confirm the domain name [`example.com`]: `example.com`
- Please provide a realm name [`EXAMPLE.COM`]: `EXAMPLE.COM`
- Directory Manager password: `Opendaylight`
- IPA admin password: `Opendaylight`
- Do you want to configure DNS forwarders? [yes]: no
- Do you want to configure the reverse zone? [yes]: no
- Continue to configure the system with these values? [no]: yes

The configurations set up will take 5 minutes.

5. We will create the OpenDaylight users and groups that will be used to authenticate the SDN environment users. Use the following command to log into the FreeIPA server under the `EXAMPLE` realm:

```
$ kinit admin@EXAMPLE.COM
```

Enter the password, `Opendaylight` as we set it in the configuration. Now use the following commands to create the OpenDaylight's group and user:

```
$ ipa group-add odl_users --desc "ODL Users"
$ ipa user-add odlAdmin --first Odl --last Admin --email
odl.admin@example.com --password
$ ipa group-add-member odl_users --user odlAdmin
```

After creating the `odlAdmin` user command, the FreeIPA server will ask you to set the user password. Set it as `Opendaylight`.

6. Now it's the time for OpenDaylight to run and authenticate the `odlAdmin` user we created in the FreeIPA server. In the host machine, start the OpenDaylight distribution using the `karaf` script. Using this script will gives you access to the Karaf CLI:

```
$ cd distribution-karaf-0.4.1-Beryllium-SR2/
$ ./bin/karaf
```

```
_____  _____  .__   .__   .__   _
_____ \ _____ \ ____ ____ _____ \ _____ ___.__.| |  |__|_   ____
 |   |   \ |  |_/  |_
 /   |   \_____ \./ _  \/ \  |  | \\_ \< |  || |  | |  |/  __\|  | \ __\
 /   |   \ |_> >  ___/|  |  \|  `  \/ _ \\__  |   ||_|  / /_/  > Y  \  |
 _____/  /   \___  >___|  /_____   (____  /  ___||___/___/__\___
      /|___| /__|
      \/|___| \/ \/ \/ \/\/ /_____/ \/
Hit '<tab>' for a list of available commands
and '[cmd] --help' for help on a specific command.
Hit '<ctrl-d>' or type 'system:shutdown' or 'logout' to
shutdown OpenDaylight.
opendaylight-user@root>
```

7. For testing the FreeIPA Server authentication, we will install the `odl-dlux-all` feature in OpenDaylight. Install the `odl-dlux-all` feature using the following command:

```
opendaylight-user@root> feature:install odl-dlux-all
```

You can check for `aaa` installed features in Karaf CLI using the following command:

```
opendaylight-user@root> feature:list -i | grep aaa
```

You should see something like this in your Karaf CLI:

```
opendaylight-user@root>feature:list -i | grep aaa
odl-aaa-api              | 0.3.2-Beryllium-SR2 | x  | odl-aaa-0.3.2-Beryllium-SR2  | OpenDaylight :: AAA :: APIs
odl-aaa-shiro            | 0.3.2-Beryllium-SR2 | x  | odl-aaa-0.3.2-Beryllium-SR2  | OpenDaylight :: AAA :: Shiro
odl-aaa-authn            | 0.3.2-Beryllium-SR2 | x  | odl-aaa-0.3.2-Beryllium-SR2  | OpenDaylight :: AAA :: Authentication - NO
CLUSTER
```

8. Now we will update the OpenDaylight `shiro.ini` configuration file to connect to our FreeIPA server and ask for user authentication. Under the `distribution` directory run the following command:

```
$ vi etc/shiro.ini
```

Update the `ldapRealm` and `securityManager` sections as follows then save the file:

```
ldapRealm = org.opendaylight.aaa.shiro.realm.ODLJndiLdapRealm
ldapRealm.userDnTemplate =
uid={0},cn=users,cn=accounts,dc=example,dc=com
ldapRealm.contextFactory.url =
ldap://<FreeIPA_VM_IP_Address>:389
ldapRealm.searchBase = dc=example,dc=com
ldapRealm.ldapAttributeForComparison = objectClass
securityManager.realms = $ldapRealm, $tokenAuthRealm
```

Now we will need to restart the OpenDaylight distribution to update its configuration. In the `karaf` console, run the following command:

```
opendaylight-user@root > shutdown -r
```

9. After the OpenDaylight distribution has been restarted, we will test the FreeIPA server authentication. In the host machine, open a browser and go to the following URL:

```
http://localhost:8181/index.html#/login:
```

Now enter the `odlAdmin` user credentials as we created in the FreeIPA server and you should be able to log in.

How it works...

We used the same configuration section in the `shiro.ini` file that we used in the previous recipe to configure OpenDaylight to connect to the FreeIPA server using the LdapRealm. However, the `LdapRealm.userDnTemplate` configuration was different based on the FreeIPA server user distinguish templates.

Index

L

L2Switch
configuring 29
label management 227, 229
legacy devices
automating 90, 92, 93
Link Aggregation Control Protocol (LACP)
links, bonding 29, 30, 31, 32, 33, 34
local.conf file
URI 142
LOG action
with NIC 241
LSP tunnels
managing, with PCEP 188, 190, 192

M

machine-to-machine protocol
using, for Internet of Things 66, 67, 69, 70, 71, 72, 73
Managed Beans (MBeans) 271
Maven archetype
used, for creating custom OpenDaylight command 259, 260, 261, 262
maximum transfer unit (MTU) 158
Metro Ethernet Forum (MEF) 46
Mininet-VM
URL 9, 22, 30, 127, 224
Mininet
URL 8
Model Driven Service Abstraction Layer (MD-SAL) 177, 227
MPLS intents
about 227, 229
failover constraint 227
protection constraint 227
MPLS VPN
multiple networks, linking across 51, 52, 54, 58
MQ Telemetry Transport (MQTT) 66
Multi Node SXP network topology
URL 118
multiple networks
linking, across MPLS VPN 51, 52, 54, 55

N

Nemo language
reference 115
NETCONF device
data store, obtaining 17, 18
mounting 11, 12, 13, 14, 15, 16, 17
netconf-connector, deleting 19
RPC, invoking 18, 19
URL 11
network bootstrapping infrastructure
securing 103, 105, 106, 107, 108, 109
network device
YANG model, updating 99, 101, 102
network Engine project
URL 120
Network function virtualization (NFV) 125
network functions virtualization (NFV) 7
Network Intent Composition (NIC) 58
Network Services Headers (NSH) 169
network virtualization
with OpenFlow 126, 127, 128, 131, 133
network-wide programming
with PCEP 193, 194, 196
network
BGP routes, adding 180, 182, 184, 186
BGP routes, removing 180, 182, 184, 186
neutron northbound (NN) 127
neutron northbound project
reference 133
NIC, features
odl-nic-console 222
odl-nic-core-hazelcast 222
odl-nic-core-mdsal 222
odl-nic-listeners 222
odl-nic-neutron-integration 222
odl-nic-renderer-gbp 222
odl-nic-renderer-nemo 222
odl-nic-renderer-of 222
odl-nic-renderer-vtn 222
NIC
commands 222, 224
features 222
firewall, setting up 224, 225, 226, 227
integrating, with OpenStack 235, 236, 237, 238

198, 199, 200, 201, 202, 203, 204
Postman collection
  URL 127
Postman
  URL 67
Provider Edge routers (PE) 51
Provider routers (P) 51
Pyretic 119

Q

QoS operation
  performing, with intents 238, 239, 240, 241
  verification 240

R

repositories
  customizing 253, 254
REST API
  used, for configuring Ethernet switch 89
role-based access control (RBAC)
  about 37, 285
  filtering for 285, 286, 287, 288, 289, 290
Routing Information Base (RIB) 176
Ryu 119

S

SDN controller server
  OpenDaylight, using as 119, 120, 121, 123
SDN Environment
  Ethernet switch, managing 86, 89
Secure Group Tagging (SGT) 115
Service Function Chaining (SFC) 221
service functions
  chaining 154, 155, 156, 157, 158, 159, 160,
    161, 164, 167, 168, 169
Service Level Agreement (SLA) 272
SFC YANG models
  URL 169
sfc103 demo
  URL 155
Simple Network Management Protocol (SNMP) 82
SNMP plugin
  using, with OpenDaylight 82, 86
SNMP simulator
  URL 83

software-defined networking (SDN) 7
source IP authorization 292, 293, 294, 295, 296,
  297
Source-Group Tag eXchange Protocol (SXP) 115
SSH access
  reconfiguring, to OpenDaylight 248, 249
start up applications
  customizing 255, 256
Subsequent Address Family Identifier (SAFI) 178
SXP capable devices
  managing, with OpenDaylight 115, 117, 118

T

TCP MD5 authentication
  enabling, for secure BGP connectivity 204, 205,
    206
  enabling, for secure PCEP connectivity 204,
    205, 206
token-based authentication 290, 291, 292
topologies
  managing, with BGP-LS 178, 180
  visualizing, with BGP-LS 178, 180
traffic redirection
  with intents 229, 230, 231, 232
Transformation Layer 268

U

UNI manager
  leveraging 46, 47
unified secure channel (USC)
  about 58
  using, with devices 58, 59, 60, 61, 63, 65
URL Handlers 268
user authentication
  modifying 34, 37
User Network Interface (UNI) 47

V

Vagranfile
  URL 37
Vagrant 1.7.4
  URL 37
virtual customer premises equipment (vCPE) 45
virtual extensible LAN (VXLAN) 147
virtual machines (VMs) 125